E. H. Mikhail is Professor of English Literature at the University of Lethbridge, Canada. He did his graduate studies at Trinity College, Dublin, and the University of Sheffield, where he received his Ph.D.

Professor Mikhail is the author of critical bibliographies on O'Casey, Synge, Wilde, Behan and Lady Gregory, and the editor of *Interviews and Recollections* on O'Casey, Synge, Lady Gregory, Wilde and Behan. His other publications include *The Art of Brendan Behan*, *A Research Guide to Modern Irish Dramatists*, *An Annotated Bibliography of Modern Anglo-Irish Drama* and *Sean O'Casey and his Critics*. He has also contributed articles to various learned journals.

The Abbey Theatre
Interviews and Recollections

THE ABBEY THEATRE

Interviews and Recollections

Edited by

E. H. Mikhail

Professor of English
University of Lethbridge

BARNES & NOBLE BOOKS
TOTOWA, NEW JERSEY

First published in Great Britain 1988 by
The Macmillan Press Ltd

First published in the U.S.A. 1988 by
BARNES & NOBLE BOOKS
81 ADAMS DRIVE,
TOTOWA, NEW JERSEY 07512

ISBN 0–389–20616–4

Printed in Hong Kong

Library of Congress Cataloging-in-Publication Data
The Abbey Theatre.
1. Abbey Theatre—Addresses, essays, lectures.
I. Mikhail, E. H.
PN2602. D82A216   1986   792'.09418'35   86–3407
ISBN 0–389–20616–4

Contents

vi CONTENTS

Acknowledgements

My gratitude is due to the following for support, encouragement, assistance, information, editorial material or notification of certain items that appear in this book: Professor William A. Armstrong, Mr Seamus de Burca, Dr F. Farag, Mr Edwin Gilcher, Miss Rosemary Howard, Professor David Krause, Dr William Latta, Mr Tomás MacAnna, Professor Mark Roberts, Professor Ann Saddlemyer, Dr Brent Shaw, Professor David Spinks, Dr Brian Tyson, Dr Richard Wall and Mr Michael B. Yeats.

The book benefited greatly from the comments and suggestions made by Dr Christopher Murray, from the translations of Gaelic texts into English by Dr Richard Wall, and from the preparation of the final typescript by Mrs Charlene Sawatsky.

Several publications have been of immense help to me, particularly those works on the Abbey Theatre or on Irish drama by Hugh Hunt, Lennox Robinson, Robert Hogan, Ann Saddlemyer, Brenna Katz Clarke and A. E. Malone.

Thanks are due to the University of Lethbridge for granting me a sabbatical leave to complete this work; and to the Social Sciences and Humanities Research Council of Canada for awarding me a Research Grant, without which this book could not have come into existence.

It is also a pleasant duty to record my appreciation to the staff of the University of Lethbridge Library; the National Library of Ireland; the Royal Irish Academy; the British Library, London; the Newspaper Library, Colindale; and the New York Public Library.

The editor and publishers wish to thank the following who have kindly given permission for the use of copyright material:

Ganesh and Co., Publishers, Madras, for the extracts from *We Two Together* by James H. and Margaret E. Cousins;

Talbot Press Ltd, for the extracts from *The Rose and the Bottle* by Seumas O'Sullivan;

The *Irish Times*, for 'The National Theatre Society' by George Roberts;

'Arthur Shields Remembers the Abbey with Pride' by Marion
Fitzgerald; 'An Irishman's Diary' by 'Quidnunc' [Seamus Kelly];
'Abbey Has Been Deteriorating for Years' by Sean O'Casey; 'Cyril
Cusack Talks' by Fergus Linehan; 'Great Days at the Abbey' by Arthur
Shields and J. M. Kerrigan; and 'The Abbey Theatre' by P. S.
O'Hegarty;

The *Irish Independent*, for 'The Irish Theatre Movement' by T. G. Keller;
the *Sunday Independent*, for 'The Abbey Theatre: Is It on the Decline?' by
Brinsley MacNamara;

The *Irish Press*, for 'My First Abbey Play' by Winifred Letts; 'Looking
Back on the Abbey' by May Craig; 'Synge and the Early Days of the
Abbey' by Maire O'Neill; 'Behind the Abbey Scenes' by Ann Treanor;
and 'The New Abbey Theatre' by Walter Macken;

Professor Ann Saddlemyer, for the manuscript 'The Dramatic
Movement in Ireland' by J. M. Synge, from her article from *Modern
Drama*, September 1981;

The Estate of Padraic Colum and the Public Administrator of the
County of New York, for 'Early Days of the Irish Theatre' by Padraic
Colum and published originally in the *Dublin Magazine*, October 1949;

Mr Séamus de Burca, for the extracts from his book *The Soldier's Song*;

Sidgwick and Jackson Ltd, for the extracts from *Ireland's Abbey Theatre* by
Lennox Robinson;

Mr Michael B. Yeats, for 'Irish National Drama', from an interview
given by W. B. Yeats in 1910;

John Murray (Publishers) Ltd, for the extracts from *Scholars and Gypsies*
by Walter Starkie;

The *Cork Examiner*, for 'Abbey Theatre Co.: Departure for America';

A. D. Peters and Co. Ltd and Methuen London Ltd, for the extracts from
Green Memory by L. A. G. Strong;

The National Theatre Society Ltd, for the extracts from *Three Homes* by
Lennox Robinson, Tom Robinson and Nora Dorman;

Mr R. Dardis Clarke, for 'My First Visit to the Abbey' by Austin Clarke;

Mr Rory Johnston, for 'The Abbey Theatre in Those Days' by Denis Johnston; © Denis Johnston 1980;

Curtis Brown Ltd, on behalf of John Child Villiers and Valentine Lamb as Literary Executors of Lord Dunsany, for the extracts from *My Ireland*; first published 1937, copyright the estate of Lord Dunsany;

Mr Sean O'Faolain, for 'Thoughts on the Abbey Theatre' and 'Meet Mr Blythe';

A. D. Peters and Co. Ltd and the Joan Daves Agency, for the extracts from *Leinster, Munster and Connaught* by Frank O'Connor;

The *Radio Telefís Éireann Guide*, for 'Great Lady of the Irish Theatre' by Shelah Richards;

Mr Tomás MacAnna, for 'Ernest Blythe and the Abbey' by Tomás MacAnna;

Drama, a British Theatre Association Publication, for 'The Death-watch Beetle' by Donagh MacDonagh;

Jonathan Cape Ltd and the Estate of Peter Daubeny, for the extracts from *My World of Theatre* by Peter Daubeny;

Ireland of the Welcomes, for 'The Abbey Theatre' by Gerard Fay;

Dr Siobhán McKenna, for 'I Modelled Joan on My Mother' by Siobhán McKenna.

The editor and publishers have made every effort to trace all the copyright-holders, but if any have been inadvertently overlooked they will be pleased to make the necessary arrangements at the first opportunity.

Introduction

The record of the Abbey Theatre will make a splendid page in the literary history of Ireland; when its curtain rose on 27 December 1904 it was to prove an epoch-making event in the world of the theatre. It was the first modern repertory theatre in the true sense of the word, having a repertory of over forty plays, any of which could be staged at a day's notice. The whole of the great movement now known as the 'little theatre' and 'community drama' took its origin from the Abbey Theatre. The Abbey's visit to Birmingham in 1907 inspired Barry Jackson and some of his friends to imitate the company and to found the Pilgrim Players, which developed a few years later into the Birmingham Repertory Theatre. When the Abbey Players visited the United States for the first time in 1911–12, one writer declared, 'The monotony of the current theatre season in America was emphatically interrupted by the advent of the Irish Players from the Abbey Theatre, Dublin.'[1] The visit caught the attention of young Eugene O'Neill and suggested a model for the Provincetown Players. The Abbey also gave Miss A. E. F. Horniman both the inspiration and the experience she needed to become, on the management side, one of the most important women in the history of the theatre in Britain. Drama critics around the world argued that their countries should emulate the example of the Abbey Theatre.[2]

Furthermore, the Abbey Theatre was the cradle of so many masterpieces and the training ground of so many artists. Hollywood, New York and London have drawn heavily on the Abbey for acting talent and have attracted several outstanding performers. Barry Fitzgerald (1888–1961) toured America in 1934 where New York critics, led by George Jean Nathan, voted him best character actor of the year for his performance as Fluther Good in Sean O'Casey's *The Plough and the Stars*. He lived in the United States from 1936, touring until 1937, when he went to Hollywood to play chiefly in films, and where he remained for over twenty years. He won an Oscar for his Father Fitzgibbon in *Going My Way*, and played in *The Quiet Man*, directed in Ireland by John Ford, with John Wayne and Maureen O'Hara. In 1915, Sara Allgood (1883–1950) accepted the lead in *Peg o' My Heart*, a comedy which was wildly successful; and in 1916, she toured Australia and New Zealand with it. Her playing of Juno in 1924 on the first night of O'Casey's *Juno and the Paycock* is part of Irish theatrical history. She gave another performance in London in 1926 as Bessie Burgess in *The Plough and the Stars*. After many successful American tours, she settled in Hollywood in 1940 and became an American citizen in 1945. In 1936, John Ford brought Arthur Shields (1896–1970) to America to play in a film version of *The Plough and the Stars*. In 1937, the Abbey Theatre gave Shields a year's leave of absence to try his luck again in America, where he spent the rest of his life, acting in films and television. Maire O'Neill (Molly Allgood) (1887–1952) played with the Liverpool Repertory Company, with Herbert Beerbohm Tree in Shakespeare in London, and with J. B. Fagan. She appeared with her husband Arthur Sinclair many times in the plays of Sean O'Casey at home and on successful American tours. F. J. McCormick (Peter Judge) (1889–1947) toured America five times, and played three major film roles. In the new Abbey Theatre there hangs a composite portrait of him entitled *The Empty Throne*. (Cecil Salkeld's picture emphasises McCormick's versatility.) Maureen Delany (?– 1961) went out to Australia and South Africa under the Tate Brothers, and toured all over England and America with the Abbey Company, appearing in *The Plough and the Stars*, *Juno and the Paycock*, *The Far-off Hills* and *The Playboy of the Western World*. In the 1950s, Jack MacGowran (1918–73) began a notable series of interpretations of the plays of Samuel Beckett. In 1961, he was named British Television Actor of the Year for his performance as Vladimir in Beckett's *Waiting for Godot*; and in 1971, he became the New York Critics' Actor of the Year for his one-man show, *Beginning to End*, based on Beckett's works – the first non-American actor to receive this award. Denis O'Dea (1903–78) starred in the films *Hungry Hill* and *Odd Man Out*. Although he went away for a while to make films, he never left the Abbey officially. His wife, Siobhán McKenna (1923–86), has acted with all the principal Irish companies and with her own production company in Ireland and abroad, and has had a large number of Broadway and London West End roles, as well as appearing in films. Cyril Cusack (1910–   ) has taken numerous leading roles in international theatres and received the International Critics' Award at Paris Théâtre des Nations Festival in 1961. His film appearances include *The Blue Veil*, *The Day of the Jackal*, *The Wild Heart* and *Jesus of Nazareth*.

For over eighty years the Abbey Theatre has known praise but also criticism, the common fate of all vital institutions. A. B. Walkley wrote in 1903 of the 'series of new thrills' he experienced from seeing the Irish actors 'playing pianissimo, hushed as in a sick-room, all grave and, as it were, careworn'.[3] 'For one whole afternoon,' Max Beerbohm wrote of the Irish Players' visit to London in 1904, 'my feet were on very verdure and there was clear, cold water for my parched throat' – one of the oases in the desert of the theatre.[4] Walkley stated at the Royal Theatrical Fund Dinner on 12 June 1910 that 'Those who may think of starting Repertory Theatres could not have a better example of a modest enterprise than that afforded by the Irish National Theatre, which they owed to Mr Yeats and his comrades.'[5] The *Pall Mall Gazette* of 13 June 1910 declared that 'It would be indeed difficult to mention any other contemporary Theatrical Repertory which has enriched the British Stage with so much modern work of a high order as that of the Irish National Theatrical [*sic*] Society.' Ford Madox Ford wrote in the *Daily News* of 20 June 1910, 'I don't think there has been anything like it in the world.'[6] Eugene O'Neill, commenting on the Abbey's first American tour, said, 'It was seeing the Irish Players that gave me a glimpse of my opportunity. I went to see everything they did. I thought then and I still think that they demonstrate the possibilities of naturalistic acting better than any other company.'[7] Stephen Gwynn concluded that 'The Abbey Theatre is, take it all in all, the most notable thing that modern Dublin has to show.'[8]

On the other hand, the Abbey Theatre – as Professor William A. Armstrong has pointed out[9] – has had its Jeremiahs. In 1912, G. Hamilton Gunning was lamenting 'The Decline of Abbey Theatre Drama'.[10] The following year, Brinsley MacNamara asked: 'The Abbey Theatre: Is It on the Decline?'[11] In 1925, Andrew E. Malone bewailed 'The Decline of the Irish Drama'.[12] In 1935, Hugh Smith posed his pessimistic question, 'Twilight of the Abbey?'[13] and in 1951, Irving David Suss completed a dissertation on 'The Decline and Fall of Irish Drama'.[14] During the years following the fire which destroyed the Abbey in 1951, its shareholders were demanding that a serious effort be made to revitalise the international reputation of the theatre: that the dirt, the frustrations, the pinched economies of the Queen's be forgotten, and that the company emerge from its exile to meet the demanding standards of international theatre.[15]

The Abbey Theatre, however, arose Phoenix-like from its ashes. When, for example, in 1968 – only two years after the new building was opened – Peter Daubeny invited the Abbey to present *The Shaughraun* at the Aldwych Theatre during the World Theatre Season, Irving Wardle wrote:

I am told that many Dubliners oppose the transfer of *The Shaughraun* to London for fear that it would project the wrong image of the country. Let me assure them that no Dublin show I have ever seen has done more to put over the idea of dynamic new Ireland than this, which at once rescues a fine dramatist from oblivion and restores the Abbey to its old status as one of the jewels of the English-speaking theatre.[16]

The same year (1968) also saw a significant international seminar organised by Carolyn Swift which sought to explore the value of the National Theatre and its influence on the international scene. Among those taking part, other than leaders of the Irish theatre, were representatives of the national theatres of Iceland, the Soviet Union, Britain, the German Democratic Republic and the Federal Republic of Germany. In calling together this distinguished gathering, the Abbey was extending its role to that of an international theatre. This new role was manifested in the following year, not only by partaking in the World Theatre Festival, but by the official visit of the King and Queen of Belgium on 16 May, and by one of the highlights of the theatre's long history – a production for the Dublin Theatre Festival of *The Cherry Orchard* (8 October), directed by Maria Knebel of the Red Army Theatre of the Soviet Union and the Moscow Art Theatre. The Abbey's international role was further marked by a visit to Italy in April of the same year when *The Shadow of the Glen* and *The Shadow of a Gunman* were presented at the Teatro della Pergola, Florence, for the city's annual festival, and by the first visit of an Abbey company to the Edinburgh Festival in September, where Tomás MacAnna's production of *The Playboy of the Western World* was presented. Further proof of the Abbey's growing international role can be found in the considerable increase in the repertoire of plays written by non-Irish writers.[17]

The history of this distinguished theatre has been abundantly recorded. George Moore's chief remarks on the Irish Literary Theatre (1899–1901) appear in his highly coloured three-volume memoir *Hail and Farewell*. The Irish National Theatre Society outlines the *Rules of the National Theatre Society Limited* (1903). Lady Gregory's personal history, *Our Irish Theatre* (1913), tersely recounts the inception and early years of the Irish dramatic movement. Cornelius Weygandt, in *Irish Plays and Playwrights* (1913), surveys 'The Dramatic Movement'. Lloyd R. Morris, in *The Celtic Dawn* (1917), gives a long sketch of the movement. Many of Ernest Boyd's opinions are fully developed in *The Contemporary Drama of Ireland* (1918), a general history of the early years of the Abbey. W. B. Yeats, in *Plays and Controversies* (1923), presents 'The Irish Dramatic Movement 1901–1919'. Dawson Byrne, in *The Story of Ireland's National Theatre* (1929), gives a casual survey. Andrew E. Malone, in *The Irish Drama* (1929), offers a more comprehensive, inspired and critical history of the period from 1899 to about 1928. Grace Plunkett, in *Twelve Nights at the Abbey Theatre* (1929) and *Doctors Recommend It* (1930), reproduces drawings and caricatures of actors and actresses. William G. Fay, in *The Fays of the Abbey Theatre* (1935), provides an autobiographical record. The thirty-eight page souvenir brochure, *The Abbey Theatre Dramatic Festival of Plays and Lectures* (1938), celebrates the two-week festival. Una Ellis-Fermor, in *The Irish Dramatic Movement* (1939), surveys 'The Early History of the Movement'. Peter Kavanagh, in *The Irish Theatre* (1946), supplies an unsystematic, very brief account of 'The Abbey Theatre'. Brinsley MacNamara, in *Abbey Plays, 1899–1948* (1949), updates Andrew E. Malone's list of plays. Micheál MacLiammóir, in *Theatre in*

Ireland (1950; with sequel, 1964), interprets well-known facts. Peter Kavanagh, in *The Story of the Abbey Theatre from its Origins in 1899 to the Present* (1950), is quite deliberately contentious, and on the period after the death of Yeats bitterly critical. Lennox Robinson, in *Ireland's Abbey Theatre* (1951), provides the official history commissioned by the theatre's authorities. Sylvester Gaffney, in *The Burning of the Abbey Theatre* (1951), offers a ballad set to music. Maire Nic Shiubhlaigh, in *The Splendid Years* (1955), covers the period 1899–1916. Gerard Fay, in *The Abbey Theatre, Cradle of Genius* (1958), concentrates on the period 1902–8. George A. Duncan, in *The Abbey Theatre in Pictures* (1963), supplies a pictorial account. Ernest Blythe, in the National Theatre Society's brochure *The Abbey Theatre* (n.d.[1965]), outlines the Abbey's policies. Both the National Theatre Society's brochure *Abbey Theatre Dublin, 1904–1966* (1966) and the Irish Tourist Board's pamphlet *The Creation of the Abbey Theatre* (1966) mark the opening of the new building in 1966. Robert Hogan, in *After the Irish Renaissance* (1967), provides a critical history of drama during the forty-year period from 1926. *Joseph Holloway's Abbey Theatre* (1967), ed. Robert Hogan and Michael J. O'Neill, covers the productions of the Abbey from 1899 to 1926, while *Joseph Holloway's Irish Theatre* (1968–70), by the same editors, covers the years 1926–44. Sean McCann, in *The Story of the Abbey Theatre* (1967), gives an informal history for the general reader. Micheál Ó hAodha, in *The Abbey – Then and Now* (1969), brings the theatre's history up to 1969. James W. Flannery, in *Miss Annie F. Horniman and the Abbey Theatre* (1970), charts the relation of this producer to the theatre movement. James Kilroy, in *The 'Playboy' Riots* (1971), recounts the incidents of the first production. Micheál Ó hAodha, in *Theatre in Ireland* (1974), supplies a short introductory critical history. Robert Hogan, in *The Modern Irish Drama* (1975–), co-edits with other scholars a multi-volume documentary history. Deirdre McQuillan, in the commemorative *The Abbey Theatre Dublin 1966–1976* (1976), records and illustrates the theatre's recent decade of productions. Hugh Hunt, in *The Abbey: Ireland's National Theatre, 1904–1979* (1979), updates the history of the Abbey to celebrate its seventy-fifth anniversary. Ann Saddlemyer, in *Theatre Business* (1982), selects and edits the correspondence of the first Abbey directors W. B. Yeats, Lady Gregory and J. M. Synge. Brenna Katz Clarke, in *The Emergence of the Irish Peasant Play at the Abbey Theatre* (1982), traces this popular form of drama.[18]

Despite the abundance of writings on the Abbey Theatre, there is still much conflict of evidence about certain points pertaining to it. For instance, the date of the formation of the Irish National Theatre Society has been inconsistently given.[19] Una Ellis-Fermor, in *The Irish Dramatic Movement*, argues that the Irish National Theatre Society, formed with Yeats as President, was a functioning organisation before the St Teresa's experiment and was responsible for the April 1902 production of *Kathleen Ni Houlihan* and *Deirdre*. The Irish National Theatre Society, however, was not formed until just before the Samhain October 1902 performances. Lady Gregory, in *Our Irish Theatre*, dates the beginning of the society as 1 March 1903, but George Russell helps to discredit Lady Gregory's dating by writing: 'She writes pleasant gossip, but it is as accurate as George Moore, almost in parts where I can check it.'[20] Lennox Robinson, in *Ireland's Abbey Theatre*, places the beginning of the Society as 1 March 1903, but there is nothing to verify that date. W. A. Henderson, in his diaries, correctly lists the inaugural performances of the Irish National Theatre Society as October 1902, but incorrectly states that they took place in Camden Street, though that location was a warehouse until December 1902. Frank Fay states that 'the W. G. Fay's Irish National Dramatic Company . . . changed to The Irish National Theatre Society after the Samhain festival',[21] but two letters concerning Yeats' Presidency of the Society disprove this. In August 1902, Fred Ryan wrote to Yeats offering him the Presidency[22] and on 28 August 1902, Frank Fay wrote to thank Yeats for accepting.[23] Yeats, therefore, was asked to be President before the October performances. Further, all the Abbey programmes and the press reports indicate that the Society was not formed until just before the Samhain performances, but definitely after the April 1902 productions. The productions in the Camden Street Theatre on 4, 5 and 6 December 1902 were, however, staged under the banner of the Irish National Theatre Society, as the playbill for these performances shows.

Another feature of the Abbey Theatre that has only recently been determined is its familiar insignia (Queen Maeve hunting) that is to be seen on its programmes, notepaper and flyleafs. Not long ago, Denis Johnston recalled, 'For years until recently, nobody has been able to say who designed it, and now I am afraid that it has slipped my memory again.'[24] How the strange combination of buildings came to be amalgamated into the original Abbey Theatre by Joseph Holloway is a matter on which little information is now available. Ernest Blythe's policies at the Abbey drew sustained criticism, and his later life as director has never been properly and fairly assessed. The tradition of acting which the Fay brothers created at the Abbey is said – particularly by spokesmen for the theatre – to have continued unabated and distinctive down to the present.[25] Whether the teaching of the Fays is still apparent in the Abbey acting of today is a point, of course, impossible to resolve.

There is also much conflict of opinions about the role the Fays played in the formation of the Abbey. George Russell says that W. G. Fay and Frank Fay 'would never have made the society famous but for the writers like Yeats, Synge and Lady Gregory coming along. But they ought to get the credit for founding the Irish School of Acting, as the writers founded the literary drama. I like Lady Gregory, but she does not know the origins of the National Theatre Society because she was not in Dublin.'[26] Lady Gregory herself seemed to support this view when she begged that an interviewer not ask her to review the history of the Irish theatre.[27] She also ends the chapter 'The Theatre in the Making' with the following sentence: 'This now, according to my memory, is how I came to work for a National Theatre in Ireland and how that Theatre began.'[28] And how exactly Yeats and the Fays came together is not quite clear. W. G. Fay stresses that 'The Abbey Theatre was first and foremost a theatrical, not a literary movement.'[29] Lady Gregory, on the other hand, says, 'They came to us at this time and talked matters over.'[30] This statement, however, does scant justice to the Fays. Lady Gregory herself wrote in 1911, when she accompanied the Abbey company on its first American tour: 'One always, I suppose, likes talking about oneself and what one is interested in.'[31] Nor is it clear exactly why the Fay brothers left the Abbey. Lennox Robinson records: 'It is difficult, thirty and more years after, to judge who was most in the right; doubtless there were wrongs on both sides.'[32] Yeats and Lady Gregory have been accused of resenting any authority other than their own in the management of the theatre. Even before the Fays departed, Edward Martyn, George Moore and George Russell had found themselves manoeuvred into positions where they could no longer continue to serve. Others argue that the Abbey would never have survived had it not been for the talent and popularity of its players. Moore's part in helping the Irish Literary Theatre – in finance, in directing, in collaboration and in publicity – is also decidedly played down by Lady Gregory in *Our Irish Theatre*. Moore recounts the facts in *Hail and Farewell*, but a somewhat different version may be found in Yeats' autobiographies. And Edward Martyn, without whose generosity the Irish Literary Theatre might never have succeeded, is chiefly remembered by the malicious, though undoubtedly witty and sometimes lovable, caricature of 'Dear Edward' in Moore's *Hail and Farewell*.

The present work is a composite biography which provides a forum to most of those who have been associated with the Abbey Theatre from the beginning to the present time: actresses (Sara Allgood, May Craig, Eileen Crowe, Siobhán McKenna, Maire Nic Shiubhlaigh, Maire O'Neill, Shelah Richards); actors (Cyril Cusack, Dudley Digges, Frank Fay, Arthur Shields, J. M. Kerrigan, P. J. Kelly, Fred O'Donovan); producers and directors (William G. Fay, Ernest Blythe, Peter Daubeny, Lennox Robinson, Tomás MacAnna, Nugent Monck); theatre benefactress (Miss A. E. F. Horniman); stage carpenter (Seaghan Barlow); house electrician (Udolphus Wright); playwrights (Lady Gregory, Sean O'Casey, Walter Macken, Brinsley MacNamara,

Denis Johnston, Paul Vincent Carroll, J. M. Synge, Winifred Letts);
poets and men of letters (Austin Clarke, Padraic Colum, James H.
Cousins, Lord Dunsany, Peadar Kearney, W. B. Yeats, P. S. O'Hegarty,
George Moore, Donagh MacDonagh, Walter Starkie, Frank O'Connor,
Sean O'Faolain, Seumas O'Sullivan, George W. Russell, L. A. G.
Strong, George Roberts, T. G. Keller); journalists (Gerard Fay); and
supporters of the theatre and enthusiasts (John Quinn, Ann Treanor).

Inevitably, limitation of space has prevented me from doing justice to
many others who have contributed to the long and eventful history of the
Abbey Theatre, and whose contributions do not appear in this
collection. It is hoped, though, that the method used in this book will
give a different impression from that of previous histories of the Abbey
Theatre, and on balance probably a truer one.

E. H. MIKHAIL

NOTES

1. 'The Players', *Everybody's Magazine* (New York), 26 (Feb 1912) 231–40.
2. John Coulter, for example, in 'The Canadian Theatre and the Irish
Exempler', *Theatre Arts Monthly* (New York), 22 (July 1938) 503–9, showed what
lessons the Canadian Theatre could learn from the Abbey Theatre; and Rudolf
Stamm, in 'Die neu-irische Theaterbewegung und wir', *Schweizer Annalen*
(Aurau), 1 (May 1944) 156–66, argued that the Swiss Theatre could benefit from
the Abbey.
3. 'The Irish National Theatre', *Times Literary Supplement* (London), 8 May
1903, p. 146; repr., slightly rev., in *Drama and Life* (London: Methuen, 1907)
pp. 309–15.
4. 'Some Irish Plays and Players', *Saturday Review* (London), 97 (9 Apr 1904)
455–7.
5. Quoted by Lady Gregory in *Our Irish Theatre*, 3rd edn (Gerrards Cross:
Colin Smythe, 1972) p. 200.
6. 'The Irish Theatre', *Daily News* (London), 20 June 1910, p. 10, in which he
endorses an appeal by W. B. Yeats and Lady Gregory for the support of the Irish
National Theatre.
7. Arthur and Barbara Gelb, *O'Neill* (New York: Harper, 1962) p. 172.
8. *Dublin Old and New* (New York: Macmillan, 1938) p. 51.
9. Preface to E. H. Mikhail, *A Bibliography of Modern Irish Drama 1899–1970*
(London: Macmillan, 1972) p. vii.
10. G. Hamilton Gunning, 'The Decline of Abbey Theatre Drama', *Irish
Review* (Dublin), 1 (Feb 1912) 606–9.
11. Brinsley MacNamara, 'The Abbey Theatre: Is It on the Decline?', *Irish
Independent* (Dublin), 9 May 1913, p. 4.
12. Andrew E. Malone, 'The Decline of the Irish Drama', *Nineteenth Century
and After* (London), 97 (Apr 1925), 578–88. Sean O'Casey's resurgent genius,
however, has belied Malone's epitaph.

13. Hugh Smith, 'Twilight of the Abbey?', *New York Times*, 31 Mar 1935, section 11, p. 2.

14. Irving David Suss, 'The Decline and Fall of Irish Drama', Ph.D. dissertation, Columbia University, 1951. Brendan Behan's resurgent genius, again, has belied Suss's epitaph.

15. Hugh Hunt, *The Abbey: Ireland's National Theatre 1904–1979* (Dublin: Gill & Macmillan, 1979) p. 193. After the 1951 fire, the Abbey company was accommodated in the Rupert Guinness Hall and the Queen's Theatre until its new building was opened in 1966.

16. Irving Wardle, 'Abbey Restored to Old Eminence', *The Times* (London), 21 May 1968, p. 6.

17. Hunt, *The Abbey*, pp. 203–19.

18. For a more comprehensive list of works on the Abbey Theatre see the Additional Bibliography at the end of this book, and E. H. Mikhail, *An Annotated Bibliography of Modern Anglo-Irish Drama* (Troy, New York: Whitston, 1981).

19. See Appendix C in Brenna Katz Clarke, *The Emergence of the Irish Peasant Play at the Abbey Theatre* (Ann Arbor, Michigan: UMI Research Press, 1982) p. 175.

20. Letter to John Quinn, 14 March 1914, quoted in *Letters from AE*, ed. Alan Denson (London: Abelard-Schumann, 1961) p. 97.

21. 'Some Account of the Early Days of the Irish National Theatre Society', MS 10953, National Library of Ireland, Dublin.

22. Letter to Yeats, August 1902, MS 13068 (13), National Library of Ireland, Dublin.

23. Letter to Yeats, 28 August 1902, MS 13068 (13), National Library of Ireland, Dublin.

24. *The Writers: A Sense of Ireland*, ed. Andrew Carpenter and Peter Fallon (Dublin: O'Brien Press, 1980) p. 70.

25. See, for example, Gabriel Fallon, *The Abbey and the Actor* (Dublin: The National Theatre Society, 1969).

26. *Letters from AE*, ed. Alan Denson, p. 96.

27. 'Lady Gregory', *Evening Post* (New York), 6 Dec 1911.

28. Lady Gregory, *Our Irish Theatre*, p. 38. See also Roger McHugh's Foreword to the 3rd edition.

29. W. G. Fay and Catherine Carswell, *The Fays of the Abbey Theatre: An Autobiographical Record* (London: Rich & Cowan, 1935) p. 106.

30. Lady Gregory, *Our Irish Theatre*, p. 146.

31. *Ibid.*, p. 99. Cf. 'Sean O'Casey's autobiographies describe Lady Gregory in her seventies and, perhaps surprisingly, reveal a rapport with her which he did not feel with Yeats or AE' (McHugh, Foreword to *Our Irish Theatre*, p. 11).

32. Lennox Robinson, *Ireland's Abbey Theatre: A History 1899–1951* (London: Sidgwick & Jackson, 1951) p. 56.

A Note on the Text

In the extracts given, spelling errors in the originals have been silently corrected, American spellings have been anglicised, and the spelling of names has been rendered consistent throughout. All titles of plays and books are in italics.

Chronological Table

1897 W. B. Yeats, Lady Gregory and Edward Martyn meet at Duras House, County Clare, and plan to found the Irish Literary Theatre.

1899 9 Jan: Edward Martyn accepts financial responsibility at a meeting of the National Literary Society for the performances, under the auspices of the Society, of the Irish Literary Theatre.
12 Jan: W. B. Yeats publishes open letter, 'Important Announcement – Irish Literary Theatre', in *Daily Express* (Dublin).
16 Jan: The Irish Literary Theatre is formally founded at a meeting of the Council of the National Literary Society.
28 Jan: AE [George Russell] publishes 'The Irish Literary Drama' in *Daily Express* (Dublin).
Apr: Edward Martyn applies to the Town Clerk on behalf of the Irish Literary Theatre.
Yeats publishes 'The Theatre' in the *Dome* (London).
23 Apr: Yeats lectures on the 'Ideal Theatre' to the Irish Literary Society, London.
6 May: Yeats publishes 'The Irish Literary Theatre' in *Literature* (London).
8–10 May: The Irish Literary Theatre presents its first season (*The Countess Cathleen* at Antient Concert Rooms on 8 May; and *The Heather Field* by Edward Martyn at Antient Concert Rooms on 9 and 10 May).
May: *Beltaine* no. 1, the organ of the Irish Literary Theatre, edited by W. B. Yeats, is published.

1900 20 Jan: James Joyce lectures on 'Drama and Life' to the Royal University Literary and Historical Society.
Jan: Yeats publishes 'The Irish Literary Theatre, 1900' in the *Dome* (London).
Yeats publishes a 'Letter to the Editor' of the *Irish Literary Society Gazette* (London).
19–20 Feb: The Irish Literary Theatre presents its second season (*Maeve* by Edward Martyn and *The Last Feast of the Fianna* by Alice Milligan at the Gaiety Theatre on 19 Feb; and *The Bending of the Bough* by George Moore at the Gaiety Theatre on 20 Feb).
22 Feb: A luncheon is given to the members of the Irish Literary Theatre by the Irish National Literary Society in the Gresham Hotel.
Feb: *Beltaine* no. 2 is published.

Apr: *Beltaine* no. 3 is published.

1901   8 Apr: Inghinidhe na hÉireann [Daughters of Erin] present tableaux and ceildh at Antient Concert Rooms.

23 June: Yeats, Sarah Purser and James Cousins meet at George Coffey's house to form a committee to work towards an Irish national theatre.

26 June: Inghinidhe na hÉireann present 'Irish Nights' at Antient Concert Rooms.

21 Oct: The Irish Literary Theatre presents its third season (*Diarmuid and Grania* by Yeats and Moore, and *Casadh an tSugáin* by Douglas Hyde, at the Gaiety Theatre). A few days before these performances, Yeats states that they mark the end of the Irish Literary Theatre.

Oct: *Samhain* no. 1, edited by W. B. Yeats, is published.

Nov: James Joyce publishes a pamphlet, 'The Day of the Rabblement', accusing Yeats and Lady Gregory of 'surrendering to the trolls' and making a plea for the production of European masterpieces as models for Irish playwrights.

1902   2 Jan: Scenes from *Deirdre* by AE are performed in the garden of George Coffey's house.

Spring: W. G. Fay's Irish National Dramatic Company is formed, including W. G. Fay, F. J. Fay, Dudley Digges, P. J. Kelly, C. Caulfield, Maire Quinn, Maire Nic Shiubhlaigh [Mary Walker], Padraic Colum, James Cousins [H. Sproule], F. J. Ryan and Brian Callender.

2 Apr: W. G. Fay's Irish National Dramatic Company presents *Deirdre* by AE and *Kathleen Ni Houlihan* by Yeats at St Teresa's Hall, Clarendon Street.

12 Apr: Yeats publishes 'The Acting at St Teresa's Hall' in the *United Irishman* (Dublin).

21 Apr: Yeats writes to Frank Fay referring to the possibility of money from 'a wealthy friend'.

26 Apr: Yeats defends the company in 'The Acting at St Teresa's Hall' in the *United Irishman* (Dublin).

25? May: Lady Gregory writes to Yeats, 'If Literary Theatre breaks up, we must try and settle something with Fay, possibly a week of little plays he has been doing through the spring, at the Antient Concert Rooms. I have a sketch in my head that might do for Hyde to work on' (*Seventy Years*, p. 413).

25 July: W. G. Fay acknowledges receiving *The Hour-Glass* and *The Pot of Broth* from Yeats at Coole.

Aug: The Irish National Theatre Society is founded. Prior to that the company was known as W. G. Fay's Irish National Dramatic Company. Although Fay hired Camden Street Hall on behalf of the INTS, it was not in fact used until 4 Dec 1902, and in the meantime the Samhain productions were billed as given by the W. G. Fay's Irish National Dramatic Company. These productions ran from 28 Oct to 1 Nov inclusively.

26 Sept: Fay brothers reject Lady Gregory's *Twenty-Five*.

Oct: *Samhain* no. 2 is published.

29 Oct: The Irish National Dramatic Company presents *The Sleep of the King* by James Cousins and *The Laying of the Foundations* by Fred Ryan at Antient Concert Rooms.

30 Oct: The Irish National Dramatic Company presents *The Pot of Broth* by Yeats at Antient Concert Rooms.

31 Oct: The Irish National Dramatic Company presents *The Racing Lug* by James Cousins at Antient Concert Rooms.

4–6 Dec: The first productions by the Irish National Theatre Society at the Camden Street Theatre; three of the Samhain plays are staged.

1903 20 Jan: Synge reads *Riders to the Sea* at Yeats' 'At Home', London.

late Jan: AE helps the Irish National Theatre Society draft a constitution, which is formally adopted at a general meeting, early Feb; a reading committee is established, consisting of Yeats, AE, Lady Gregory, F. J. Ryan, Padraic Colum, Arthur Griffith and Maud Gonne.

3 Mar: Synge's *Riders to the Sea* and *In the Shadow of the Glen* are read out at Lady Gregory's flat in London.

14 Mar: The Irish National Theatre Society presents *The Hour-Glass* by Yeats and *Twenty-Five* by Lady Gregory at the Molesworth Hall. Between the plays Yeats lectures on 'The Reform of the Theatre'.

22 Mar: The Irish National Theatre Society appoints individuals to posts concerned with printing and business matters, costumes and properties.

29 Apr: The general meeting of the Irish National Theatre Society adopts an additional rule (V.k) prohibiting members from performing elsewhere without permission.

Apr?: Prospectus of the Irish National Theatre Society is distributed.

2 May: The Irish National Theatre Society performs, under the auspices of the London Irish Literary Society, at the Queen's Gate Hall, South Kensington, London.

2 June: The Irish National Theatre Society accepts AE's amendment concerning a reading committee and Yeats, AE, Colum and the Fay brothers are selected; Yeats protests against Cousins' *Sold*.

Sept: Maud Gonne's political work becomes so exacting that she resigns from the Irish National Theatre Society.

8 Oct: The Irish National Theatre Society produces *The King's Threshold* by Yeats and *In the Shadow of the Glen* by Synge at the Molesworth Hall; Maud Gonne, Maire Quinn and Dudley Digges leave in protest over Synge's play.

24 Oct: The *United Irishman* publishes Maud Gonne's 'A National Theatre', and Yeats' defence of Synge.

3 Dec: The Irish National Theatre Society produces *Broken Soil* by Padraic Colum at the Molesworth Hall.

12 Dec: Miss Horniman writes to George Roberts, Secretary of the Society, concerning the possibility of a theatre.

30 Dec: Rules of the Irish National Theatre Society are registered, signed by W. G. Fay, F. J. Fay, P. J. Kelly, F. J. Ryan, Helen Laird, Maire Walker, James Starkey, George Roberts.

1904   1 Jan: Miss Horniman writes to George Roberts saying that she has received 'a sum of money unexpectedly' and intimates that it will go towards a theatre.

14 Jan: The Irish National Theatre Society presents Yeats' *The Shadowy Waters* at the Molesworth Hall.

26 Mar: The Irish National Theatre Society, sponsored by the London Irish Literary Society, performs at the Royalty Theatre, London, the company's first appearance on a legitimate stage.

6 Apr: Amendment slip to Rules promises that the signatories will continue as members of the Society for at least one year if resident in Dublin; signed by W. G. Fay, H. F. Norman, P. Colum, G. Roberts, F. Ryan, U. Wright, Maire Nic Shiubhlaigh, Prionnsias Mac Siubhlaigh [Frank Walker], F. J. Fay, Sara Allgood, J. S. Starkey, M. Nic Gharbhaigh; witnessed by AE; expulsion of P. J. Kelly for joining Dudley Digges and Maire Quinn to perform at the St Louis International Exhibition (the first break in the original team).

8 Apr: Yeats sends to AE Miss Horniman's formal offer of a theatre.

23 Apr: AE resigns as Vice-President, remaining member of the Irish National Theatre Society.

11 May: The Irish National Theatre Society signs acceptance of Miss Horniman's formal offer of a theatre.

6 July: Miss Horniman returns signed contract to Society; W. G. Fay is hired to oversee the renovations to the Abbey Theatre.

20 Aug: Patent is granted in the name of Lady Gregory for six years.

27 Dec: The Abbey Theatre officially opens with *On Baile's Strand*

by Yeats, *Spreading the News* by Lady Gregory and *Kathleen Ni Houlihan* by Yeats.

1905 24 Oct: The Irish National Theatre Society is disbanded and replaced by the professional National Theatre Society Limited, which is registered under the Friendly and Industrial Societies Act; the directors of the new company are Lady Gregory, W. B. Yeats and J. M. Synge, who hold the bulk of the shares, while Sarah Allgood, Vera Esposito, Udolphus Wright, W. G. Fay and Frank Fay have one share each.

Dec: Maire Nic Shiubhlaigh resigns from the Abbey Theatre, and with her go Honor Lavelle, Emma Vernon, Maíre Garvey, Frank Walker, Seamus O'Sullivan and George Roberts (the second exodus from the company).

1906 May: Edward Martyn and Stephen Gwynn call a meeting of the seceding members and other politico-cultural groups to discuss the formation of a new society.

6 June: The Theatre of Ireland is formed as an amateur organisation with similar aims to those of the National Theatre Society.

Autumn: J. M. Kerrigan joins the Abbey company.

1907 26 Jan: The Abbey Theatre presents Synge's *The Playboy of the Western World*, which creates the first major riot in the theatre.

Mar: Ben Iden Payne, at Miss Horniman's insistence, joins the Abbey Theatre as producer; this eventually leads to William G. Fay's resignation.

1908 13 Feb: William G. Fay and Frank Fay leave the Abbey Theatre.

1 Oct: Dr J. F. Larchet is appointed musical director.

1909 24 Mar: J. M. Synge dies leaving a three-act play, *Deirdre of the Sorrows*, not quite completed.

25 Aug: The Abbey Theatre puts on Bernard Shaw's *The Shewing-up of Blanco Posnet*, which could not be performed in London because the Lord Chamberlain had withheld his licence.

Dec?: Lennox Robinson is appointed producer (director of plays) and manager of the Abbey Theatre.

1910 May: Miss A. E. F. Horniman withdraws her subsidy from the Abbey Theatre because it did not close when King Edward VII died on 6 May. A legal dispute over payment of the subsidy then outstanding is settled in favour of the Abbey (29 Apr 1911). Miss Horniman's connection with the Abbey then ceases.

1 Nov: Miss Horniman relinquishes her control on the Abbey Theatre on the expiration of the six years' patent granted to her for the theatre. The directors pay £1000 owning to her, for transfer of ownership.

2 Nov: Lady Gregory takes over the reins of patentee for the Abbey Theatre's new lease of life for twenty-one years to come.

1911 Sept: The Abbey Theatre makes its first American tour, which lasts until Feb 1912.

1912 Dec: The Abbey Theatre makes its second American tour, which lasts until May 1913.

1914 Feb: The Abbey Theatre makes its third American tour, which is to be the last for many years.

June: Lennox Robinson resigns as manager of the Abbey Theatre; he is to be recalled to the Abbey five years later.

1915 July: A. Patrick Wilson, the manager, is dismissed for 'turning to his own purposes, offers that were intended for us'; he is succeeded by St John Ervine.

Oct: The financial situation is such that the players' salaries have to be reduced.

1916 24 Apr: The Easter Rising takes place. The Abbey is closed down, cancelling the production of a new play, *The Spancel Death*, by T. H. Nally. Several Abbey actors take part in the Rising, and one, Sean Connolly, is killed in the attack on the Dublin Castle.

May: Arthur Sinclair, Sydney Morgan, Harry Hutchinson, J. A. O'Rourke, Kathleen Drago, Eithne Magee and others leave the Abbey Theatre to form their own touring company, the Irish Players.

July: St John Ervine resigns; he is succeeded by J. Augustus Keogh.

1918 Lennox Robinson founds the Dublin Drama League under Yeats' Presidency with himself as Secretary; the League continues giving occasional productions until 1929.

Dec: Fred O'Donovan informs Joseph Holloway that he is thinking of going to America and in the following Feb he leaves the Abbey Theatre; with him go the last remnants of the old company.

1921 Spring: The Abbey Company is dismissed by Lennox Robinson due to the financial position of the theatre as a result of the Curfew order during the time of 'The Trouble'.

May: J. B. Fagan arranges four lectures in his London home to launch an appeal to help the Abbey Theatre.

9 Dec: Yeats writes to Lady Gregory suggesting that the Abbey Theatre be handed over to the Provisional government.

1922 The state of the Abbey Theatre's finances is such that the directors can only afford to engage three of the players on full-time salaries, the remainder being 'part-timers'.

1923 12 Apr: The Abbey Theatre presents Sean O'Casey's *The Shadow* *of a Gunman*, which (together with *Juno and the Paycock*) saves the theatre from bankruptcy.

1924 15 Apr: Lennox Robinson is appointed a Director of the National Theatre Society.

27 June: Lady Gregory and W. B. Yeats write to President Cosgrave offering to hand the Abbey Theatre over to the government.

Dec: The Abbey Theatre is granted an annual subsidy by the Irish Free State, and so becomes the first state-subsidised theatre in the English-speaking world.

1925 27 Dec: The Abbey Theatre celebrates its twenty-first birthday.

1926 8 Feb: The Abbey Theatre presents O'Casey's *The Plough and the Stars*, which creates the second major riot in the theatre. (The first major riot occurred when *The Playboy* was presented in 1907.)

5 Mar: O'Casey packs his bag and goes to London.

Nov: The Peacock Theatre, designed to be used for experimental productions and for performances by pupils of the Abbey School of Acting, is planned in a house adjoining the Abbey; it opens on 13 Nov 1927.

1927 Ninette de Valois forms the Abbey School of Ballet.

1928 Apr: The Abbey Theatre rejects O'Casey's *The Silver Tassie*.

1931 June: The directors of the Abbey Theatre offer a prize of £50 for the best full-length play.

Oct: The Abbey Company resumes its visits to America with a mammoth coast-to-coast tour of seventy-nine centres; three more tours were to follow (Oct 1932–May 1933; Sept 1934–Apr 1935; Aug 1937–Apr 1938).

1932 23 May: Lady Gregory dies.

1935 9 Mar: F. R. Higgins, Brinsley MacNamara and Ernest Blythe are appointed directors of the Abbey Theatre.

Aug: Hugh Hunt comes over from England as producer.

Oct: Brinsley MacNamara resigns in protest over the production of *The Silver Tassie* and is replaced by Frank O'Connor.

1937 Apr: The Abbey's Experimental Theatre is started under Ria Mooney's direction.

1938 Aug: The Abbey Theatre Dramatic Festival is held in Dublin.

Sept: F. R. Higgins is appointed managing director of the Abbey Theatre.

Nov: Hugh Hunt leaves the Abbey Theatre; he is replaced by Louis D'Alton in Jan 1939; D'Alton resigns in May 1939 to be succeeded by Frank Dermody.

1939 28 Jan: W. B. Yeats dies.

1940 May: Frank O'Connor resigns.

Oct: Roibeárd Ó Farachain is appointed to the Board.

1941   Jan: F. R. Higgins dies; in his place the Board appoints Ernest
Blythe as managing director.

1942   May: The Minister of Education directs that the work of An
Comhar Dramaíochta, which is subsidised to produce plays in
Irish, should thenceforward be done through the Abbey
Theatre.

1944   13 Mar: Joseph Holloway dies after keeping a record of the
Dublin theatres for forty-eight years.

1945   26 Dec: The Abbey Theatre presents its first pantomime in Irish.

1947   Apr: F. J. McCormick dies ('a shattering blow to our Theatre' –
Lennox Robinson).
7 Nov: The poet Valentin Iremonger and the university lecturer
Roger McHugh protest at the low standards of production
during a performance of *The Plough and the Stars*, thereby sparking
off a controversy.

1948   Jan: Ria Mooney is appointed producer.

1951   18 July: The auditorium and backstage of the Abbey Theatre are
gutted by fire; offers of alternative accommodation come from
many different sources, and the company occupies the Rupert
Guinness Hall for eight weeks.
24 Aug: The Abbey Theatre leases the Queen's Theatre for five
years.

1954   27 Dec: The Abbey Theatre celebrates its Golden Jubilee.

1957   After long and difficult negotiations, additional space adjoining
the site of the old Abbey Theatre is purchased, and it becomes
possible to make a satisfactory plan for the new building.

1958   14 Oct: Lennox Robinson dies; he is replaced on the Board by
Gabriel Fallon.

1959   An act of the Oireachtas is passed authorising the Minister for
Finance to contribute £250,000 towards the rebuilding of the
Abbey Theatre.

1961   Plans for the new Abbey Theatre are finally passed by the Dublin
Corporation and approved by the government.

1962   Feb: Tenders for building the new Abbey Theatre are invited.
15 June: The lowest tender submitted by A. J. Jennings & Co.
Ltd is accepted and the contract for the new building is signed.

1963   3 Sept: The President of Ireland lays the foundation stone of the
new Abbey Theatre.

1964   Apr: The Abbey Theatre presents *Juno and the Paycock* and *The
Plough and the Stars* at the Aldwych Theatre in London as part of
the 1964 World Theatre Season.
18 Sept: Sean O'Casey dies.

1965   Nov: The Board appoints Walter Macken as artistic adviser and
assistant manager.

1966 June: Macken announces his resignation; in his place Micheál Ó hAodha is appointed.

18 July: The new Abbey Theatre is opened (on the fifteenth anniversary of the burning of the old Abbey).

Dec: The position of artistic adviser is taken over by Tomás MacAnna.

1967 23 July: The new Peacock Theatre is formally opened.

31 Aug: Ernest Blythe retires as managing director of the Abbey Theatre; he remains an influential member of the Board until 1972. Phil O'Kelly is promoted from deputy manager to manager but without a seat on the Board.

1968 Apr: The Abbey Theatre's international role is marked by a visit to Italy where *The Shadow of the Glen* and *The Shadow of a Gunman* are presented at the Teatro della Pergola, Florence, for the city's annual festival.

Sept: For the first time an Abbey company visits the Edinburgh Festival.

30 Sept–8 Oct: Carolyn Swift organises an international seminar to explore the value of the National Theatre idea and its influence on the international scene.

Oct: Tomás MacAnna retires to take up an appointment as visiting professor in Minnesota; he is succeeded by Alan Simpson, who serves for only one year starting 1 Dec as his contract is not renewed. His departure brings to a head the question of the relationship between the Board and its artistic officer.

1969 Aug: Sir Tyrone Guthrie directs his first play for the Abbey Theatre, Eugene McCabe's *Swift*.

1 Dec: Hugh Hunt consents to succeed Alan Simpson on condition that the title be changed to that of artistic director; Sean Cotter is appointed as assistant artistic director.

1970 Mar: The Abbey production of *Borstal Boy* is presented in New York.

May: The Abbey production of *The Hostage* visits Antwerp, Zurich, Frankfurt, Cologne and Vienna.

3–8 Aug: The Abbey Company is the guest of the British National Theatre at the Old Vic with the production of *The Well of the Saints* and *The Dandy Dolls*.

1971 Dec: Lelia Doolan is appointed artistic director of the Abbey.

1972 June: Kathleen Barrington becomes the first player to sit on the Board of directors; in the same month Tomás MacAnna is also coopted.

23 Nov: The Abbey production of *Richard's Cork Leg* is presented at the Royal Court Theatre, London.

1973 The Abbey production of *The Silver Tassie* is presented in Helsinki and Brussels.
Sept: The Abbey production of *King Oedipus* is presented at the Edinburgh Festival.
Lelia Doolan resigns as artistic director.

1974 The Abbey Theatre accepts a recommendation by a subcommittee to appoint a literary editor; the first literary editor to be appointed is Denis Johnston.

1975 25 Jan: Ernest Blythe dies; his place on the Board is taken by Tomás MacAnna.

1976 The Abbey Company is invited to take part in the American Bicentennial celebrations by presenting MacAnna's Golden Jubilee production of *The Plough and the Stars* in New York, Philadelphia, Washington and Boston.

1977 Nov: The Abbey production of *Talbot's Box* is presented at the Royal Court Theatre, London.

1978 29 May: The Abbey production of *You Never Can Tell* is presented at the Malvern Festival.
Nov: The Board accepts the advice of Tom Kilroy and others that the literary editor must be a full-time and adequately paid member of the Abbey Theatre's staff. Sean McCarthy is appointed such.

1979 27 Dec: The Abbey Theatre celebrates its seventy-fifth anniversary.

1982 Aug: Ulick O'Connor is appointed to Board of directors.
Oct: Joe Dowling is reappointed artistic director (having served since end of 1977).

1983 Jan: Sean McCarthy resigns as literary editor, and is replaced by Christopher FitzSimon.

Irish Drama Arrives*

JAMES H. COUSINS

On 23 September (1901) I attended the one and only meeting of the committee of the Irish Literary Theatre;[1] and on 21 October its third and last season opened,[2] again in the Gaeity Theatre.[3] Heretofore the actors had been chosen individually from the English stage; but on this occasion the main piece was put in the hands of the Benson Shakespearean Company. *Diarmuid and Grania*, the first title on the bill, was announced as under the joint authorship of W. B. Yeats and George Moore. The partnership was regarded by certain of Yeats' admirers as a descent into Hades. But some consolation for the degradation of a spiritual poet to the companionship of a literary scavenger, as Moore was then considered, was attempted to be found in the hope that the fall of Yeats might bring about the redemption of Moore. Moments of poetry elicited the whispered exclamation, 'Ah! that's Willie.' Other phrases were attributed to 'dirty George'. But it came out, as a disturbing rumour, that the typical poetical Yeatsian patches were by Moore, and this typical Moorish splashes of realism were by Yeats. Be this as it may, some interchange of quality was apparent in the succeeding independent works of the collaborators. Moore passed from *Esther Waters* and bald ugliness to *Evelyn Innes* and beauty-spots; Yeats passed from *The Countess Cathleen* to heroic endeavours towards modernity in throwing chunks of ugliness into *Deirdre*. Neither of them proved a success at being the other.[4] The first night of *Diarmuid and Grania* was a great social event. Everybody who was anything, and a great many who were nothing but wished to be something in the Ireland of ideas, was present. The play passed on to an applauded conclusion; but there were strings of discontent in the minds of many at the end of the first act. At the end of the second act the discontent was vocal among the auditors. The old bardic tale, with its picturesqueness and chivalry, was evidently undergoing a reversion of the process of bowdlerisation; it was being vulgarised into a mere story of a young man breaking faith with his host and abducting his wife. In addition to this disqualification in the view then prevailing in Ireland, the play disclosed the defects, so contrary to the Irish temperament, of being dull and slow. There were calls for the authors at the final curtain. Yeats, being the less garrulous but more

We Two Together (Madras: Ganesh, 1950) pp. 62–5.

1

explanatory of the duad when opportunity offered, came before the curtain, and spoke of the efforts of the promoters of the Irish Literary Theatre to break down the 'vulgarity' of the English commercial theatre. Some of the audience took this as a subtle joke, and laughed. But Yeats was deadly serious.

Then followed an event unique in the history of an imaginative and active people, the first performance on the regular stage of a play by an Irish author in the Irish language performed by native Irish speakers. In a land of enthusiasm there have been few occasions to excel that one in the expression of a national hope. It had nothing to do with politics: all shades of political opinion were in the auditorium. It had nothing to do with religion: Catholic priests and Protestant parsons sat under the same roof: the actors were Catholics, the author a Protestant. It was a simple upsurge of a unifying wave from the depths of a race's consciousness, and it touched everyone with the joy of regeneration. Something had come to life, something that was experiencing birth in its body and rebirth in its soul. The play that thus opened up the authentic drama of Ireland, that is, drama dealing with the actual life and imagination of the people, written in the speech of the people by one of themselves and played by the people, was a one-act play, *The Twisting of the Rope*, by Dr Douglas Hyde, the President of the Gaelic League,[5] who himself played the part of Hanrahan. This person had set his heart on the girl of a house where he was a caller. It was desired to get rid of him, and a plot to that end was arranged. An imaginary accident made it necessary for a hay-rope to be twisted. Hanrahan's known pride as a rope-twister was played upon, and he was set to work with his back to an open door. As he twisted the rope and bragged and flirted, he had to move backwards, until he finally went through the open doorway. The door was slammed upon him, and the curtain fell on his vociferous curses. A simple story; but its dressing and dialogue and the energy and delight of the actors were irresistible, and a scene of ungovernable enthusiasm followed, in which I too was carried away.

So ended the three annual seasons experiment of the Irish Literary Theatre; and it was manifest that it was not an end but a beginning. It had not brought out any work or author of transcendent dramatic genius; but it had stirred up public expectation, and created a need for national expression and given some indication towards its fulfilment; above all, it had put the Irish language on the stage.[6]

In the week following the last season of the Irish Literary Theatre, on 1 November, 1901, Lady Gregory was 'at home' at 9 Merrion Row to those connected with the adventure. All the celebrities were present. Yeats spoke on 'Art'. The movement was given a social status. But the question some of us asked one another was, whether its 'status' was a 'standing' where it had come to terminus, or the pause that is part of stride.

NOTES

James H. Cousins (1873–1956), poet and playwright. In 1897, he moved from Belfast to Dublin, where he met AE [George Russell], W. B. Yeats, Edward Martyn, Douglas Hyde and other writers of the Irish literary revival. In 1901, he met William G. Fay and Frank Fay, and learning of their desire to produce Irish plays, introduced them to AE, who had written the first act of his *Deirdre*. Cousins wrote a number of plays, among them *The Sleep of the King* (1902), *The Racing Lug* (1902) and *The Sword of Dermot* (1903). Some of his short pieces were poetic versions of Irish short stories and, except in quality, were not unlike some of the early plays of Yeats. Yeats, however, deplored 'too much Cousins', succeeded in squashing a production of Cousins' comedy *Sold*, and firmly detached him from the theatre movement. Cousins is more interesting as a personality than as a writer. Although he was a catalyst in the early days of the Irish theatre movement, he is most memorable as an engaging and enthusiastic eccentric. See Alan Denson, *James H. Cousins and Margaret E. Cousins: A Bio-bibliographical Survey* (Kendal: Alan Denson, 1967), and *Lost Plays of the Irish Renaissance*, ed. Robert Hogan and James Kilroy (Newark, Delaware: Proscenium Press, 1970).

1. The history of modern Irish drama usually begins with the formation of the Irish Literary Theatre in January 1899. In 1897, W. B. Yeats, Lady Gregory and Edward Martyn had met at Duras House, Kinvara, near Galway. The meeting has been considered as momentous as that of Nemerovich-Danchenko and Stanislavski; both gave rise to a new theatre.

2. The first season opened on 8 May 1899; the second, on 19 Feb 1900.

3. The first season opened at the Antient Concert Rooms; the second, at the Gaiety Theatre.

4. On the collaboration between Yeats and George Moore see Ray Small, 'A Critical Edition of *Diarmuid and Grania* by William Butler Yeats and George Moore', Ph.D. dissertation, University of Texas, 1958; and Donald M. Michie, 'A Man of Genius and a Man of Talent', *Texas Studies in Literature and Language*, 6 (Spring 1964) 148–54.

5. The Gaelic League was founded in 1893, with Douglas Hyde (1860–1949) as its moving spirit and first President.

6. *Casadh an tSugáin (The Twisting of the Rope)* was the first Gaelic play to be produced in any theatre. However, 'Tadh Saor', by An tAthair O Laoghaire, had been produced in Maroon in 1900 by Gaelic League members. Also the Fay brothers had produced *Eilis agus an Bhean Deirce*, by Peadar MacFhionlaoich, on 27 Aug 1901 at the Antient Concert Rooms before *Casadh an tSugáin*.

The Irish Literary Theatre*

GEORGE MOORE

The future, if any, of the Irish Literary Theatre has been the subject of much speculation, and of varied prophecy. Whether the experiment of three years holds out sufficient hope to warrant an attempt to establish a permanent theatre; what should be the aims of such a theatre; how to establish it, and how to carry it on are questions discussed with interest by many people. No name has been more prominent in the recent history of the Irish Literary Theatre movement than that of Mr George Moore. The fact that he is something of a storm-centre for criticism lends additional interest to his views. An interview with Mr Moore could not fail to be entertaining reading, so we have interviewed Mr Moore. He is no longer a mere visitor to Dublin, occupying a room in a hotel or a 'pied-à-terre'. He has come over to Ireland for good – for what good time will show us – and is a ratepaying resident with a house in Ely Place.[1] The interview is, as will be seen, somewhat one-sided, the interviewer confining his attention to eliciting Mr Moore's opinions, and giving them as closely as possible in his own words.

INTERVIEWER. In *Samhain* Mr Yeats said[2] that the Irish Literary Theatre has completed its term of three years. If I remember rightly he says that he may be writing an epitaph. Is that a likely contingency?

MR MOORE. I hope not, for the Irish Literary Theatre is the outward sign of the awakening of intellectual life in Ireland. What Mr Yeats meant was that the three years during which we undertook to carry on the theatre whether we succeeded or failed have come to an end. Our success with *Grania*[3] has made the future more safe. We hope to be able to carry on the theatre. We shall try to carry it on until the nation is ripe for a national theatre.

INTERVIEWER. What are your plans for the immediate future?

MR MOORE. We decided this year to produce a play by Dr Douglas Hyde,[4] with Hyde in the principal part, and for next year we are trying to get a play by a priest to produce in our next session. I have written to Father O'Leary for leave to produce his play if possible. He has given me leave, but the play is in several scenes, and will have to be reconstructed, I think.[5]

INTERVIEWER. Will Father O'Leary alter his play for you?

* Freeman's Journal (Dublin), 13 Nov 1901, p. 5.

MR MOORE. That I cannot say. I shall have to write to him on the subject.

INTERVIEWER. There is Father Dinneen; I hear that he has nearly completed a new play?[6]

MR MOORE. So I have heard.

INTERVIEWER. And is your mind set upon a play by a priest?

MR MOORE. If Ireland is to have a national theatre it must be frequented by all classes – by all who believe in Irish nationality. We want to bring the priests into the theatre.

INTERVIEWER. But there is a rule forbidding . . .

MR MOORE. Yes, and that rule I want rescinded. The theatre needs purification. I want to redeem it from the counting-houses and the various immorality that the counting-house brings in its train. The Archbishop has spoken against the detestable musical comedies, but his words lose force, for he is speaking from hearsay.

INTERVIEWER. Am I to understand that you are seeking to establish a censorship?

MR MOORE. Yes; a censorship, and I think I can have no better censor than the Church. I am glad the Irish Literary Theatre has decided to have a play by a priest next year, for I want a censorship. There is no law forbidding a priest to write a play, though he is forbidden to attend the performance of a play.

INTERVIEWER. And the anomaly created by the performance of a priest's play will, you think, result in the rescinding of the established rule?

MR MOORE. I hope so. And with the rescinding of the rule the censorship will come.

INTERVIEWER. But I should have supposed that a censorship would be resented by you – that you would think it likely to interfere, shall I say, with what you call 'the pursuit of art for art's sake'.

MR MOORE. I do not contemplate writing anything the Church will condemn. I am sure Mr Yeats and Mr Martyn do not. I do not know what the committee of the Literary Theatre think about it, but I am convinced that a censorship is necessary. The admirable Middle Ages prove that. I am willing, so far as I am concerned, to submit the national theatre, should it be established, to the censorship of the Church. I plead that in the interests of art the Church may undertake this task. The intelligent censorship of the Church will free the stage from the unintelligent and ignorant censorship of the public, the censorship of those without personal convictions, and of those whose ideas are the conventions and the gossip of the little coterie they frequent. It is from that censorship that I wish to rid the stage, nor is this a new idea of mine. So long as ten years ago I wrote an article[7] defending the London censorship against Mr Archer,[8] who attacked it. The London censorship is a lay censorship, and a lay censorship is almost futility; but the ecclesiastical censorship would be an ideal state of things. It would confer upon art the limitations which art enjoyed in the Middle Ages. I do not approve of the publication of letters in the papers regarding the morality of the stage. I do not believe in these pretences of opinion, for they are not opinions – they are the prejudices of the moment, the gossip of the neighbours. Not one man in a thousand is capable of forming an independent opinion regarding the morality of a work of art. The ordinary man has no time to think on such subjects, and his spasmodic letter of protest does no good. It only attracts people's attention to the consideration of subjects which it would be much better for them not to consider at all. I have noticed that when these letters appear the writers generally protest against plain speech. So long as the conventions and the gossip of Brixton and Rathmines[9] are respected the stage indulges in the most shockingly degrading spectacles. But the moment the dramatist ventures to break the conventions and to disregard the idiom of respectable circles the morality of the play is called into question. It matters not how noble and how faithful the treatment may be. The dramatic critics are not any better than the public. Do they not all think that Mr Pinero has been influenced by Ibsen? As well might you talk of the influence that Michelangelo exercises upon the pavement artist. Now, ecclesiastical censorship would redeem us from all this. Ecclesiastical censorship would put limitations upon art, and art has never suffered from limitations. Art suffers from indefinite licence. Above all ecclesiastical censorship would free us from the intolerable censorship of public opinion regarding morals.

INTERVIEWER. You do not apparently anticipate any quarrel between you and the priest about what is right and wrong in art?

MR MOORE. One quarrels with a fool about art, one never quarrels with an intelligent man about it, whether he is priest or lay man. If any difference of opinion should arise regarding a phrase I should never consider it a hardship to make a sacrifice for someone's convictions. I prefer to make a sacrifice for the sake of someone's convictions than to make a sacrifice for the sake of someone's prejudices or someone's pocket.

INTERVIEWER. Nobody doubts that the cleansing of the stage and the raising of public taste are necessary to the establishment of a national theatre.

MR MOORE. Yes; the stage must be redeemed from the counting-house. Money is the original vice, and it is the placing of the theatre on what is called a commercial basis that has brought about the licence and the vulgarity of the musical comedy. Every year the theatre makes an appeal to the desire of amusement, every year the theatre is moved further out of ideas and more into scenery and stockings. If Shakespeare is presented, scenery and dresses and songs and dances make atonement for the ideas. Some time ago, I think about a month ago, you published a long letter on the subject of a national theatre. Your correspondent at first seemed to me better informed than the usual correspondent is, but the value of his letter was discounted by his suggestion that a national theatre might be run 'on commercial lines'. He spoke of £5000 subscribed, and instanced a theatre in Berlin, and his letter vexed me much, for it was an example of the almost hopeless obtuseness we have to deal with. If this matter is to be discussed we must begin by agreeing that a national theatre is quite a different thing from a brewery, and cannot be expected to pay dividends any more than a national library or a national gallery or Trinity College. The moment a theatre is expected to pay dividends there is nothing for the manager to do except to look out for a musical comedy like *The Shop Girl*, or *The Runaway Girl*, or *Kitty Grey*, or for a farcical comedy like *Charley's Aunt*[10] and to run it as long as it will run in town, and to send out companies to gather up all that money that can be gathered in the villages. If the question of the national theatre is to be discussed, let all those who discuss it be agreed regarding one thing, that a national theatre gives people an interest in the town in which they live, and that it is an educational and ennobling influence, and far more necessary, more far-reaching in its effects than a picture gallery, or even a library. Although the national theatre will not pay dividends upon the money subscribed, any more than Shamrock II, a national theatre would be of enormous pecuniary value to Dublin. Some months ago I raised this question in your columns;[11] I pointed out that we poor Dubliners, overtaxed, exhausted by unjust financial burdens as we are, are not only foolish to buy goods that the foreigners import into this country, but foolish enough to pay, perhaps, £150,000 a year to English companies for our amusements. The national theatre would be supported by the priests, and would gradually bring about the ruin of these travelling companies who take, at least – think of it – £150,000 a year out of Ireland; and a national theatre would not only stop this leakage, but it would give employment to a number of young people with talent for acting, for scene-painting, for writing and for music. I have been criticised lately for accepting the most beautiful music from an English musician.[12] I was told I should have paid an Irishman to write the music for me. When Dublin has decided to stop this fearful leak of £150,000 a year, and to amuse itself, instead of importing amusements, it will have the right to tell me that (if I should be with the management of the national theatre) I must employ more native talent, actors, scene-painters, and musicians. No one will be more willing to comply with this demand than I shall be; no one will recognise its justice more completely. The present moment is opportune for such a theatre. The national language is being revived.

Dr Hyde's play was an enormous success; it delighted everyone; and, as I am being very much criticised at this moment, I will take this opportunity of saying that I knew how to make sacrifices for the language. I remained in Dublin to rehearse Dr Hyde's play, instead of going to Birmingham to rehearse Mr Yeats' and my own. I was determined that at all costs Dr Hyde's play should be well performed. Everything has to be paid for, and I can say with truth that it was I who paid for the admirable performance of the Irish play. But to return to the matter in hand – the establishment of a national theatre. The plays performed there would be performed under the direct censorship of the Church. They would consist of selections from the masterpieces of the world, some Russian, some Flemish, some Scandinavian, some French masterpieces, but the central idea of the theatre would be the restoration of the Irish language. A short Irish play would be given constantly, perhaps every night. I daresay some enthusiasts would wish the whole of the performance to be in Irish, and would denounce the theatre because it was not. I am afraid these people would cause me many a sigh, and not a little irritation, but these enthusiasts would be useful, and though they sometimes prove a little trying, we would not be without them.[13]

INTERVIEWER. Now, Mr Moore, will you tell me how you propose to get money for this national theatre?

MR MOORE. It would be an easier thing for me to tell you first about how much it would cost. I think I could manage to do a great deal if the theatre were given to us rent free, rates, gas and policing paid for us, and a subscription of a thousand a year. Sir Thomas Lipton spent a quarter of a million of money trying to do something which is already forgotten, building a vessel which no one would live in, a sort of toy boat which is now up for sale. For this sum of money he could have given London an endowed theatre equal to the Comédie Française; for much less he could give Dublin a national theatre, and a national theatre would secure to a man much more permanent and more vital immortality than a museum or a picture gallery, or I may say anything else in the world.

INTERVIEWER. Then your hope, Mr Moore, is in the millionaire?

MR MOORE. I cannot say that it is. Money is vice, and he who has got money does not see far; his sight is short. A university would not reach as many as a theatre, whose concern was with ideas, whose ambition was to present life from a high, noble, intellectual point of view. I am afraid it will take some time for the Corporation to see that a theatre of the kind I have indicated would be of great moral, intellectual and pecuniary benefit to Dublin. But one never knows from what side help may come. I do not think I have got anything more to say on this question.

INTERVIEWER. But you have not told me, Mr Moore, what are your plans for the next performance to be given by the Irish Literary Theatre.

MR MOORE. Mr Martyn has written a new play, *The Enchanted Sea*,[14] I think that this should be performed. I saw him last night on the subject, and I told him that we were all agreed that this play should be performed. I proposed to him the revival of *The Heather Field*,[15] because this play when originally acted in the Antient Concert Rooms was a very great success. I think the revival of the play would prove more successful. I think every one would like to see it again. I should like to see *The Heather Field* performed for three nights and *The Enchanted Sea* for three nights, and I should like to see *The Heather Field* preceded or followed by a play in Irish by Father O'Leary, and I should like to see *The Enchanted Sea* preceded or followed by a play by Father Dinneen. I am now awaiting Mr Martyn's answer.[16]

NOTES

The Irish Literary Theatre was founded on 16 Jan 1899 by W. B. Yeats, Lady Gregory and Edward Martyn, who were later joined by George Moore (1852–1933). Its history is well known and has been well told by the original leaders and founders. W. B. Yeats and Lady Gregory both wrote accounts of various parts of it in *Dramatis Personae* and *Our Irish Theatre*, respectively. George Moore contributed full description of certain episodes in *Hail and Farewell*, though his impression of events does not necessarily tally with those of his colleagues.

1. Moore had been living in London. By 1901, however, circumstances had compounded to make the move to Ireland – his 'messianic mission', as he called it – very attractive. From 1901 to 1911, he lived at 4 Ely Place, adjacent to St Stephen's Green, East. Although he left Ireland again in 1911, Ireland and Irish speech rhythms coloured much of his work thereafter.

2. W. B. Yeats, 'Windlestraws', *Samhain* (Dublin and London), no. 1 (Oct 1901) 3.

3. *Dairmuid and Grania*, by George Moore and W. B. Yeats, had its first production by the Irish Literary Theatre on 21 Oct 1901.

4. Douglas Hyde (1860–1949), scholar, poet, translator, founder of the Gaelic League and first President of the Republic of Ireland. His play *Casadh an tSugáin* [The Twisting of the Rope] – the first Gaelic play to be produced in any theatre – had its première by the Irish Literary Theatre on 21 Oct 1901.

5. Father P. O'Leary's play was not produced by the Irish Literary Theatre. However, Joseph Holloway recorded on 14 Feb 1903 in his *Impressions of a Dublin Playgoer* that a performance was organised by the Central Branch of the Gaelic League and that 'the audience was sufficiently lulled to rest to be sufficiently awake to enjoy the homely humours of Father O'Leary' comedy . . . *An Sprid* [*The Ghost*]'. See *Joseph Holloway's Abbey Theatre: A Selection from His Unpublished Journal 'Impressions of a Dublin Playgoer'*, ed. Robert Hogan and Michael J. O'Neill.

6. The Irish Literary Theatre did not produce any play by Father Dinneen.

However, in 1901 W. G. Fay directed Dinneen's *An Tobar Draoidheacta* [*The Enchanted Well*] for an autumn *feis* organised by Cumann na nGaedheal in which members of the Ormond Dramatic Society took part.

7. 'The Dramatic Censorship', *New Review* (London), Oct 1890, pp. 354–62.

8. William Archer (1856–1924), English drama critic.

9. Brixton is a district in London; Rathmines, in Dublin.

10. *The Shop Girl* (1894), by Henry J. W. Dam; *The Runaway Girl* (1898), by Seymour Hicks and H. Nichols; ?*Kitty Clive* (1895), by F. Frankfort Moore; and *Charley's Aunt* (1892), by Brandon Thomas. Dates are of first performances.

11. George Moore, 'The Irish Literary Theatre', *Freeman's Journal* (Dublin), 24 Apr 1901, p. 4.

12. Edward Elgar (1857–1934), who wrote, at Moore's request, the incidental music, including the 'Funeral March', for *Diarmuid and Grania*. In an earlier interview – 'Mr George Moore and Irish Composers', *Weekly Freeman* (Dublin), 21 Sept 1901 – Moore had given a detailed explanation of the choice. See also Eileen Kennedy, 'George Moore to Edward Elgar', *English Literature in Transition*, 21, no. 3 (1978) 168–87.

13. On the same day of this interview, however, the *Freeman's Journal* published a leading article which attempted to refute a number of Moore's points. 'It seemed that no matter what rigorously patriotic or moral stance Moore might adopt, he could never quite hope to quell the suspicions which his previous writings and reputation had aroused in his countrymen' (Robert Hogan and James Kilroy, *The Irish Literary Theatre*, 1899–1901 (Dublin: Dolmen Press, 1975) p. 125.

14. *The Enchanted Sea*, by Edward Martyn, was presented for the first time by the Players' Club at the Antient Concert Rooms on 18 Apr 1904.

15. *The Heather Field*, by Edward Martyn, opened by the Irish Literary Theatre at the Antient Concert Rooms on 9 May 1899.

16. For more on the Irish Literary Theatre see Denis Gwynn, 'The Irish Literary Theatre', in *Edward Martyn and the Irish Revival* (London: Jonathan Cape, 1930), pp. 109–70; Hogan and Kilroy, *The Irish Literary Theatre*; Harold Williams, 'The Irish Literary Theatre', in *Modern English Writers* (London: Sidgwick & Jackson, 1925) pp. 193–6; Stephen Gwynn, 'The Irish Literary Theatre and Its Affinities', *Fortnightly Review* (London), 76 (Dec 1901) 1050–62; George O'Neill, 'The Inauguration of the Irish Literary Theatre', *New Ireland Review* (Dublin), 11 (June 1899) 246–52; Moira L. Ray, 'Birth of Ireland's National Drama', *Theatre Magazine* (New York), 3 (July 1903) 167–8; W. B. Yeats, 'Plans and Methods', *Beltaine* (London), no. 1 (May 1899) 6–9; W. B. Yeats, 'Irish Literary Theatre', *Irish Literary Society Gazette* (London), 1 (June 1899) 5–7; and J. A. A. Stokes, 'The Non-Commercial Theatres in London and Paris in the Late Nineteenth Century and the Origins of the Irish Literary Theatre and Its Successors', Ph.D. dissertation, University of Reading, 1968.

How Our Theatre Began*

SEUMAS O'SULLIVAN

Great things were happening at the turn of the last century. AE[1] and Horace Plunkett,[2] with the Agricultural Organisation Society; Griffith,[3] with the young giant, *Sinn Fein* (still in its cradle, but already with more than one slain serpent to its credit), the Fay brothers,[4] with the beginnings of what should have been a national theatre. The air was, indeed, to use the worn-out phrase, electric. 'It was the best of times; it was the worst of times.'

Our theatres were flooded with the third-rate overflow of the London stage, but the Fay brothers were already getting into their stride. Many books have been written on the Irish National Theatre, but they have one and all made the initial, and, to me, unforgivable, mistake of attributing the movement to one man only.

Yeats had, it is true, in 1899, with his performance of *The Countess Cathleen* in the Antient Concert Rooms,[5] directed our thoughts to the possibility of producing plays by Irish authors in Dublin; but his company consisted entirely of English men and English women. That first performance of *The Countess Cathleen* was, nevertheless, a memorable occasion.

'The event', writes Ernest Boyd, 'was marked by one of those demonstrations of aesthetic illiteracy which have from time to time conferred a certain notoriety upon works deserving of more serious fame. The first charge was based upon the language of the demons, the second upon the theme itself. It was argued that no Irish woman would sell her soul to the devil, and that the personages of the play, natural and supernatural, referred in too irreverent fashion to sacred subjects.'[6]

I was, by chance, in the gallery, and at the fall of the curtain a storm of booing and hissing broke out around the seats in which I and a few enthusiasts were attempting to express our appreciation of the magnificent performance. But close to me, and at the time unknown to me, was a lad who vigorously contributed his share to the applause. It was James Joyce, who was later on to face an even greater storm of disapproval when he published his *Ulysses*.

In the following year the Literary Theatre continued its good work

---

*Condensed from *The Rose and the Bottle* (Dublin: Talbot Press, 1946) pp. 116–26. Editor's title.

with the production of George Moore's *The Bending of the Bough*,[7] Martyn's *Maeve* and *The Last Feast of the Fianna*,[8] by Alice Milligan; and in 1901 I was present in the Gaiety Theatre when the Literary Theatre gave their final performance – *Diarmuid and Grania*, by Yeats and Moore, and the *Casadh an tSugáin* of Douglas Hyde.

No praise can be too high for Yeats and those who were with him against every opposition and difficulty during those three years of pioneer work. But the real beginning of a national theatre came in 1902, when, in a little hall in Clarendon Street, the brothers Fay produced *Kathleen Ni Houlihan*, by Yeats, and AE's *Deirdre*.[9] Those who had the privilege of being present on that occasion will remember it as long as they live.

I have never since seen an audience so moved as when Madam MacBride, who played the title role in Yeats' play, spoke the closing words as she turned away from the cottage door. I was with Arthur Griffith, and I can still see his face as he stood up at the fall of the final curtain to join in the singing of what was then our national anthem – *A Nation Once Again*.

On the same evening I was first introduced to the Fay brothers and to the other members of the little company, and when they repeated their performance, in the Antient Concert Rooms, I, too, was 'impressed' into the cast,[10] and after a gruelling course of 'voice-production', etc., at the hands of Frank Fay, made my bow as an actor in the part of Ainle in AE's *Deirdre*.

Most of our rehearsal work was done, at this time, in a house in High Street, but in 1903 [*sic*][11] we managed to secure a little hall behind a grocer's shop in Camden Street, and here we set to work seriously on the preparation of plays by Column and Synge and others. All the 'set pieces', scenery and even the forms on which the audience were to sit, had to be made by ourselves. Very often the actors at the far end had to raise their voices to drown the noise of hammer and saw. But it was all glorious enjoyment, and we were, I think, convinced that our enthusiasm was, indeed, 'making history'.

In addition to the members of the company, who never failed to turn up on rehearsal nights, and generally after a full day's work at their respective jobs, we had other visitors. John B. Yeats[12] would sometimes turn up after his day in the studio, and Synge, who was then living in Rathmines, and George Moore, too, came there to read out French verse or prose as he thought it should be spoken, for Frank Fay was almost fanatical in his worship of the French stage.

Yeats, of course, was a frequent visitor, and so was Lady Gregory, although as a rule Lady Gregory preferred the comfort of the Nassau Hotel. She was a most hospitable hostess, and refreshed the company with claret cup – even, on special occasions, champagne.

Sometimes, on summer evenings, Fay used to bring his company out to the hills above Dublin, to 'try out' our speeches across the little stream that runs by the foot of Kilmashoge. At that time the only way of getting to our chosen place on the hillside was by train to Dundrum, and from that on foot to Kilmashoge. One such evening, as we players of 'minor' parts were toiling up the steep hillside, we were overtaken and passed by a *vis-à-vis*, in which were seated Dudley Digges, Marie Quinn (afterwards Mrs Dudley Digges), and one or two others of our 'star' actors and actresses, and I can still hear our ribald rejoinders as they waved to us magnificently from their carriaged ease.

But we were in truth a very democratic company. All had their particular work to do, and all did it consistently and enthusiastically. No theatrical company was ever freer from those jealousies and bickerings which mar so many projects – especially of the histrionic sort. This I am inclined to attribute to two facts. First, that no member of the company was paid. Second, that every member of the company had a vote in its conduct and proceedings. On two occasions we wandered further afield – inaugurated, in fact, the idea of a touring company, which was later to prove so successful with the Abbey Players.

On the first occasion we gave an open-air performance of *Deirdre* in the grounds of the beautiful old house, Dun Emer, near Dundrum – a house which is now famous as the original home of the Dun Emer Press, and of the Dun Emer Guild, which is still producing rugs and carpets known the world over.

Another performance of *Deirdre*, and with it Yeats' *The Pot of Broth*, was given at the Town Hall in Loughrea. This last was a glorious expedition. I can still remember the magnificent 'spread' which was prepared for us by the hospitable parish priest and his curates. As we sat there eating and drinking of the best, we heard the ringing of a bell in the street, and looking out through the window we saw the town-crier walking solemnly, with bell in hand, and shouting in a voice well-trained for the purpose the announcement that the players from Dublin were that night performing in Loughrea Town Hall.

On the following morning our generous hosts had, we found, provided for us a pair of carriages, in which we drove in state around that 'Grey Lake' which has been immortalised by Seumas O'Kelly in his novel, *The Lady of Deerpark*.

NOTES

Seumas O'Sullivan [James Sullivan Starkey] (1879–1958), poet, bibliophile, a leading and influential figure in the Irish literary revival, and a friend of Arthur Griffith, James Joyce, George Russell, Oliver Gogarty and W. B. Yeats. In 1923 he founded the *Dublin Magazine*. See L. A. G. Strong, 'Seumas O'Sullivan', *Irish Writing* (Cork), no. 13 (Dec 1950) 54–8.

1. AE [George William Russell] (1867–1935), poet and painter, and friend of Yeats. He joined the Irish Agricultural Organisation Society under Sir Horace Plunkett in 1897 and became editor of its organ, *The Irish Homestead* (1905–23). His gifts as a writer and publicist gained it a wide influence in the cause of agricultural cooperation. From 1923 to 1930 he was editor of the *Irish Statesman*.

2. Sir Horace Curzon Plunkett (1854–1932), pioneer of agricultural cooperation, and first President of the Irish Agricultural Organisation Society in 1894.

3. Arthur Griffith (1871–1922), political leader and first President of the Irish Free State. He founded and edited the *United Irishman*, which he used to preach failure of the Home Rule policy and to demand total separation from Britain. When it ceased publication in 1906 as a result of a libel action, he started a new paper, *Sinn Fein*.

4. William George Fay and Frank Fay.

5. The Antient Concert Rooms in Great Brunswick Street (now Pearse Street) later became the Academy Cinema.

6. Ernest Boyd, *The Contemporary Drama of Ireland* (Dublin: Talbot Press; London: T. Fisher Unwin, 1918) p. 58. One sentence, however, is omitted from the quotation after 'serious fame': 'A politician, a cardinal, and a newspaper combined forces in order to stir up opposition to the play, on the ground that it was blasphemous and unpatriotic.'

7. *The Bending of the Bough* was presented for the first time by the Irish Literary Theatre at the Gaiety Theatre on 20 Feb 1900.

8. *Maeve* and *The Last Feast of the Fianna* were performed for the first time by the Irish Literary Theatre at the Gaiety Theatre on 22 Feb 1900.

9. *Kathleen Ni Houlihan* and *Deirdre* had their premières by W. G. Fay's Irish National Dramatic Society in St Teresa's Hall, Clarendon Street, on 2 Apr 1902. After these performances the Fays decided to make a permanent society of plays; and so, in Aug 1902, the Irish National Theatre Society was founded, its President being W. B. Yeats.

10. There were in the company some who were simply 'impressed' into acting, because there were no others to be obtained.

11. August 1902, actually.

12. John B. Yeats (1839–1922), painter; father of W. B. Yeats. He painted several of the leading personalities of the Irish dramatic movement, and the paintings still adorn the lobby of the Abbey Theatre.

How We Began the Abbey*

W. G. FAY

When Seumas O'Sullivan saw at the Antient Concert Rooms, Dublin, the first performance of W. B. Yeats' verse play, *The Countess Cathleen*, amongst the audience was James Joyce. What neither of them was aware of, as they watched the performance of *The Countess Cathleen*, was that it was to be responsible for the formation of the Irish Players and the founding of the Abbey Theatre.

Appreciation of poetry was not one of my best points at that time, but my brother Frank insisted that for the good of my soul I should come with him to see the play. It was a fatal suggestion, for it led to our inflicting on our innocent country a theatre which it did not want.

For a performance on a fit-up stage of a verse play it was very much hampered, but it got over and we enjoyed it. However, on our way home we came to the conclusion it would have been much more effective if the actors knew what they were talking about. Frank said that if there was to be a modern Irish drama at all it must be played by Irish actors, for English actors could never get the atmosphere right.[1] As chief of the Ormond Dramatic Society[2] he believed that if we could get a play his team could give a performance that would be 'Irish and proud of it too!' I said: 'Let's go to it.'

He kept well informed of all theatrical events both in England and on the continent and told me how a clerk in a Parisian gas works who, with some friends, wanted to act but had no money, managed to hire a small hall in Montmartre and began productions that in a few years were so successful that Antoine[3] was able to open a theatre in Paris – the Théâtre Libre. If Antoine could do it in Paris, why could not the same idea be used in Dublin?

Some time later a friend of Frank's drew his attention to two acts of a play called *Deirdre*, published in Standish O'Grady's *All Ireland Review*, signed AE, which, his friend said, was the pen name of George Russell. When I read it I saw at once that, given a third act, it was just the sort of material the Ormond Dramatic could give a production, and suggested he should interview Mr Russell, whom he had met at Lady Gregory's with Mr Yeats.

It was useless, for AE told Frank that he had no knowledge of, or interest in, the theatre. He wrote because he wanted to see what the

Irish Digest (Dublin), 28 (Oct 1947) 30–2.

greatest of 'The Three Sorrows of Story Telling' would look like in play form. It was a great blow to us, but Frank said to me: 'I've tried; now you go and see if you can persuade him. I'll fix an interview for you.'

My principal reading from the time I was fifteen was the Restoration drama, which we could buy off the stalls on the quay at twopence a copy – bound in calf and tooled in gold – and that, helped by cutting and altering plays on tour when we had not enough cast to play them completely, made me a not inefficient play doctor.

I very nervously agreed to visit AE and try to get him to finish the play, and met for the first time a man who was to be an inspiration to me for the rest of my life. When AE told me the background of the *Deirdre* story it was quite evident that the third act was the return to Ireland of Fergus with Deirdre and the sons of Usna; their murder by Concobar; and the death of Deirdre. We roughed out a scenario and he promised to finish the play.

We had a play. How could we produce it? Frank put in £5 and I emptied the teapot and found another five. So the original finance of the Irish National Theatre was £10!

Where could we stage it? We had played many times to help the Temperance Society attached to St Teresa's, Clarendon Street. They had a large hall with a good stage. We asked if we could have the use of it for a week. We could have it for a month and welcome!

When W. B. Yeats heard we were going to stage *Deirdre* he offered us a short play he had written, called *Kathleen Ni Houlihan*, on condition that Maud Gonne (Madam MacBride) played Kathleen. What a bit of luck for us! Miss Gonne was the living embodiment of Kathleen.

I made the scenery and painted the cottage. AE designed the costumes, made by Helen Laird[4] assisted by Miss Gonne, and painted the sets for *Deirdre*. Strenuous days followed, for we could only work in the evenings when time was our own, but on Wednesday, 2 April 1902, at St Teresa's Hall, Clarendon Street, Dublin, W. G. Fay's Irish National Theatre Company[5] produced *Deirdre*, a play in three acts by AE, followed by Miss Maud Gonne in *Kathleen Ni Houlihan*, by W. B. Yeats.

The production was so successful that we determined to keep together and we formed the Irish National Theatre Society to produce Irish plays. The President was AE; Vice-Presidents, Miss Maud Gonne and Dr Douglas Hyde; Secretary, Fred Ryan, and the following members: Maire T. Quinn, Maire Nic Shiubhlaigh, Helen Laird, Seumas O'Sullivan, George Roberts, Frank J. Fay, Dudley Digges, P. J. Kelly, T. Keohler, J. H. Cousins, Padraic Colum, Henry Norman, Frank Walker and W. G. Fay.

Having formed a society, the next thing was to find a location, which we did at 34 Lower Camden Street. A bare hall at the back of a provision merchant's on the one side and a butcher's shop on the other, made it a perilous voyage for the audience to reach the box-office on a Saturday night.

We had to make our own stage, scenery and seats, but we produced four [*sic*]⁶ plays there before we decided it would only do for rehearsals. We then produced plays at the Molesworth Hall, making the receipts of one show pay for the next.

The production of W. B. Yeats' verse play⁷ brought his friend, Miss A. E. F. Horniman, over to Dublin to design the costumes and pay for the making of them. She grew interested in our adventure and came again to costume *On Baile's Strand*, the play that opened the Abbey Theatre, for which she had paid £7000.

The first time we met, during conversation I asked her if her hotel was comfortable. She said it was. At breakfast her table was a bit rickety and she called the waitress's attention to it. The girl said: 'It's real sorry I am, ma'am', crossed to the sideboard, cut a thick slice of bread and propped it under the short leg.

The next time she visited us I asked if the bread was still there. She said: 'Yes, but they have toasted it!'

NOTES

William George Fay (1872–1947), with his brother Frank, set out to make a career on the stage and formed their own small company. They joined Yeats and Lady Gregory in founding the Abbey Theatre and evolved the style of acting identified with it. After a difference with the Abbey directors in 1908, the Fays went to the United States and produced a repertory of Irish plays. See Gabriel Fallon, 'The Genius of W. G. Fay', *Irish Monthly* (Dublin), 75 (Dec 1949), 505–8; T. G. K[eller], 'The Fays of the Abbey Theatre', *Dublin Magazine*, 10 (Oct 1935) 89–90; Gabriel Fallon, 'Tribute to the Fays', *Irish Monthly* (Dublin), 73 (Jan 1945) 18–24; and W. G. Fay and Catherine Carswell, *The Fays of the Abbey Theatre: An Autobiographical Record* (London: Rich & Cowan, 1935).

1. In 'The Irish Literary Theatre', *United Irishman* (Dublin), 6 (2 Nov 1901) 2, Frank Fay argued against English actors performing Irish plays.

2. For a while the Fay brothers took on the stage names of W. G. Ormond and Frank Evelyn, and in 1892 the name 'Ormond Dramatic Society' was adopted for their company. In 1902, the 'W. G. Fay's Irish National Dramatic Company' was founded.

3. André Antoine (1858–1943), the first of the distinguished line of directors. His Théâtre Libre, founded in 1887, operated for only nine seasons, but this period was long enough to establish his revolution and to create a standard for the type of realistic production which is the basis of the modern French theatre.

4. Helen S. Laird [Honor Lavelle] was also one of the first official founders of the Irish National Theatre Society.

5. The company was called W. G. Fay's Irish National Dramatic Company.

After the success of these performances, the Fays decided to make a permanent society of players; and so the Irish National Theatre Society was founded.

6. Not four plays, but three. The playbill for the performances of the Irish National Theatre Society on 4, 5 and 6 Dec 1902 announces the programme as: *The Laying of the Foundations*, by Fred Ryan; *The Pot of Broth*, by W. B. Yeats; and *Elis agus an Bhean Deirce*, by P[eadar] T. Mac Fhionnlaoich.

7. It is not clear what Fay means by 'verse play' since he does not say 'latest verse play'. Actually, the play was *The King's Threshold*, first staged at the Molesworth Hall on 1 Oct 1903. Miss Horniman financed the production, designed and made the costumes.

The National Theatre Society*

GEORGE ROBERTS

The foundation members of the Irish National Theatre Society [*sic*][1] were: W. G. Fay, Frank Fay, Dudley Digges, P. J. Kelly, Maire [Mary] Walker, Sara Allgood, Maire T. Quinn, Padraic Colum, Fred Ryan, James H. Cousins, James Starkey, George Roberts, George Russell [AE], Frank Walker.

The election of officers was then proceeded with. There was some discussion as to whether AE or W. B. Yeats should be elected President, and it was subsequently decided to approach W. B. Yeats. Dr Douglas Hyde, Maud Gonne and Edward Martyn were proposed as Vice-Presidents, but Martyn declined. The first need of the new society was a hall, and W. G. Fay was strongly in favour of obtaining one, however small, which we could rent and in which we could give performances. After some search we found a little place in Camden Street, which was made by roofing over a yard, at the back of a provision shop. It measured about twenty feet by forty, and we obtained it for a rental of 10 shillings a week. Almost immediately arrangements were made with Cumann nGaedheal[2] for us to take part in a week's performance at their Samhain festival.

The Irish National Theatre Society, although founded as stated, did not give any performances until the Samhain festival was finished. These performances were given by the Fays' original Irish Dramatic Company. The plays given at the Samhain festival were:

Irish Times (Dublin), 14 July 1955, p. 5.

Tuesday, 28 October 1902 – *Deirdre*, by AE; *Kathleen Ni Houlihan*, by W. B. Yeats.

Wednesday, 29 October 1902 – *The Sleep of the King*, by J. H. Cousins; *The Laying of the Foundations*, by Fred Ryan.[3]

Thursday, 30 October 1902 – *The Pot of Broth*, by W. B. Yeats; *Deirdre*, by AE.

Friday, 31 October 1902 – *The Racing Lug*, by J. H. Cousins; *The Laying of the Foundations*, by Fred Ryan.

Saturday, 1 November 1902 – *The Laying of the Foundations*, by Fred Ryan; *Kathleen Ni Houlihan*, by W. B. Yeats; *The Pot of Broth*, by W. B. Yeats.

Artisans

For these performances we netted £60, and it was decided we should fit up our little hall with a stage, curtains and seating accommodation, and hold performances there. Seating was our first problem, but Willie Fay, with his admirable resource, discovered where casts to form the iron framework of seats could be obtained very cheaply. Accordingly, we ordered a quantity of these, and some timber, and for the next few weeks all the male members of the company became carpenters – except Frank Fay, who looked with impatience at the interruptions of his teaching us to get all our energy and resource in bawling 'Oh' and 'Ah.'

It was doubtless this state of affairs which gave rise to the legend that the company was formed of a number of artisans. I was much amused in hearing myself referred to in a newspaper paragraph as a foreman carpenter. Yeats often referred to us to his English friends as 'The Artisans' Theatre'.

Our Theatre

As soon as we had the seats finished we gave a performance in our 'own' hall, or as we proudly called it 'our theatre', putting on *The Laying of the Foundations* and *The Pot of Broth*. Judging by the audiences we had at St Teresa's Hall and the Samhain festival and the small size of our theatre, we carefully made ample provision for several members to be at the door to prevent overcrowding; but we were bitterly disappointed when two ladies of the general public made a noisy entrance by knocking over a pile of empty boxes in the narrow passage of the provision shop. As the making-up and dressing had to be accomplished behind the scenery at the side of the stage, and the scene-shifting and dressing went on simultaneously, performing under these conditions was more than even our enthusiasm could endure, so the idea of holding further performances here was abandoned, and we decided to use the hall for rehearsal only and to use the Molesworth Hall for performances.

About this time we were invited to play at Loughrea by an unconventional priest, Father O'Donovan.[4] We arrived at Loughrea one Saturday morning and had arranged for two performances, one in the afternoon and one in the evening. We played *Deirdre* and *Kathleen Ni Houlihan* and *The Pot of Broth*.

The next morning we were to meet Yeats, who had come with us, at the hall. Yeats read to us extracts from *The King's Threshold*, a play he was then writing. The atmosphere of the hall became so stuffy that he attempted to open the window which had apparently not been opened since the hall was built, and a small portion of the window frame came away in his hands. This incident appeared in his next volume of essays dealing with '*The Decay of Life in Ireland*,' where he says: 'I was in the West of Ireland, and on attempting to open a window the whole casement came away in my hand'[5] – a typical example of Yeats' overstatement.

To London

We were amazed when later we received an invitation to play in London. It came from Stephen Gwynn, the Secretary of the Irish Literary Society in London. We accepted this in fear and trembling. It was one thing to give performances to a few people whom we all more or less knew, but to face the London critics was a horse of another colour. However, in spite of Frank Fay's moody prognostications, we resolved to take the opportunity, and to hell with the consequences.

Crossing the channel by night (most of us were limited for time because of our daily jobs), Frank Fay spent the time in pacing the deck to and fro in most violent agitation, and if anyone of us had the temerity to speak to him he snarled an inarticulate reply. But not so Willie, who was in great heart, laughing and joking with all the members of the company and ready to face an audience of 10,000. We duly arrived in London and put up in a small hotel in Soho. Having left our baggage there we went to inspect the Queen's Gate Hall,[6] where we were to play. Though this was larger than our own hall in Dublin, our voices carried quite well to the back of the gallery, and this restored Frank Fay's good humour.

We then all became so busy making preparations for the first house on Saturday afternoon that in our hurry and excitement our nervousness was completely forgotten. We scarcely had time even to think where we were until we found ourselves on the stage, and then we slogged into it. Were we not performing to a London audience! Were not the foremost critics of the day there to slate us! Well, we were out to dour damndest and to hell with anyone who shirked.

The next morning we all met at breakfast. The man selling newspapers readily disposed of all his stock, and we settled down expecting to be either damned, or worse still, to get a little indulgent patting on the back. But no. The critics were full of praise. William Archer wrote in the *World*: 'It is a weakness of mine to be intolerant of the amateur in art. . . . Consequently it was not without misgiving that I went to the Queen's Gate Hall to witness a performance . . . by the Irish National Theatre Society. . . . I remained, if not to pray, at any rate, to applaud and admire with the utmost sincerity. In almost all of them there was a clear vein of talent, while the work they presented was all of it interesting, and some of it exquisitely and movingly beautiful.'[7]

NOTES

George Roberts (1873–1953), one of the founders of the Irish National Theatre Society and its first Secretary. 'The Roberts Papers', comprising letters, notebooks, etc., are in the National Library of Ireland.

1. Actually, the name of 'Irish National Theatre Society' was not adopted until Aug 1902. The group first called itself the 'Irish National Dramatic Company' or the 'Irish National Dramatic Society'.

2. A political party, later called Fine Gael.

3. Roberts omits *Eilis agus an Bhean Deirce*, which played on 29 and 31 October 1902.

4. Probably Father Jeremiah O'Donovan (1871–1942) [the novelist Gerald O'Donovan], who served as administrator of the Loughrea parish from 1897 to 1904, and who was a prominent member of the Irish Agricultural Organisation Society. The year of the visit was 1903.

5. *Discoveries* (1906), in *Essays and Introductions* (New York: Macmillan, 1961) p. 261.

6. On 2 May 1903, the Irish National Theatre Society, under the auspices of the London Irish Literary Society, performed the following plays from the repertoire at the Queen's Gate Hall, South Kensington, London: *The Hour-Glass*, *Twenty-Five* and *Kathleen Ni Houlihan* (matinee); *Kathleen Ni Houlihan*, *The Pot of Broth* and *The Laying of the Foundations* (evening).

7. William Archer, 'Irish Plays', *World* (London), 12 May 1903, 784–5.

The Irish Theatre Movement: Some Early Memories*

T. G. KELLER

I have often thought that it would be interesting to jot down some memories of the beginnings of the Irish theatrical movement, which resulted in the establishment of the Abbey Theatre, as I was casually connected with it from the start.

I have a natural antogonism to dates, and as I have no written or printed records of any sort, these notes must be of quite an informal nature. They will be merely the setting down of little incidents and items caught in the net of memory. Big things often pass us by unnoticed, while trifles sometimes stick as a life-long possession.

Energetic Brothers

My dominant memory of those days is of the buoyant, effervescent, indoubtable energy of the Fay brothers. They were the motive power that moulded the Irish theatrical movement at its source. Whatever it possesses of strength or weakness at the present time may be traced to their influence. For above all the Fays were great personalities, and they impressed themselves imperishably on a theatre development which has since flung itself all over the world.

Frank Fay was the Napoleon of this little missionary theatre group. His word was law, and, loyally aided by his brother, he saw that it was carried out. He was fundamentally and temperamentally a classic. He knew what tragedy and comedy were, as interpreted by the masterminds of his art. He really wanted nothing new, only the old august, mellowed triumphs of established art. But his standards of excellence were astonishingly high, and he never faltered in his insight, even when working with the raw, fresh, crude material (in actors) with which he had to deal.

W. G. Fay was almost in every respect the exact opposite of his brother, except in his devotion to theatre art – a consuming point of

* *Sunday Independent* (Dublin), 6 Jan 1929, p. 7.

interest in which they were both united. But while Frank was cautious, careful, anxious, almost to a fault, Willie was the very incarnation of the seemingly easy-going, take-it-as-it-comes, nature; with this little difference that under his apparent pliability there was a sort of canny circumspection that knew almost unconsciously what it wanted, and invariably managed to get it. And the goal of his insouciance was exactly the same as that of his more serious-minded brother. It was the excellence of classic art. But while Frank was satisfied with the compact realisation of normal tragedy or comedy, Willie added the illusory ray of romantic imagination – a ray that destroys most of its devotees, but when caught reveals a new star in the theatrical firmament.

A Modest Birthplace

It was in the little hall in Camden Street that I first felt the invigorating power of the Fays. This was the merest ramshackle construction in one of Dublin's busy but poor-class streets. And yet many pioneer spirits of the day, attracted by the vitalising art magnetism that radiated from the Fays, found their way there. One or two public performances were given there, but were not encouraging. I do not wonder, because the stage and the auditorium were both equally bleak and desolate. But it really achieved its right to a fundamental position in the history of the twentieth-century theatrical movement in Ireland by the fact that, while it lasted, it was a centre and meeting-place for anyone interested in creative art.

The little rickety notice-board of rehearsals and other matters soon became crowded with sketches of the actors done by visiting artists. AE [George Russell], a constant attendant, was responsible for many of these, which are now treasured possessions of various people interested in the movement. Gradually these pictures overflowed the bounds of the notice-board, and soon the walls were dotted with a remarkable assemblage of lightning impressions of rehearsals and portraits of the leading personalities.

Joyce as Tenor Singer

There was a piano there, and occasionally the now famous Mr James Joyce, wandering in, would be induced to sing, displaying a tenor voice of rare quality. But Joyce was always careful to disassociate himself from the movement.[1] He probably failed to sense the reality of its mission. And when he left Dublin he was particular to emphasise this fact in the farewell poem he had printed and distributed to his friends. In this he stated:

> But I must not accounted be
> One of that mumming company.

And then he picked out in delicate outline the idiosyncracies of one or two of the leading members, who happened to be poets like himself.

Budding Dramatist

Padraic Colum and James H. Cousins, both poets and dramatists, were members from the beginning, and were frequently to be seen. Fred Ryan, a democrat and litterateur, long since dead,[2] was a prominent personage. His chief ability was displayed in articles on economic and political matters, which illuminated a little periodical called *Dana*,[3] edited by him in conjunction with John Eglinton. But he contributed one Ibsenish play[4] to the movement, a forerunner of the native impetus which later on collided into Edward Martyn's *The Heather Field*.[5]

Seumas O'Sullivan was an enthusiastic adherent, and very prominent in his unwavering fidelity. He acted with distinct success in many of the plays produced, and, with the exception of the Fays, he probably knows more about the problems and trials of those early days than anyone else. In referring to him my only regret is that he never set himself to the task of writing a play for the Irish movement. He can still remedy this if he will. With his Irish lineage, his passionate national feeling and his powers of lyrical expression he could readily add something that has not yet been achieved.

Moore Chary of the Cigars

There were other intellectual and artistic activities connected with this little centre of enlightenment situated in what might almost be described as a Dublin slum. George Moore came down one night to talk about French poetry. I remember the anxiety displayed in securing some cigars to offer him. None of the company knew anything about cigars. But a purchase was eventually effected, and when the wise Moore, running no risks, emphatically and politely refused to smoke, a wave of depression obscured the horizon of the company for many days.

It was a severe rebuff. George Moore could depend on them for a good play, but when it came to cigars – that was a different matter. It did not, however, interfere with the fervour he displayed in declaiming Verlaine, or with his intimate knowledge of the subject about which he discoursed so fluently.

Yeats on Nietzsche

Mr Yeats on another occasion lectured on Nietzsche. It was just at the time when this philosopher was adjusting age-old truths to the jargon of twentieth-century intellectual snobbery. Yeats thought him something ultimate then. And he gave us a beautiful moonshine parade of reality. It is all too dazzling in memory to reconstruct. Nietzsche may or may not have been responsible for the Great War. But at least he helped to put the Irish dramatic movement on its feet, for Yeats, its dominant force, was at that time under his thumb.

My only clear memories of Lady Gregory at Camden Street are connected with her first play – *Twenty-Five* I think it was called (she has long since disowned it), and the huge barmbracks she used occasionally to send down to sustain the company during the exhausting work of rehearsal.[6]

Putting Plays to the Vote

One of the early rules of the society was the regulation that any play proposed to be produced should be read at a general meeting, and its acceptance or rejection decided by vote. I do not think this was always carried out. But I recollect a few interesting meetings of this nature. At one of them a play which Mr Yeats had either written or submitted was judged as not suitable and put aside. I do not remember the name of this play.[7] But the incident is quite clear in my mind. Mr Yeats was not present, as he was on his way to America at the time for a lecturing tour.[8]

Another meeting which was held in the Nassau Hotel stands out prominently in perspective. Lady Gregory and, I think, Mr Yeats, used to stay occasionally at this hotel, and more meetings were held there to suit their convenience. At this one Mr Yeats told us about Synge for the first time, and *Riders to the Sea* and *The Shadow of the Glen*, being read, were unanimously passed for performance.

Too Much Unanimity

I think it was at this meeting – if not this one some other at the Nassau Hotel – that an American visitor commented caustically upon the amazing complacency of the members of the company. Every notion put before the meeting was passed with hardly a remark of approval or dissent from any one. He could not understand every one agreeing without a word of discussion, especially in a society whose rules were so evidently based on democratic principles, and he remarked that it would be impossible to find such complete docility anywhere in the whole continent of America.

At the Nassau Hotel I have also a clear recollection of meeting Dr Gogarty[9] for the first time. He was not a member of the society, but he was on intimate terms with the Yeats–Gregory group. His own dramatic development came in after years. At this period he was a willing helper, and could call cabs for Lady Gregory on a wet night at the Abbey with unequalled reliability.

Outstanding Lady Artist

The leading lady actor of these days was Miss Maire Nic Shiubhlaigh[10] – in English, Miss Walker. She had a refined and beautiful talent of delicate and poetic fabric, and she heralded a lofty and spiritual art into which the movement never developed. She did her work and passed into obscurity, but there has never been anyone else like her at the Abbey Theatre. She represented something of Mr Yeats' first early dreams of dramatic beauty and imagination which have never been realised. Another prominent lady was Miss Quinn, now Mrs Dudley Digges, whose talent lay in the region of a caustic and stimulating realism.

Frank Fay and W. G. Fay, in their respective spheres, filled most of the prominent parts, but in addition there was Dudley Digges,[11] now a prominent figure in America, and Mr P. J. Kelly,[12] who has also obtained considerable reputation there. I recall a very solemn conclave in Camden Street at which Mr Kelly was expelled because he had broken a rule by acting for another society without permission.[13] I wonder does he remember the incident? Mr Frank Walker was also conspicuous as an adaptable actor who could be relied upon for sincere work with a distinct and admirable Irish flavour.

NOTES

Thomas G. Keohler [later Keller] was a foundation member of the Irish National Theatre Society. See Henry F. Norman, 'Unheard Music: In Memory of Thomas Goodwin Keller', *Dublin Magazine*, 17 (Oct–Dec 1942) 26–31.

1. In Nov 1901, Joyce published a pamphlet, 'The Day of the Rabblement', in which he said that 'The Irish Literary Theatre must now be considered the property of the rabblement of the most belated race in Europe.' See Ann Saddlemyer, 'James Joyce and the Irish Dramatic Movement', in *James Joyce: An International Perspective Centenary Essays*, ed. S. H. Bushrui and Bernard Benstock (Gerrards Cross: Colin Smythe; Totowa, New Jersey: Barnes & Noble, 1982).

2. Since 1913, at the age of thirty-nine. Ryan was first Secretary of the Irish National Theatre Society.

3. *Dana* ran from May 1904 to Apr 1905.

4. *The Laying of the Foundations*, which was first presented by the Irish National Dramatic Company for the Cumann na nGaedheal in the Antient Concert Rooms on 29 Oct 1902. Only Act Two of this two-act play has survived, and is available in *Lost Plays of the Irish Renaissance*, ed. Robert Hogan and James Kilroy (Newark, Delaware: Proscenium Press, 1970).

5. *The Heather Field* was first staged by the Irish Literary Theatre in May 1899;

so Ryan's play cannot really be called its 'forerunner', if this is what the writer means.

6. Cf. 'It was in Camden Street during a rehearsal of her play *Twenty-Five* that she instituted what was later to become one of the most popular features of Abbey Theatre first nights – the "Gort barmbrack suppers". The Gort barmbrack was a huge cartwheel of a fruit-cake, filled with the richest ingredients, made specifically by her own bakers at Gort for the casts of any of her new plays' (Maire Nic Shiubhlaigh, *The Splendid Years* (Dublin: James Duffy, 1955), pp. 31–2).

7. Cf. 'A few days later Frank Fay wrote again to say that *The Hour-Glass* had been put aside because it was not thought possible to give it the preparation necessary for such an important piece. At the same time, in spite of Rule Six and the Reading Committee the brothers jointly turned down Lady Gregory's *Twenty-Five*. Obviously they either relented or were over-ruled for the play was put on a few months later with W. G. Fay in the leading part' (Gerard Fay, *The Abbey Theatre, Cradle of Genius* (Dublin: Clonmore & Reynolds, 1958) p. 48). Yeats' play, *The Land of Heart's Desire*, was also rejected, this time on religious grounds. The Fays feared that the reference to a crucifix, bearing the figure of Christ, as a 'tortured thing', might lead to the resignation of Dudley Digges, one of their most valued actors. Yeats' first lecture tour to America was in Nov 1903. This is one year later than the delay over the production of *The Hour-Glass*.

8. This early rule, however, was eventually to lead to the dissolution of the society; it was inevitable that Yeats would never submit to placing power to accept or reject the plays of Synge, Lady Gregory and himself with a meeting of players whose artistic judgement he already had reason to distrust.

9. Oliver St John Gogarty (1878–1957), surgeon, wit and writer.

10. See her recollections in this book, p. 40.

11. See his recollections in this book, p. 31.

12. See his recollections in this book, p. 48.

13. In 1903, at a meeting of the Irish National Theatre Society, P. J. Kelly and Dudley Digges notified the group that they had been engaged to act in a revival of *The Heather Field*. The society agreed, but cautioned that in the future longer notice should be given. In 1904, however, the society had been approached by the organisers of the International Exposition to perform in the St Louis Exhibition. It was decided that they could not leave Dublin for a stay of several months, but three players chose to go as individuals – Dudley Digges, Maire Quinn and P. J. Kelly. Digges and Quinn had already resigned in protest over the Dec 1903 performance of *The Shadow of the Glen*, and Kelly was expelled from the company in April.

The Origin of the Abbey Theatre*

A. E. F. HORNIMAN

I sat alone here in my flat[1] making the costumes for the Irish Players to wear in *The King's Threshold*.[2] I was thinking about the hard conditions in which they were working, and the idea struck me that if and when enough money were to turn up, I would spend it on hiring or building a little hall where they could rehearse and perform in fair comfort. I wrote at once to W. B. Yeats, who was then in Ireland. He was not very enthusiastic on the subject. Time went on, and being in Dublin I searched to see if there were any possible places there. Some money came to me quite unexpectedly[3] – enough for me to hire the hall of a derelict Mechanics' Institute in Marlborough Street. There was no space for a vestibule, but the deserted Morgue of the City of Dublin was adjoining, so I hired that from the Corporation.

The building eventually was called the Abbey Theatre, and Dr Moore,[4] my lawyer, was busy making inquiries as to getting it licensed when he discovered that in Ireland the law in regard to theatres was not the same as in England, and that I must apply for Royal Letters Patent. That was about to be done, and then Dr Moore found that the petitioner must be domiciled in the country. I could not consider leaving my abode in London, so he suggested 'a man of straw'. Mr J. B. Yeats,[5] RHA,[6] was first suggested, but he was not suitable as he lived with his daughters; then Lady Gregory was considered and asked to petition in my place.[7] She consented by telegraph, and her lawyer arranged that I should sign a deed indemnifying her up to £200 if thereby she incurred any pecuniary loss. In his investigations Dr Moore discovered that she was legally *Dame* Gregory for such a document. She was not present at the Castle[8] when the petition was presented, and various people witnessed on my behalf, Sir Horace Plunkett amongst them. The Dublin Theatres had three counsels and I had two, and was severely cross-examined as to my intentions. It was my first experience of public speaking.

The architect, Mr Joseph Holloway,[9] still lives in Dublin. I remember that he was present; I could not remember the name of the builders and referred to him as being the right person to ask. It is a long time ago, but I

* *John O'London's Weekly*, 20 Aug 1932, p. 741.

think that the official who acted as Judge was the Solicitor-General, and that he afterwards became Lord Campbell. Lady Gregory actually published in a book that she made the Abbey Theatre, but I did not contradict it; indeed, I only laughed at the time, as I fancied that she had come to believe it herself. Various friends have urged me to publish the facts, but it is hard to believe that after such a long time anyone would be interested. Yet, in a way, the Abbey Theatre was the first of the many 'little theatres' which are sprinkled all over the world. From the financial point of view, I have my old Dublin pass-books, which are clear evidence.

NOTES

Annie Elizabeth Fredericka Horniman (1860–1937), English theatre manager and patron, one of the first to organise and encourage the modern repertory theatre movement, and a seminal influence in the Irish and English theatres at the beginning of the twentieth century. Her father, of Horniman's Teas, Manchester, had considerable wealth. She was interested in the Irish dramatic movement and acted for some time as unpaid secretary to W. B. Yeats. In 1903 she went to Dublin and there built and equipped the Abbey Theatre, with which she remained connected until 1910, when she disposed of it to a Board of trustees. The present recollections were written in the form of a 'Letter to the Editor' in response to a correspondent's request for information on the origin of the Abbey Theatre. See also James W. Flannery, *Miss Annie F. Horniman and the Abbey Theatre* (Dublin: Dolmen Press, 1970); Rex Pogson, *Miss Horniman and the Gaiety Theatre, Manchester* (London: Rockliff, 1952); Edward Malins, 'Annie Horniman, Practical Idealist', *Canadian Journal of Irish Studies*, 3 (Nov 1977) 18–26; and 'Miss Horniman's Offer of Theatre and the Society's Acceptance', *Samhain* (Dublin), no. 4 (Dec 1904) 53–4. Miss Horniman's collection of ten-volume extracts from periodicals, 1903–17, relating to the Abbey Theatre, are in the John Rylands Library, Manchester, England.

  1. In Montagu Mansions, London.
  2. *The King's Threshold*, by W. B. Yeats, was first performed at the Molesworth Hall, Dublin, on 8 Oct 1903. According to Yeats, Miss Horniman staged the play at her own expense, and also designed and made the costumes. This production marked a change in Yeats' work, and for many years he turned deliberately to Irish legends, especially to the Cuchulain legend.
  3. On 1 Jan 1904, Miss Horniman wrote to George Roberts saying that she had received 'a sum of money unexpectedly' and intimated that it would go towards a theatre. Her Hudson Bay shares had risen spectacularly.
  4. Of Whitney and Moore, Solicitors.
  5. John B. Yeats, W. B. Yeats' father.
  6. Royal Hibernian Academy of Arts.
  7. On 20 Aug 1904 patent was granted in the name of Lady Gregory for six years. In those days in Dublin, plays could not be performed anywhere but in a theatre that held a patent from the Lord Lieutenant.

8. Dublin Castle, centre of British rule.

9. Joseph Holloway (1861–1944), architect and theatre-goer who became known as a Dublin 'character' attending every theatre performance in the city. He kept a daily journal which eventually reached the massive proportions of 221 manuscript volumes, now in the National Library of Ireland.

New Dublin Theatre*

Those who were yesterday afternoon privileged to be present at a private view of the newly completed Abbey Theatre must have been very agreeably surprised at what they saw. As if by a wave of the harlequin's wand, an old and unsightly structure in Lower Abbey Street and another in Marlborough Street have all but disappeared, the stone front of the latter only having been utilised; and the two have been transformed into a stylish new theatre, capable of seating 562 persons. This addition to our places of dramatic entertainment has been made at the sole cost of Miss A. E. N. [sic] Horniman, an English lady, who is very deeply interested in the cultivation of the dramatic art in general and of Irish dramatic art in particular. This aesthetic object is solely what she has had in view, any element of a political or religious nature being entirely excluded. She herself remains the lessee of the theatre; but it will be available without charge to the Irish National Theatre Society, who will give the opening performance on Tuesday, 27 December. The entrances are from Marlborough Street, the central one being sheltered by a verandah. The visitor on going in finds himself in a large carpeted porch, the walls of which are hung with portraits, painted by Mr W. B. Yeats [sic],[1] of Mr William Fay, the stage manager of the theatre, Mr Frank Fay, Miss Maire Nic Shiubhlaigh and Miss Horniman, proprietress of the theatre. In the greenroom at one side are portraits of Dr Douglas Hyde and Mr George W. Russell, Vice-Presidents of the Irish National Theatre Society, also by Mr Yeats, and a portrait of Mr Yeats himself, painted by Madame Troncy, of Paris. Descending a carpeted stairway, one arrives at the stalls which seat 178 persons. Behind these are 186 pit seats. Both stalls and pit are ranged on an upward slope so that every occupant of a seat will be enabled to obtain a perfect view of the stage, and there will be no such thing as a bad seat. A large balcony extends round the interior above the lower seats, and this is fitted to accommodate 198 persons, the same care having been taken to construct

*Freeman's Journal (Dublin), 1 Dec 1904, p. 5.

the seating so that those occupying back seats can see the stage. Polished brass work separates each seat in every part of the house from those adjoining it on each side, and all the upholstering is in scarlet leather. There is no gallery over the balcony. All the passages within the interior, and also leading into it, are richly carpeted. Electric lighting prevails everywhere. A large light is in the centre of the ceiling of the interior, and round about the theatre are fourteen triple lamps. The walls are painted in colours, which harmonise well with the rest of the details, and on the walls are large medallions exhibiting the city arms, the Irish harp, and other devices appropriate to the national character of the entertainments to which the theatre is to be devoted. Room for a band, when that is required for any performance, will be augmented in front of the stage by the removal of the front row of stalls. All the requirements of the Corporation with respect to lighting, heating, ventilation and the safe ingress and egress of the audience have been strictly complied with; and there is, of course, a safety curtain, such as exists in all our other Dublin theatres. All the materials used in the building and fitting up of the theatre are Irish, with a trifling exception. There is no bar; but at a buffet tea and coffee will be supplied.[2]

NOTES

On 8 Apr 1904, Yeats sent to AE [George Russell] Miss Horniman's formal offer of a theatre – 'I have a great sympathy with the artistic and dramatic aims of the Irish National Theatre Company, as publicly explained by you on various occasions' – and on 11 May the Company signed their acceptance. W. G. Fay was hired to oversee the renovations to the theatre which progressed during the autumn. On 27 Dec 1904 the Abbey Theatre officially opened. To mark the occasion, a reception was held earlier to show the theatre's refurbishing, a description of which can be obtained from this account.

1. By John B. Yeats, W. B. Yeats' father.
2. For another description of the building see William Archer, 'Things in General: The Irish Theatre', *Morning Leader* (London), 5 Dec 1908, p. 4.

A Theatre Was Made*

DUDLEY DIGGES

The history of the beginning of the Irish Theatre has been abundantly written. My contribution to the story is from the actor's angle; in a

*Condensed from the *Recorder: Bulletin of the American Irish Historical Society* (New York), 10 (1 July 1939), 15–18. Editor's title.

theatre which was dominated by poets and dramatists, mystics and philosophers, passive resisters and physical-force men, you can imagine that the poor Thespians were put to it to defend their ancient right to a place upon the stage.

However, it is no exaggeration to say that the Irish theatre was primarily an actors' theatre, and if at the right moment there had not been in Dublin a group of young people like myself who had had considerable training in the rudiments of acting, the theatre could not have come into existence at the time it did, and in fact it really might never have happened at all.

I have no desire to appear any older than I am, but I was sadly reminded of the years the other day when I looked in an old Dublin magazine and saw that on 17 March 1900, in the Coffee Palace Hall, in Townsend Street, Dublin, I gave a commendable performance of the part of Charles in *The Irish Tutor*.

That was two years before the production of AE [George Russell]'s *Deirdre* and Yeats' *Kathleen Ni Houlihan*, which launched the Irish theatre, and I can remember that at that time we had a round of old farces with which at a moment's notice we could delight the denizens of Dublin, Dalkey or Blackrock.

Paddy Miles' Boy, That Rascal Pat, The Boots at the Swan, Who Speaks First, The Kiss in the Dark, Bamboozling, Advice Gratis, The Secret, My Wife's Dentist, Box and Cox, His Last Legs: we had been drilled in all those plays for years, and though we were only amateurs we were well drilled, for the devil two such slave drivers have I ever worked under as Frank and Willie Fay.

Now, the early story of the theatre is briefly this. It came after the failure of some efforts on the part of Yeats and Martyn and Moore to establish an Irish Literary Theatre. They abandoned the idea completely.[1] You see, they had had to engage some English professionals to act in that last and most translated of their plays, *Diarmuid and Grania*. It had been through four languages before it was produced, English, Irish, French and Kiltartan and, as you can imagine, the unfortunate English players had great difficulty in adjusting their tongues to the intricacies of the Irish idiom in which it finally emerged.

I mean, 'It is what I am saying to you, Grania', 'Let you not be listening to myself now, Grania.' As usual, the poor actors got most of the blame, and it was given out that English voices were impossible in Irish plays, and the whole thing was dropped.

A year or so passed and then a political organisation of women,[2] headed by Maud Gonne, wanted to raise money for some project or other. Anyway, they had been given a short play by a northern poet, Alice Milligan, dealing with the escape of Red Hugh from Dublin Castle and written in a kind of measured prose.[3]

Now, Frank Fay was in touch with this organisation and his little company of contemptible amateurs were entrusted with the production. Yeats was invited to the performance, and he was so delighted with the efficiency of the performers and their ability to act that he said at once: 'Here are the players for our Irish theatre', and inside a very short time we were off.

AE gave us his *Deirdre* and Yeats offered his *Kathleen*, provided Maud Gonne would play the part. She was not an actress, but a tall, beautiful and conspicuous figure in the national politics of the day. She hesitated to give the loyalists a chance to ridicule her and say: 'Ah . . . yes . . . of course . . . the stage, that's where she belongs', but she wanted to raise money for little nationalist children, and she yielded.

Life took on a new excitement for us all, the plays were produced in the hall of the St Teresa's Total Abstinence Society and were a tremendous success; and next morning Dublin woke to find itself with a national theatre on its hands. Then, of course, we had to organise!

We were great believers in the democracy of art. Everyone was to have a vote in everything. In fact, we nearly democratised the theatre to death. There were some who had strong feelings about political matters and wanted to see the theatre develop along propagandist lines.

Without much effort I could point my finger at the culprit who brought in an innocent but deadly little anti-recruiting play which nearly threw everything into what Fluther Good would call 'a state of chassis',[4] and caused one poet to lift his hands to Heaven and declare that 'the Irish Theatre would go down in a sea of fists'.[5]

In a cold, draughty little hall in Camden Street we performed prodigious feats of production on a stage twelve feet by eight. Willie Fay built the scenery, and out of rough lumber made the benches on which about sixty people could sit and shiver. The critics came and complained about the uncomfortableness of everything, and begged us 'for God's sake if we were going to have an art theatre to have it somewhere they wouldn't freeze to death'.

At Samhain time, the old Irish festival, we had a repertoire of several new plays and gave them for a week in a well-lighted and comfortable hall known as the Antient Concert Rooms, famous for the fact that the owner stuck to the old way of spelling it 'Antient' and would be damned if he'd change it, and there were we young people working in offices, pounding ledgers all day, but going down to the theatre to perform seven times a week with real joy in our hearts, just like real actors; but it was all for love of Ireland and art, and I was far happier than I have ever been since.

I should like to say a word or two about the personalities of some of those men with whom we worked, some whose names are perhaps not so well known to you. Apart from the labour at which they earned their bread, most of them were thinkers and dreamers who found expression for their ideas in Arthur Griffith's journal, the *United Irishman*, afterwards *Sinn Fein*.

Being an actor, my first thoughts turn to those two men who taught me my trade, Frank and Willie Fay. In the daytime Frank was an expert shorthand writer and typist, and at night he was an authority on French and English drama, an able elocutionist who gave me lessons at sixty cents a month, and a passionate lover of the theatre.

Working too hard for the boss was never a ferocious passion in leisurely easy-going Dublin, and somehow Frank used to find time in that office where he was employed to type out all parts for actors in the theatre. He was an able talker on the subject, but was especially strong on the French, Elizabethan and eighteenth-century drama. I can see him now, a little man, walking down the long street to his work in the morning, a long black coat almost to his heels, a small black derby hat, and his nose glued to the pages of a book.

He had a consuming adoration for his brother, Will. Willie was the black sheep who had run away and joined a circus, travelled with an Uncle Tom show, joined the fit-ups and toured in Irish melodrama. In his brother's eyes this contact with the profession lifted him to heights poor Frank never hoped to reach. He always spoke of Will with bated breath, and what the brother said was gospel, for he had had experience. Willie was a less fluent but more positive personality than his brother and became the chief director of the Abbey.

If there was time I could tell you more about Fred Ryan, an auditor by day, a student of international affairs by night, whose articles on British Imperialism caused great discomfiture in Dublin Castle. He gave us our first satirical comedy, *The Laying of the Foundations*, a satire on municipal politics, the manuscript of which has unfortunately been lost; of James H. Cousins, a poet from Belfast, who subsequently succeeded to a chair of English literature in Tokyo; of George Roberts, another northerner who always seemed to me to be writing complaining poetry about Dagda and Dana,[6] but who later established the publishing house of Maunsel & Co., and brought out so much of the literature which followed this period; of Seumas O'Sullivan, whose delicate lyrics you will find in *The Golden Treasury of Verse*; and of Padraic Colum.

There were seven great giants of that era, six of whom are gone. Dr Douglas Hyde, that scholar and apostle of the Irish language, has lived to occupy the highest place of honour his country could bestow on him.[7] Our greatest poet, William Butler Yeats, in his last years seemed to me like some old sentinel, standing at the portals of the Abbey, guarding its integrity and the freedom of its artistic soul.

I remember the words he used on that opening night when he asked for a theatre in which 'all Ireland might walk the stage' and sounded a call to all young artists to 'be bold, be bold, but not too bold'.

Under his guiding inspiration the dramatic genius of our people has awakened the delight and admiration of the world. It is for those into whose hands the guidance of the Irish theatre has now passed to guard well those ideals of artistic freedom and integrity which Yeats has left to them, so that nothing which is merely vulgar shall ever soil its name and nothing artistically true and worth of its place shall ever be excluded from its doors.

NOTES

At the annual dinner of the American Irish Historical Society in New York, the Gold Medal of the Society for 1939 was presented to Dudley Digges (1879–1947), 'in recognition of his part in the creation of the Irish Theatre, and in tribute to his career of distinction on the American stage'. In reply, Digges delivered the address condensed here. See also Padraic Colum, 'The Dead Player', *Dublin Magazine*, 29 (July–Sept 1953) 1.

1. In May 1902, Lady Gregory wrote to Yeats, 'If Literary Theatre breaks up, we must try and settle something with Fay' (*Seventy Years 1852–1922*, ed. Colin Smythe (Gerrards Cross: Colin Smythe, 1974) p. 413).

2. Inghinidhe na hÉireann [Daughters of Erin], founded by Maud Gonne in 1900.

3. *The Deliverance of Red Hugh*, by Alice Milligan, was presented by Ormond Dramatic Society and Inghinidhe na hÉireann on 27 Aug 1901.

4. This was said by Captain Boyle in Sean O'Casey's *Juno and the Paycock*, not by Fluther Good in *The Plough and the Stars*.

5. This was said by AE during a rehearsal of his play *Deirdre* at which W. G. Fay and Frank Fay flew at each other. There is a line in the play that said, 'I foresee that the Red Branch will go down in a sea of blood.'

6. Dagda, in Irish mythology, is 'Good', God of Earth's fertility; Dana, his daughter, is the 'earth-mother', of the Celtic race.

7. Douglas Hyde became the first President of Ireland.

My First Abbey Play*

WINIFRED LETTS

Recently I was reading Lady Gregory's *Journals*[1] edited by Lennox Robinson. Old memories came flooding back as I read the book.

*Condensed from *Irish Writing* (Cork), no. 16 (Sept 1951) 43–6.

I was young again; I was rocking at the top of the old Dublin–Dalkey tram; I was going to the Abbey Theatre. I cannot now recall how or why I went there first, because we were by the tradition of that day people who went to the Gaiety – people who would never miss a Shakespeare revival, or fail to see *Trelawney of the Wells*, or, in lighter mood, *Charley's Aunt*. Perhaps it was because I could then get a seat for sixpence, a convenient sum in youth.

I forget the details of the day, only remembering that the play was *Riders to the Sea*, that Sara Allgood was the mother and William Fay the son, that Maire O'Neill and Brigid Fay were the two daughters.[2] This was not a play, it was life: it was the eternal battle of man with the sea, the sea as they know it in the western coast, not our polite sea that lets us bathe so safely at Blackrock Baths. This was tragedy as the Greeks knew it.

I cannot remember any applause, only that hush which falls on supreme art. The small audience had a discretion, a sense of tragedy, that purges through pity and through fear.

Gradually I came back to the normal day. There was Lady Gregory in the stalls, wearing her black mantilla. With her was W. B. Yeats; I see him in a grey velvet coat – or do I dream that? I was already under the spell of the early Yeats, the lyrical Yeats of the 'Celtic Twilight' and the 'Secret Rose'.

In dreeps of western rain and on a most treacherous bicycle I had followed his footsteps to Drumcliffe, to Lisadell and the Rosses, to the shores of Lough Gill and to Dromahaire. Now I looked at him with the loving awe that belongs to youth.

I went home, still dazed, still entranced, to the suburban placidity of Blackrock. But the spell of Synge's speech and tragedy lay upon me. I was eager to write something in the same medium. Of course it was a poor little play, something that could be parodied and torn to pieces. I called it *The Eyes of the Blind*;[3] it concerned a murder on a Wicklow bog.

I must concede myself one dramatic moment when my blind beggar saw the ghost of the murdered man behind the murderer's chair. Frank Fay told me later that his own part as the blind man had meant something significant to him. To my great surprise the play was accepted. I now had an entry to the world behind the stage, so entirely strange, awesome, exciting in the humdrum of suburban life.

The manager at that time was Iden Payne.[4] I recall him as a rather harassed young man with pockets bulging with papers. Better I remember the two Fays, Frank and Willie. To see these people rehearsing my own play as I sat in the darkness of the auditorium was wonderful to me. No one else was in the least impressed, but they were all kind and casual.

On the first night there [were] no shouts for author, no bouquets on the last night. Indeed my verdict came from an old woman in the pit. I sat behind her at the matinee, anxious to test reactions there. She wore a black bonnet with bugles and they shook as she turned to her companion. 'I don't think much of that', she said. But, woman of the bugles, you did get a thrill when the blind man saw the ghost, for the bugles were frozen for that moment.

What matter? The play was not the thing for me, but it had been the 'Open Sesame' to the regions behind the stage. I had shared Lady Gregory's big barmbrack in the greenroom. I had learnt something of the ways of producers at rehearsals. It was so that I first saw Mona Limerick, an actress of a strange, exotic quality that fitted her perfectly to her part of the lovely fated Deirdre.[5] To me she remains the ideal Deirdre, the lovely woman fated to the tragedy that she foresees.

I knew – what a joy that was – the two Fays and their families. Their charm was to be just the same off the stage as on it. What Yeats called the beautiful fantasy of William Fay's playing of the fool in *On Baile's Strand* seemed to follow him into daily life.

I remember a drive with him to The Scalp. We were seated on an outside car. During that drive he described to me the detailed arrangement of the universe. I remember that the dwellers in the moon act only with a group-will, all moving alike – a perfectly trained chorus. 'When we die we go to a White House and gain in knowledge' – it must be a happy white house now you are in it, William Fay.

Like all that group of Irishmen, they charmed the bird from the bough with their talk, did the Fays.

By now they were welcome guests at our quiet home in Blackrock. My mother, who never went to a theatre, had the temperament, responsive and passionate, that discerned the quality of artists. She loved the Fays and they loved her. Indeed hers was a sharp criticism of another visitor: 'No. I can't like him. I had expected him to be like Willie Fay and he isn't.'

Memories of others I have in plenty. I see Kerrigan[6] as the dead Naisi in Synge's version of the Deirdre legend. Mrs Pat Campbell[7] as Deirdre was lying across his chest. One wondered if the weight equalled the glory of the moment.

I seem to see Synge, sitting there, dark, inscrutable as Fate. Of a poverty in the human spirit he was well aware; ruthlessly he dragged it before the footlights. *The Well of the Saints* was to prove his point; better, he says, be blind beggars living in a world of beauty and nobility than have seeing eyes to discern the ugliness of the actual. In those days I loved to follow his tracks in the Wicklow mountains, in Glenmalure and Glen Imaal where the 'shadow of the glen' falls coldly.

Of Michael Dolan[8] I have many theatre memories: as schoolmaster, priest or maybe as shopkeeper in a Shiels[9] comedy. Always he was excellent, always so fitted to that team-work that was so noteworthy in the Abbey. Later it was my good fortune to see him in the quintessence of all these parts – I saw him as Noah. It was the translation of the French play *Noé*[10] by André Obey.

This was the first time I had realised Noah as a man and not the little painted wooden figure of our childhood's Noah's Ark. But there was Noah the man, *the* man at the crossroads of life from whence the roads descending the mountain to strange lands where his sons would father the white and coloured races who would fight each other to this day.

How perfectly Maureen Delaney [*sic*][11] filled her part as the kindly inadequate Mrs Noah; how poignantly human is her search for her little cat and her lonesomeness for the neighbours who had filled her life before the Flood.

Was ever actress so beloved on or off the stage as Maureen Delaney? It irks one to see Maureen in the parts she can, one admits, play so well where she is unlovable, evil. Her public counts her the embodiment of everything most humorous, most lovable, motherly, home-making in Irish life.

We who have youthful memories of the old Abbey still cherish them, good and bad. The great copper-framed mirrors on the walls, the intense discomfort of the seats in the upper circle to anyone tall – but what can you expect for half-a-crown?[12] The O'Casey plays made me forget any discomfort. We shall never see Sara Allgood[13] as Juno again, the perfect tribute to all the selfless, sainted charwomen of Dublin.

We shall never see McCormick[14] in every part that he made so noteworthy. What an artist he was, modest, selfless, a dreamer of dreams, always striving towards an achievement still beyond. He was a man who loved the sea, and there seems there a symbol of his power as an actor, sometimes a jolly beggar, often a king, terrible as in Oedipus, puerile as in Joxer, cruel, gay, tragic – his range was only cut short by death.

A Phoenix will arise from the ashes of the old Abbey,[15] and younger audiences will feel the thrill and the wonder that we felt long ago – but for the old Abbey the old Irish prayer: 'God be with the days.'

NOTES

Winifred M. Letts (1882–1972), poet, playwright and fiction writer. Her other writings on the Abbey Theatre include 'The Fays at the Abbey Theatre', *Fortnightly* (London), no. 978 (June 1948) 420–3; 'Early Days at the Abbey', *Irish Digest* (Dublin), 31 (Sept 1948) 8–11; and 'When the Abbey Was Young', *Ireland of the Welcomes* (Dublin), 1 (July–Aug 1952) 9–11.

1. Lady Gregory, *Journals, 1916–1930*, ed. Lennox Robinson (London: G. P. Putnam, 1946).

2. *Riders to the Sea*, by J. M. Synge, was first presented by the Irish National Theatre Society at the Molesworth Hall on 25 Feb 1904. Sara Allgood was not the mother (Maurya), but the daughter Cathleen. Winifred Letts is probably referring to a later revival at the Abbey Theatre.

3. *The Eyes of the Blind*, a play in one act by Winifred Letts, was first produced at the Abbey Theatre on 1 Apr 1907.

4. By early 1907, Miss Horniman and Yeats were growing a little dissatisfied with the Abbey Theatre. Miss Horniman thought that a more professional producer should be imported from England. As a result, Iden Payne joined the Company as producer. However, his encounter with the Abbey was brief and unhappy, and after producing Maeterlinck's *Interior* and Scawen Blunt's *Fand*, he resigned to embark on a distinguished career at Miss Horniman's Gaiety Theatre in Manchester and later at the Stratford Shakespeare Memorial Theatre.

5. Mona Limerick was Iden Payne's wife. In a revival of Yeats' *Deirdre* on 1 Apr 1907 Payne cast his wife in the title role to the fury of Sara Allgood.

6. J. M. Kerrigan. See his recollections in this book, p. 133.

7. Mrs Patrick Campbell (1865–1940), English actress who became one of the leading theatrical figures of her day. Bernard Shaw – who calls her 'perilously bewitching' – wrote for her the part of Eliza Doolittle in *Pygmalion*.

8. Michael J. Dolan (1884–1954), a distinguished actor at the Abbey Theatre, who took over management from Lennox Robinson in Dec 1923. See Christopher Murray, 'Three Letters from Lady Gregory', *Prompts* (Dublin), no. 1 (June 1981) 5–7.

9. George Shiels (1881–1949), playwright. In 1921, the Abbey Theatre accepted his one-act comedy *Bedmates*. From that time until 1948, it staged one or more of his plays almost every year. The Abbey celebrated his centenary in 1981 with a production of *The Passing Day*. His portrait, by Jack Wilkinson, was presented to the Abbey by the Ballymoney Drama Festival to mark the centenary also. See Daniel J. Casey, 'George Shiels: The Enigmatic Playwright', in *Irish Renaissance Annual IV*, ed. Zack Bowen (Newark, Delaware: University of Delaware Press, 1983) pp. 17–41; and Micheál Ó hAodha, 'The Amazing Mr Shiels', *Irish Times* (Dublin) 14 May 1981, p. 10.

10. *Noah* was presented at the Abbey Theatre on 11 Nov 1935.

11. Maureen Delany (?–1961) joined the Abbey Company in 1914, when she made her first appearance in Edward McNulty's comedy *The Lord Mayor* (13 Mar). She is famous for her Widow Quin and her Maisie Madigan. See R. M. Fox, 'Maureen Delany Takes a Bow', *Irish Digest* (Dublin), 29 (Dec 1947) 21–3; Kees Van Hock, 'Vignette: Maureen Delany', *Irish Times* (Dublin), 5 Aug 1950, p. 4; and Maeve Barrington, 'Queen of the Abbey Theatre', *Irish Digest* (Dublin), 54 (Oct 1955) 29–31.

12. A half-crown in old currency, before decimalisation was introduced in 1971, was two shillings and sixpence. One could buy a paperback book for that sum as late as the 1960s.

13. For a note on Sara Allgood and her recollections see p. 87.

14. F. J. McCormick (Peter Judge). For a note on him and his recollections see p. 179.

15. In 1951, the old Abbey Theatre was destroyed by fire.

The Irish National Theatre Society*

MAIRE NIC SHIUBHLAIGH

It was about this time – June 1902 – that we acquired what we intended to be a modest theatre at Lower Camden Street – the back shed of an egg and butter store, ingeniously and inconveniently hidden from its neighbours behind piles of provisions and other miscellaneous wares. It was hard to find, small, draughty and uncomfortable but beggars could not be choosers and though our independent spirit just kept us out of the former category, we were in no position to make demands. Bad and all as the place was, the rent – about 10 shillings a week – was quite outside our slender means, and it was with some trepidation, and several invocations to the gods in favour of theatrical pioneers, that we took it over.

I may say here that Camden Street is one of the busiest shopping quarters in Dublin. It straggles in a southerly direction across the centre of the city and pursues a course through a maze of smaller streets towards Rathmines. Along its narrow way, shops big and small jostle each other, and marketers throng narrow pavements. At that time, no one in his proper senses would have expected to find a theatre here, and even if he had, it would have required an expert guide versed in the intricacies of Dublin streets to discover the whereabouts of ours. Its entrance – an open hall door – peered shyly at passers-by from between the prosperous shop-fronts of a butcher and a family grocer.

It was a wet, windy day when I went down to see it. With considerable difficulty and several false starts I managed to find it, stumbled down an inky passageway full of interesting smells, reminiscent of sawdust and onions, and came out into a fair-sized room where Willie Fay, covered in dust and wearing a delapidated boiler-suit, hammered away at what looked like the beginnings of a stage.

Willy Fay, as I said before, could get work out of anyone. It was only a matter of minutes before I was shaking the dust out of a pile of frowsy old curtains, and holding wood for him to saw. As the others arrived, they were rapidly enlisted to help with the other jobs Willie had been thinking out while he worked. That first night in Camden Street was a memorable

*Extracted from *The Splendid Years: Recollections of Maire Nic Shuibhlaigh, As Told to Edward Kenny* (Dublin: James Duffy, 1955) pp. 23–6, 47–51, 56–9, 64–6.

one. There was many a crookedly driven nail in the framework of our stage, and many a swollen thumb in the company. When we had begun to get tired, Fay leaned back with a hammer in his hand and said: 'It's not such a bad little place, is it? . . . Well, not *very* bad, anyhow?'

Not very bad . . . it was about fifty feet long by thirty wide. One of the walls was lime-washed, one was papered, and the others still bore traces of a deep-green paint in the places where damp had not reached. If there was an intact pane of glass in the windows it was not visible. The roof complained noisily in the breeze; there were no seating arrangements; the ceiling leaned intimately towards us and looked as though it leaked. The only comfort to be derived from the scene was the sight of a rusty stove, pushed into a corner with the jagged end of a chimney-pipe protruding from its rear. We hoped it was still workable. In dismay we glanced at Fay. 'A little bit of hard work will do wonders', he said, and scratched his head.

The next night we brought a carpenter friend down to 'do the hard bits', as Fay said, rolled up our sleeves, and got to work. Frank, with four or five others, adjusted the intimate roof, pushed putty into the more noticeable cracks and replaced the broken window-panes with boards. We painted the walls green and bordered the plywood proscenium of the stage with cream. Fay brought some planks and converted them into benches for the audience to sit on. The stage was ridiculously small – little bigger than a rostrum – with tiny cubicles on either side in which to dress and make up.

In a fortnight we had done all in our power to make the place presentable, but finished, it could by no stretch of the imagination be termed beautiful. It was austerely practical in its appointments. Joseph Holloway, one of our more prominent associates, writing later of it, said, 'It breathed the air of unsophisticated Bohemianism, and, somehow or other, gave the impression that if high art blossomed here, it did not mature in very luxuriant surroundings.' He was one of our admirers, but he could not, in truth, have said more in favour of the place. There was a truly primitive air about it.

But whatever its shortcomings, this little hall became the first Irish theatre. Though, as we later discovered, it was completely unsuitable for public performances, it became our first headquarters, not merely a rehearsal room, but a meeting-place where, with complete freedom, we discussed our ambitions with each other and the many outsiders who became interested in our work. Here, more than anywhere else, were the foundations of the theatre laid. It was here that we gathered around us that homogeneous collection of politicians, artists, poets and dramatists who formed the core of the movement. In many ways our meetings bore little resemblance to those of a theatrical company. Rehearsals, to the casual onlooker, seemed to form merely a small part of our activities. It was only with the approach of new plays that time was given over wholly to preparations for an appearance, and a space cleared amidst a chaos of props, scenery, work-tables and draperies, where we could more easily enact a scene. In the intervals between productions Frank Fay held his elocution classes in one corner, Willie prepared his scenery in the next, and around the stove, in a wide circle of benches, the remaining members of the assembly sat and deliberated gravely and youthfully on topics of the day. It was here, too, that we received our first touring offer; that we discussed the opening of the Abbey.

Meanwhile, our first London visit was bearing fruit in a way we had not envisaged. Something was happening which, in the excitement of the production of Synge's play – and the success of Colum's – was inclined to be overlooked. We heard of a wealthy Englishwoman with an interest in the theatre who had seen our performances at the Queen's Gate Hall and become interested. 'She is anxious to do something for us', said Yeats.

She was. Hearing that we intended to produce a new Yeats play with *The Shadow of the Glen*, she came to Dublin and offered to dress the production for us. Her name was Miss A. E. F. Horniman. It was Miss Horniman who built the Abbey Theatre, and gave us the use of it.

Miss Horniman was a tall, quiet Englishwoman, a member of a wealthy Manchester commercial family, well-known as a patron of the drama in England, where she had already done much for the experimental theatre. Through Yeats, whom she knew in London, she had visited the Queen's Gate Hall on the occasion of our appearance there, and had been sufficiently attracted by our work to make it known that she wanted to assist us. She came to Dublin about the summer of 1903, took rooms in a large hotel, imported bales of the most expensive dress materials, engaged a team of English theatrical costumiers, and began fitting us out for the production of a new Yeats play, *The King's Threshold*.

Few of us ever got to know her intimately, although she was an extremely likeable person who made a point of meeting us all and never tired of advising us wisely on stage matters. During her stay in Dublin she frequently came down to rehearsals at Camden Street with Yeats, evincing at all times the greatest interest in our methods and sitting near the stove talking in her quiet witty way. It may be said here that her interest in us never had anything to do with the national aims of the society. Miss Horniman, who merely hastened the ultimate destination of our movement by building the Abbey the following year, was interested merely in the development of drama. It is questionable, too, if during these first years of her association with us, she fully realised the basis upon which the National Theatre Society had been established originally. If she had, she might have thought twice before financing it. Her interest in us was not as an Irish national cooperative movement, but as a society with a fresh approach to the drama which, therefore, deserved encouragement. Since she had already financed a number of such groups in England, she regarded our group as yet another small company in which by her aid she would receive a governing interest. In view of subsequent events, it was a pity that her position was not sufficiently clarified at the outset. When, after the foundation of the Abbey, she began unwittingly to exert her influence in the affairs of the theatre, she indirectly brought about the death of the original National Theatre Society.

But in 1903, none of us could see into the future. As far as most of us were concerned, Miss Horniman's offer was heaven-sent. Before her arrival in Dublin, our career, even if it had proved to us that there was a future for what we were doing, in the city, had not been very profitable financially. The National Theatre Society might at last have been exciting interest, but it was certainly not making money. The arrival of a complete outsider who was prepared to assist us materially by dressing even one of our productions, was something which it would have been foolish to ignore. We blessed our new-found friend who, as it turned out, spared neither time nor money upon the society. Miss Horniman was generosity itself; she gave wholeheartedly and with an almost embarrassing readiness. Certainly it would be untrue to say that the Irish theatre does not owe her a debt of gratitude. Her assistance, which only began with the dressing of Yeats' play, placed the Irish National Theatre Society on its feet. There is little doubt that if she had not helped us when she did, it would have been many years before we could have emerged from the small halls in which we were playing at that time.

From the start, she was as good as her word. Miss Horniman dressed *The King's Threshold* expensively and elaborately. The play, a dramatisation of the legendary silence of Seanchan, was staged very effectively by Fay, who made use of draperies in a manner reminiscent of *The Hour-Glass*. The scene on the steps of the king's palace was devoid of all unnecessary decoration and provided an austere effect of greens and greys which contrasted well with the dresses of the characters, most of which were richly jewelled. Very sincerely we thanked Miss Horniman and she returned to England. Soon she became a pleasant memory. Our surprise can be understood when, a few months later, Fay called us around him and announced that she wanted to help us again. 'Miss Horniman wants to build a theatre in Dublin', he said 'and give us the use of it.'

Not unnaturally, most of us were overjoyed; although, at a debate held later on the matter, there were certain murmurings against Miss Horniman's proposal. Some members, who were perhaps more discerning than the rest of us, foresaw a danger of the national ideals of the movement being shelved if an outsider was allowed in. But older heads on the committee counselled acceptance of the offer. The society replied agreeing to perform in any theatre which Miss Horniman might provide for the purpose in Dublin. She answered by return asking Fay to find a suitable building or site. 'I can only afford to make a very little theatre, and it must be quite simple', she said later. Nevertheless, we believed that she was prepared to provide up to £1,000 for the project; a sum which would have been ample for the conversion of a small hall near the centre of the city at that time. In actual fact the figure for the acquisition and alteration of the building which became the old Abbey Theatre was, I think, something in the region of thirteen or fourteen hundred pounds, but Miss Horniman provided the extra money without complaint.

We set about finding a suitable site. The object, of course, was to get one as close to the centre of the city as possible. As it happened, our luck was in. Owing to a recent Corporation by-law which stipulated that all theatres in the city should undergo extensive alterations in order to install safety-devices in the case of fire, a number of the smaller Dublin halls were closing down. One of these – attached to the Mechanic's Institute in Abbey Street and within easy reach of the tramway terminus – closed its doors a few weeks before we began our search. It happened to be on the site of one of the oldest theatres[1] in Dublin. The remains of the original building had been razed and a small theatre erected where popular plays had been performed up to about the middle of the last century. This had degenerated through the years into a cheap music-hall, which had been closed by the authorities. Later the building was taken over by the Mechanics' Institute, which had rented it about ten years later to a well-known theatrical company. The directors of the latter, after fighting a losing battle against a government law which demanded an enormous fee for the patenting of serious theatres had bowed to the inevitable and mixed its dramatic entertainments with music-hall turns. 'The Mechanics', as it was widely known in Dublin, was a popular if rather noisy place, typical of a number of small music-halls in the city. When the new Corporation fire law was enforced, it had found it impossible to carry on, and closed down altogether. Being already fashioned as a theatre, the place suited our needs admirably. The advice of a well-known Dublin architect, Joseph Holloway, was sought, and after some legal difficulties had been overcome, the lease was acquired, together with that of an adjoining building in Marlborough Street – formerly the old Dublin City Morgue. It was estimated that the task of making both buildings one and decorating the interior would take about eight or nine months. Work was begun early in 1904. It was hoped that the opening night would be in December of the same year.

In comparison with the other theatres in Dublin at that time, the original Abbey Theatre was very small; in fact, it must have been the smallest down-town hall in the city. But for us, emerging from the out-of-the-way Molesworth Hall, with memories of our earlier appearances in Camden Street still vivid, it was wonderful to be able to play in a real theatre at last. We had a 'greenroom' – a sort of common room where we could meet and wait between the acts of plays – a stage, which, even if it was not very big, was reasonably well equipped, and we had a more or less draught-proof auditorium that would not offend those people who were used to the comforts of the bigger theatres. We could at least be sure that there would never again be murmurs about hard chairs and cold breezes.

The theatre opened for the first time on a Tuesday, 27 December 1904. It is easy to describe.

The building took up most of a corner, the pit entrance looking into Abbey Street within sight of Nelson Pillar, the door to the main vestibule stalls and balcony opening on to Marlborough Street. Passing through the double glass doors here, one entered a tiny lobby, to the left of which was the greenroom, later taken into the lobby to give extra space and allow for the provision of a coffee bar.

Around the vestibule, which held the booking-office and cloakrooms, hung portraits of Lady Gregory, Miss Horniman, Willie Fay and myself. The lobby was a cramped space in those days, little more than ten or twelve feet in width, and hardly much longer.

The auditorium seated something like 500, not much more, but it was an attractive little place. Always it had that atmosphere which led to a feeling of intimacy between player and auditor. Standing on the Abbey stage, the feeling, absent in so many other theatres, of being one with the audience was always present. Actually it had been the intention to have a projecting platform in the manner of the Elizabethan theatre, but it was found that this would occupy too much space. The actual stage, although small, proved big enough for us. None of our sets were elaborate..

The decoration of the house had been carried out in nearly every case by Irish workers, although some of the articles, such as the carven figures of the electroliers, came from the continent. Two stained-glass windows, fashioned in the image of a tree in leaf, on either side of the Marlborough Street entrance, were the work of Miss Sara Purser.[2] A picture of Sara Allgood, which later hung in the vestibule, was also her work. J. B.

Yeats, the poet's father, painted pictures of Miss Horniman, Lady Gregory, Frank and Wille Fay and myself, also for display in the lobby.

As was only to be expected on such an occasion, we had a full house. It was the most fashionable theatrical event of the year. Distinguished-looking visitors kept drifting into the tiny vestibule, scrutinising the fittings and discussing the history of the society, standing in little knots on the stairs. Yeats was impressive in evening dress, and kept coming behind the scenes every few minutes to see how things were getting along.

Backstage, Willie Fay, dressed for his part in one of the new plays, a wild wig slipping sideways over his elfin face, swung unexpectedly from a baton high in the flys, arranging the lighting. Beneath him passed an endless procession of figures carrying ladders, tools, canvas screens, draperies. Idlers at the back of the drawn hessian curtain eyed the swelling audience; a muffled mumble of voices rose from the auditorium.

Standing as far out of the way as possible, those of us who were unoccupied, ate a scrap meal of bread and cocoa. It was all we had had to eat for hours. Every member of the society had been in the theatre since early afternoon.

In between bites we watched the auditorium through a crack in the curtain. The pit and gallery were full. The stalls were slower in filling, but the crowd was increasing all the time. A number of people sitting in front seemed oblivious of the pre-curtain chatter as they listened to the violin music of Arthur Darley,[3] our one musician.

Darley was a great addition to the little company. A violinist of note, he was a well-known collector of traditional Irish airs. Yeats had taken him along to play between the acts when we were in the Molesworth Hall. He used to stand in the corner of the stage, just outside the curtain, fondling his violin self-consciously and playing plaintive little pieces much appreciated by audiences. Few reviews would have been complete without mention of him. It turned out later that he had known Synge in Paris before the writer came to us. Both had played in the same orchestra.

The sound of a familiar voice drew our attention backstage again. In a dark corner, sitting on an upturned property-basket, sat Synge himself, rolling the inevitable cigarette.

'God bless you', he said. 'I hope you're as happy as I am. I'm so honoured that my little play should be chosen for the first week.'[4]

In early Abbey and Camden Street days lack of funds forbade the purchase on any extensive scale of a permanent wardrobe collection, and our ingenuity knew no bounds. Most of our most effective properties and dress accessories were created by ourselves, mostly from cardboard, papier-mâché, tin (in the case of shields and spears in period pieces) and odd pieces of paste jewellery picked up occasionally in the city. In these early times, too, before the theatre acquired the well-known gong which, hanging behind the stage, is beaten before the start of a play, the rise of the curtain was heralded in a less musical, but none-the-less effective manner by three solemn knocks delivered to the floor behind the proscenium by whoever happened to be idle. Dignity at all costs, as we used to say.

When we came into the Abbey and the gathering of a part-time theatre staff became necessary, it was from amongst the non-acting associate members of the society that it was drawn. Usherettes, ticket-checkers, booking-clerks and technicians were appointed, and a number of these provided the nucleus of the full-time theatre staff employed after the company became professional. Most of them remained with the theatre in this capacity all their lives. One of the most notable personalities was the late Nellie Bushell, usherette in the stalls until her death, who, during the years of the Black-and-Tan[5] war, often turned the torn-ticket box into a miniature arsenal, concealing the arms of fugitives who sought a few hours' refuge in the theatre. Originally a poplin-weaver, she had always been actively associated with the political clubs, being a member in later years of Madame Markievicz'[6] Fianna na hÉireann, the original Irish scout force which had headquarters after its foundation in 1909 at our old premises in Camden Street. Backstage, too, under the direction of Willie Fay, there were plenty of helpers who looked after the technical side of productions, and there was the beginning of a permanent staff of technicians in Seaghan Barlow and Udolphus Wright, the stage carpenter and house electrician respectively, both of whom gave up much of their spare time in the first days of the movement to work both as players and scene-shifters and were appointed, whole-time, to both these jobs in later years.

Of course, like dramatic societies everywhere, we had a faithful, if small, following of our own in these first years, drawn from amongst the play-going public. There were a number of people quite outside the dramatic movement, who had seen our first performance in 1902 and had followed our career closely afterwards. Many of these friends – they were friends as well as auditors; it would have called for a degree of friendship to stick by us during the ups and downs of those first two years – many of these friends turned up for every new play we gave; in fact, some of them came to see the company each time it appeared, whether the play was a new one or not. One or two of them followed us night after night, occupying a place in the auditorium for as often as three or four nights in succession, as long as a play ran.

I think, of all the people who occupied a place in our first night life at this time, the most interesting was Joseph Holloway, the Dublin stage-diarist and the man who had supervised the conversion of the old Mechanics' building for Miss Horniman. Indeed, Holloway was probably one of the most colourful of all the many figures who moved on the fringe of the dramatic movement after 1903 or 1904.

NOTES

Maire Nic Shiubhlaigh [Mary Walker] (1888–1959), a notable Abbey actress and a founding member of the Irish National Theatre Society. She was the first Irish player to use the Irish form of her name for stage purposes. See Alice Tracy, 'Maire Nic Shiubhlaigh of the Abbey Theatre', *Carloviana* (Dublin), 1 (Dec 1962) 10–11; and S[usan] L. M[itchell], 'Dramatic Rivalry,' *Sinn Fein* (Dublin), 4 (8 May 1909) 1 (berates Yeats for letting Maire go).

1. The New Princess Theatre of Varieties, in the Mechanics' Institute, Lower Abbey Street, was built on the site of the Theatre Royal, Abbey Street, and opened in Nov 1874 under the management of J. S. Lofthouse: see Peter Kavanagh, *The Irish Theatre; Being a History of the Drama in Ireland from the Earliest Period up to the Present Day* (Tralee, Ireland: Kerryman, 1946) p. 391.

2. Sarah Purser (1848–1943), artist.

3. Arthur Darley, descendant of poet George Darley. He excelled in his traditional Irish airs, which he played in front of the curtain; and when he left the Abbey, J. F. Larchet took up his baton.

4. *The Shadow of the Glen* was billed for the second night.

5. The Black-and-Tans were auxiliaries supplied by the British in 1920 during the Anglo-Irish conflict.

6. Countess Constance Markievicz, née Gore-Booth (1868–1927), revolutionary.

The Early Days of the Irish National Theatre*

P. J. KELLY

Some account of the beginnings of the Irish national theatre movement, together with intimate portraits of its founders, is here given by P. J. Kelly, an actor now playing in *Dark Rosaleen*.[1] Mr Kelly lived with the great Irish dramatic movement in its early and struggling days; he knew intimately the men and women who founded it – John Millington Synge, William Butler Yeats, Lady Gregory, George Moore, Edward Martyn and others – and his recollections of these people and their work are of peculiar interest. When the representatives of the Irish National Theatre

* *New York Times*, 1 June 1919, section 4, pp. 2–3.

came to this country some years ago as the Irish Players, they had already begun to cater in considerable degree to the popular taste in their selection of plays, and of this trend, and of those responsible for it, Mr Kelly here speaks frankly and openly.

Mr Kelly was born and educated in Dublin, and grew up, as he describes it, in a dramatic atmosphere.

'Dublin', he began – this in the nature of a prelude to the matter in hand – 'has always been interested in the drama. A hundred years ago that city teemed with dramatic clubs and dramatic papers, just as it does today. It was only the other day that a writer in a Dublin paper pointed out that the recent appearance there of two new dramatic weeklies was no innovation, for a century ago there were periodicals which concerned themselves with the drama alone, as well as a daily paper that was issued in the interests of the theatre. This paper was called the *Theatrical Observer*, and it boasted a critic who didn't give a hang for anybody. To prove it the present-day journalist quotes from a critique written by this gentleman a hundred years ago as follows:

> We would wish that the musicians would leave their hats in the music room, and not offend our eye by cumbering the stage with them. Also that they would wait until the act be quite over before they return to the orchestra.

'A few weeks later the critic again commented in his paper:

> We observe that the gentlemen of the band have not wholly abstained from bringing their hats into the orchestra and placing them upon the stage. Do they think that the effluvia of a greasy hat can be welcome to the ladies in the dress circle?

'Since there is no more reference to "the gentlemen of the band", one does not know just the effect had upon them by this pointed criticism, but from it one does glean some idea of the attitude of the press toward the theatre in Dublin a century ago. In subsequent years the interest in dramatic art increased to such an extent that Ireland was more than ready for the establishment of a national theatre in 1902, when a group of intellectuals intimately concerned with the Irish literary renaissance organised a society for the production of plays which they considered real literature, but which, for commerical reasons, the theatrical managers declined to produce.

'I was just nineteen when I became a member of the Irish National Dramatic Company. Our first production was *Deirdre*, a play by George Russell, the mystic poet and painter. A little later W. B. Yeats gave us his *Kathleen Ni Houlihan*, a peasant play in one act. These plays were presented for the first time on 2 April, 1902, at St Teresa's Hall, Clarendon Street, Dublin. Both plays were rehearsed by W. G. Fay; the scenery was painted by Mr Russell and Mr Fay, and the dresses for *Deirdre* were designed by Mr Russell and made in Dublin by some of his friends.

'Among those in the cast presenting these two plays were Dudley Digges (now playing here in *John Ferguson*[2]), Mrs Digges,[3] Maud Gonne (a lady of great beauty and talent), Padraic Colum and myself. The success of these two plays was such that those engaged in presenting them felt it would be a great pity to let work so enthusiastically begun, drop at this point. There being no money, however, to go on with the project, we took up a collection among ourselves and rented a little hall at 34 Lower Camden Street, where we stored the scenery and properties we possessed and began rehearsal again under the direction of W. G. Fay. Our repertoire this time included besides *Kathleen Ni Houlihan* and *Deirdre*, a farce by Mr Yeats entitled *The Pot of Broth*. This is the bill which formed the programme of the Samhain festival, the company presenting them having been known up to that time as W. G. Fay's Irish National Dramatic Company. After this the title was changed to the Irish National Theatre Society. It was hoped to make Mr Russell, who had given them their first play, the first President, but he insisted that this honour should go to W. B. Yeats.

'In the modest beginning of the Irish National Theatre Society, which is now directed by Mr Yeats and Lady Gregory, and which owns the Abbey Theatre, Dublin, we all worked gratis, and worked with all the love of the art there was in us as inspiration. No task was considered too menial to undertake by any member of that first little company of players and producers. Playwrights, actors and producers combined in building props, painting scenery, constructing with our own hands everything that was necessary, even down to building the chairs upon which the audience sat. A new member of the company was usually handed either a paintbrush or a hammer and bag of nails.

'Of our first performance Mr Fay wrote to a friend: "We took in four pounds, fifteen shillings, on our opening night, so we saw no reason to complain financially."

'In addition to Mr Yeats the roster of the Irish National Theatre Society included such distinguished names as George W. Russell, Lady Gregory, George Moore, Edward Martyn and John Millington Synge, with many other equally brilliant men and women. The society, and my association in it with these great artists, was a veritable wonderland to me. I confess that it is so yet. I often turn in thought from these more commercial days in the theatre to my work in this splendid literary movement of Ireland, and remember with a never dying interest the many amusing incidents along the way of its growth, particularly those pertaining to the brilliant folk associated with it.

'Probably the most interesting figure in the Irish literary renaissance is W. B. Yeats. Mr Yeats is a man of lofty idealism, as his writings all show. It was sometimes extremely difficult, however, to follow his thought. I remember one instance in particular. Mr Yeats was collaborating with George Moore in writing a three-act play called *Diarmuid and Grania*, which was produced in Dublin by the Benson Shakespearean Company prior to the formation of the Irish National Theatre Society. During the collaborations Yeats explained to Moore that the first act must be horizontal, the second act perpendicular and the third act circular.

'"When is an act perpendicular, horizontal, or circular?" George Moore demanded to know, whereupon Yeats gave him a look of disgust and made no further effort to explain. In his own mind his meaning was evidently clear enough, but no one else ever found out what he meant by the application of such terms to a play.

'Yeats is also an extremely absent-minded man. At a social gathering I once saw him pour a jug of milk into a teapot instead of the hot water necessary to make the tea. This incident is typical of the man, whose thought was so occupied with the creation of literature that he was quite liable to forget to go to bed.'

Speaking of the late John Millington Synge, Mr Kelly said:

'I can half close my eyes and see him now as I used to see him at rehearsal. He was a man of medium height; rugged in appearance; wore a black moustache, and carried a heavy stick. Silent, kindly in manner, Synge was a figure which suggested tremendous power. I had the privilege of appearing[4] in his first play, *The Shadow of the Glen*, which received a somewhat dubious approval when produced by the Irish National Theatre Society. The central figure symbolises freedom, reminding one a bit of Ibsen's *A Doll's House*. The plays of Synge resemble those of Yeats in that they are universal in theme, and it is my opinion that he never wrote a greater one than *The Shadow of the Glen*, despite the antagonism it stirred in some quarters.[5] His next play to be produced by the society met with greater favour. It was his one-act tragedy, *Riders to the Sea*.

'Of the others instrumental in the establishment of the Irish National Society, Lady Gregory has remained, with W. B. Yeats, the most loyal. She is still with Mr Yeats in Dublin, combining her effort to his to turn the tide of commercialism which has in recent years swept over the project.

'Not so loyal has George Moore proven. A great novelist and art critic, I remember him as a man with singularly flaxen hair and a tremendous penchant for controversy. One one occasion I rehearsed under Mr Moore's direction in two plays which were presented at the Queen's Theatre, Dublin. One was Ibsen's *A Doll's House*, and the other *The Enchanted Sea*, by Edward Martyn. During rehearsals Martyn and Moore fought so many intellectual battles that it was impossible for the company to understand what it was all about. It seemed to me almost a miracle that the plays were successfully produced.

'While George Moore was born and brought up in Ireland, he lived for many years in Paris and London, finally tiring of the commercialism of the theatre in those cities however, and returning to Ireland to lend his activities to the literary renaissance of his own land. He was quite childlike in his prejudices, and his eccentricities were many. As an example of the latter he left the Roman Catholic Church, assigning as his reason that he "didn't like the stained glass windows". Moore lived at Ely Place, a most respectable neighbourhood in Dublin. He was much interested in studying the Gaelic language. During the period of his absorption in its mastery he had his hall door painted a bright green, and left it thus, the observed of all observers. Mr Moore, as well as the Fays, are now in London and no longer connected with the Irish theatre movement.

'Edward Martyn also deserted the ranks of the artists instrumental in the establishment of the society, piqued because Mr Yeats and Lady Gregory disagreed with him regarding the permanent literary quality of his plays. Martyn was a man who never sought publicity, who was a great lover of music, and generous to a degree where his interests were involved. It was once thought that he would endow the Irish National Theatre Society, but instead he gave £50,000 to the establishment of a boy choir in the Catholic Cathedral in Dublin, inspired to do so by his great dislike of female voices.

'So it came about that the Irish National Theatre Society had at last to turn for financial support to someone other than those responsible for its inception. Miss Horniman of Manchester came to the rescue of the organisation with sufficient backing for its continuance.'

Mr Kelly's reminiscences of the first years of this famous theatrical organisation include many interesting experiences, one of them being an incident attending the production of Yeats' *The Pot of Broth*. The occasion was the presentation of this little play in Foynes, a little village in County Limerick, near the banks of the Shannon. The audience was composed largely of farmers and fishermen, who sat through the farce without a smile.

'At the end of the performance Lord Monteagle, a landowner who took a keen interest in the welfare of his tenantry from both an economic and intellectual standpoint, explained to our astonishment that the play had not been understood. His Lordship was most apologetic, and assured us that the fault was not ours. The fact was that seeing a play for the first time was such a tremendous experience for our simple audience that it sat dumbfounded. So our stage director, Mr Fay, stepped before the curtain and in the simplest possible language told the story of the play, after which we began at the beginning and gave it all over again. This time our audience never missed a laugh.

'We had another amusing experience upon one occasion when we played in County Galway. Having no money to pay for admission, practically the entire audience came to the door of the hall in which we were to play laden with eggs and vegetables. There was considerable consternation in the company, but it was finally decided to accept them, and the play was given. The beginnings of the society which has become such a splendid influence in the theatrical world – or had until recent years, when financial success was placed above artistic achievement – were filled with just such quaint experiences.'

Asked if he believed the Irish National Theatre Society will again entirely revert to its policy of producing plays of permanent literary values, regardless of their chance of popularity with the masses, Mr Kelly gave it as his opinion that it will.

'With W. B. Yeats and Lady Gregory working to that end, it cannot be otherwise', he said.

NOTES

1. By W. D. Hepenstall and Whitworth Kane. Joseph Holloway, in his diary for 15 July 1940 wrote that *Dark Rosaleen* 'had a very successful run in New York'.
2. By St John Ervine.
3. Maire Quinn.
4. As Michael Dara (a young herd).
5. *In the Shadow of the Glen* displeased Synge's fellow countrymen because the fickleness of the wife might be construed to be an attack on Irish women; it will be remembered that Maud Gonne and Dudley Digges had walked out of the Molesworth Hall on the first night of the play.

The Dramatic Movement in Ireland*

J. M. SYNGE

The Irish plays which were produced in Manchester the other day[1] are the result of a dramatic movement which has been going on in Ireland for some years. In 1899, Mr W. B. Yeats, Mr Edward Martyn, Mr George Moore, Lady Gregory and some others founded the Irish Literary Theatre, and for the next three years, Irish plays were performed for one week annually in Dublin. The first performances took place in May 1899, when two remarkable plays were produced, *The Heather Field* by Mr Edward Martyn and *The Countess Cathleen* by Mr W. B. Yeats. They were played by English actors in a concert hall fitted up for the occasion, and *The Countess Cathleen*, a poetical and delicate play, suffered a good deal from bad scenery and a not very satisfactory delivery of the verse. One part however – that of the poet, Aleel – played by Miss Florence Farr was most musically spoken. The other play which had to do with modern life in Ireland was more easy to perform and was in every sense a success. The following year three plays were given, *The Bending of the Bough* by Mr George Moore; *Maeve* by Mr Edward Martyn; and *The Last Feast of the Fianna* by Miss Milligan. *The Bending of the Bough* had a sort of actuality which gave it a hold upon the audience; but the other two plays were not of much importance. Finally in the autumn of 1901, the Irish Literary Theatre wound up its career by giving two plays in the Gaiety Theatre, Dublin, *Diarmuid and Grania*, written by Mr W. B. Yeats and Mr George Moore in collaboration, and a small one-act comedy in Gaelic written by Dr Douglas Hyde. The first play was acted by Mr Benson's company and the second by amateurs with Dr Hyde himself in the principal role as the wandering folk poet. This little play was in some ways the most important of all those produced by the Irish Literary Theatre, as it alone has had an influence on the plays that have been written since, and have made up the present movement. The other plays had many good qualities but none of them had the germ of a new dramatic form or seemed to have found any new store of the materials of drama. *The Countess Cathleen* differed more in the peculiar beauty and distinction of its writing from the many verse plays that were written in

*Manuscript in the National Library of Ireland; edited by Ann Saddlemyer.

England since the time of Wordsworth and Shelley than in its essentially dramatic qualities. The plays of Mr Edward Martyn and Mr George Moore, on the other hand, were closely related to those produced by the school of Ibsen. *The Twisting of the Rope* however (Dr Hyde's play), slight as it was, gave a new direction and impulse to Irish drama, a direction towards which, it should be added, the thoughts of Mr W. B. Yeats, Lady Gregory and others were already tending. The result has been a series of little plays with Irish peasant life which are unlike, it is believed, anything that has preceded them.

Before each series of performances of the Irish Literary Theatre, a small review was edited by Mr W. B. Yeats. The first two numbers were called *Beltaine* (the Irish name of the spring festival) and the third, which was produced in autumn, was changed to *Samhain*, an autumn festival of the Gaels. This name has since been retained for the review which has appeared annually for some years, and must be consulted by those who wish to become familiar with the opinions of Mr W. B. Yeats – opinions more or less fully shared by those who work with him – on the dramatic movement in Ireland. In the first *Beltaine*, published in May 1899, Mr Yeats thus explains the aims of the Irish Literary Theatre,

> The Irish Literary Theatre will attempt to do in Dublin something of what has been done in London and Paris; and if it has even a small welcome it will produce, somewhere about the old festival of Beltaine at the beginning of every spring, a play founded upon an Irish subject. The plays will differ from those produced by associations of men of letters in London and in Paris because times have changed, and because the intellect of Ireland is romantic and spiritual, rather than scientific and analytical, but they will have as little of a commercial ambition. Their writers will appeal to that limited public which gives understanding and not to that unlimited public which gives wealth; and if they interest those among their audience who keep in their memories the songs of Callanan and Walsh or old Irish legends, or who love the good books of any country, they will not mind greatly if others are bored.

Works written with these aims and produced by English actors were hardly likely to produce a dramatic movement of much real vitality, but fortunately, at the end of the three years' work, of the Irish Literary Theatre, a little company of Irish actors was discovered which had been brought together by two brothers, who were much interested in the stage. One of these gentlemen, Mr W. G. Fay had many years' experience as a professional actor, and then for some [time] he had directed a little company that produced farces and other simple plays in various halls in Dublin. This little company first acted plays relating to the movement of the Irish Literary Theatre in the spring of 1902 when it produced a little play by the poet AE [George Russell] on the saga of Deirdre and the Sons of Usnach and *Kathleen Ni Houlihan* by Mr W. B. Yeats, one of the most interesting of all the plays that the movement has produced. Since then the actors, writers and a part at least of the audience, have been intimately related and the movement has lost all resemblance to the movements fostered by purely artistic cliques in London and Paris. The problem the writers have now to master is the one always present in the greater arts, the problem, that is to say, of finding a universal expression for the particular emotions and ideas of the personality of the artist himself. How far this has been done in the plays that have been produced hitherto it is hardly possible to say but in dealing with the movement the popular aim which it includes should not be forgotten.

To resume however the story of the movement itself. In the autumn of 1902 Mr Fay's company produced various plays, *Deirdre*, *Kathleen Ni Houlihan*, *The Racing Lug*, by Mr Cousins, *The Pot of Broth* by Mr W. B. Yeats, and some months later, Lady Gregory's *Twenty-Five* and *The Hour-Glass* by Mr W. B. Yeats.

In May 1903 the company played five plays in the Queen's Gate Hall, Kensington, with a great deal of success, obtaining with other notices the following review from Mr Walkley in the supplement to *The Times* —

Stendhal said that the greatest pleasure he had ever got from the theatre was given him by the performance of some poor Italian strollers in a barn. The Queen's Gate Hall if not exactly a barn can boast none of the glories of the ordinary playhouse and it was here that only a day or two ago a little band of Irish men and women, strangers to London and to Londoners gave some of us, who for our sins are constant frequenters of the regular playhouses, a few moments of calm delight quite outside the range of anything which those houses have to offer. They were members of The Irish National Theatre Society, which consists, we understand, of amateurs all engaged in daily work who can devote only their leisure time to the stage. That was the case, it will be remembered, with the enthusiasts who helped Antoine to found his Théâtre Libre, but there is this difference that while the French enterprise was an artistic adventure and nothing else, the Irish Theatre is that and something more. It is part of a national movement. It is designed to express the spirit of the race, the 'virtue' of it in the medium of acted drama. That is an excellent design. If the peculiarities of Irish thought and feeling can be brought home to us through drama, we shall all be the better for the knowledge; and the art of drama, too, cannot but gain by a change of air, a new outlook, a fresh current of ideas. But with these larger aspects of the matter we are not now concerned. Our present business is to record the keen pleasure which an afternoon with The Irish National Theatre has afforded us, and to do our best to analyse that pleasure.[2]

He speaks then of the pleasure given him by the accents of the Irish actors, their quietness on the stage and passes on to speak of the plays themselves.

The following winter, a considerable number of new plays were produced by the company at the Molesworth Hall, Dublin, including *The King's Threshold* and *The Shadowy Waters* by Mr W. B. Yeats; *Broken Soil* by Mr Colm; *Riders to the Sea* and *The Shadow of the Glen* by the present writer. About this time the company rented a small hall[3] entered by two dark passages in a poor street in Dublin, and there the members rehearsed two or three evenings of the week during the winter. Sometimes as at the rehearsals of *The King's Threshold* and *The Shadow of the Glen* the little hall was half filled with scenery and customes and at one end a carpenter was hammering a movable platform and 'fit-up' while at the other end the actors were rehearsing the elaborate verses of Mr Yeats. Many of the costumes were made in the hall also by the ladies of the company during the intervals of their rehearsing and since the members have moved on to more comfortable quarters, many of them look back not unkindly at the little ramshackle hall where the rain came in through the roof on wet nights and drunken wanderers[4] used sometimes to be found asleep in the long passages when it was time to go home.

The following spring another visit was made to London and several plays, *The King's Threshold*, *The Shadow of the Glen*, *Riders to the Sea*, and *Broken Soil* were given with much success at the Royalty Theatre. Not long afterwards Miss Horniman, with great generosity, fitted up the Abbey Theatre, Dublin, for the use of the company and from that time forward this theatre has been their home. About the same time, Mr Yeats brought out a double number of *Samhain*, in the autumn of 1904, in which he explained at length his views on the various aspects of our movements. Our plays, he says, must be literature or written in the spirit of literature. The modern theatre has died away to what it is, because the writers have thought of their audiences instead of their subjects. We must have appropriate stage management, that is, a stage management which will keep us free from gestures, movements and intonations which have lost their meaning and vitality. Again we must have a new kind of scenic art in which the background will be of as little importance as the background of a portrait group and when it is possible of one colour or of one tint with the persons on the stage. The experiments of the National Theatre Society, he adds, will have of necessity to be for a long time few and timid, and we must often, having no money, and not a great deal of leisure, accept, for a while, compromises and much even that we know to be redeemably bad. One can only perfect an art gradually, and good playwriting, good speaking and good acting are the first necessity.

During the last eighteen months, most of the new plays that the company has produced in the Abbey Theatre have been rather longer than those that preceded them. Lady Gregory has produced two historical plays in three acts[5] which have much interest, although perhaps less vitality than her two admirable farces *Spreading the News* and *Hyacinth Halvey*. *The Land* by Patrick Colm; *The Eloquent Dempsey* and *The Building Fund* by Mr Boyle; and *The Well of the Saints* by the present writer are in three acts also. Fresh aid has been given to the company during the last session by the admirable staging of Mr Robert Gregory and the music of Mr Arthur Darley whose playing of traditional Irish music on the violin has brought an element of beauty into many programmes.

Outside Ireland

Several of Mr Yeats' plays have been produced in America, and not long ago *The Well of the Saints* was played in German at the Deutsches Theatre, Berlin, and *The Shadow of the Glen* in Bohemian in the theatre at Prague.

Several new plays are in hands for the company's next season in Dublin which will open in September or October next.

NOTES

John Millington Synge (1871–1909), playwright.

1. The Irish National Theatre Society performed in Manchester, England, on 23 and 24 Apr 1906.

2. A. B. Walkley, 'The Irish National Theatre', *Times Literary Supplement* (London), 8 May 1903, p. 146. Reprinted, slightly rev., in *Drama and Life* (London: Methuen, 1907) pp. 309–15.

3. Camden Hall.

4. One of whom undoubtedly was James Joyce.

5. *Kincora* and *The White Cockade*.

Early Days of the Irish Theatre*

PADRAIC COLUM

Some years ago one of these demons who write books on special subjects wrote to me: she was making a study of the theme of 'The Children of Lir', and in her ransacking of all languages and literatures she discovered that half a century ago I had published in the *Weekly* [*Irish*] *Independent* (Dublin) a short play entitled *The Children of Lir*, and she wanted me to send her the text. I thanked whatever saint there is who bestows oblivion on the juvenilia of poets and dramatists and wrote back that my forgetfulness of the matter was almost complete. But she, being a determined researcher, did not leave it at that: she then sent me a picture showing the special hell that those who baulked researchers were cast into, implying that my escape from it depended on my recalling something about that publication. And this started the train of recollection whose stages form this lecture.

Well, this was the first work I ever got published – and paid for, I am happy to say. But for me the significant result was that it brought about my meeting with Miss Mary Quinn who was afterwards Mrs Dudley Digges, and through her with the group that initiated the National Theatre Society.

Something of that very early literary effort came back to me in the train of my recollections. I found that there were three good lines in it. I remembered them distinctly because when they came to me I said to myself – I remembered this, too, 'It can't be but this is poetry.' The four children of Lir speak of the witch who is to transform them into swans, and one says:

> The lonely spirit
> Who haunts the rath and makes the night bird cry
> I do not dread so much as I dread Aoife.

And now you will want to know why a person of eighteen wanted to write a play on such an untheatrical subject as the legend of 'The Childred of Lir'.

---

* Dublin Magazine, 24 (Oct 1949) 11–17; 25 (Jan 1950), 18–25.

The answer is that I knew nothing whatever about the theatre. I had seen *The Colleen Bawn*, *The Shaughraun*,[1] and some plays put on by amateurs, and once I had gone to the Gaiety Theatre, and spent a whole shilling for a seat in the pit – I could have got into the gallery for sixpence – to see Mr and Mrs Kendal in a play called *The Elder Miss Blossom* . . . I think the real reason why the theatre did not impress me was because at the age of seventeen I had discovered and read two plays of Ibsen's – *The Master Builder* and *Hedda Gabler*. That great northern dramatist whose plays were so remote from any life I knew entered my mind like the bombardment that displaces the atom. I bless the person who left these two plays in a dusty corner in the public library in Dunleary; they took possession of my mind; they left no room for anything that was not designed, that was not solid.

I seem to be straying away from *The Children of Lir* published in the *Weekly Irish Independent*. But the overall subject of my talk to you is the early days of the Irish theatre, and Ibsen, still alive, still to publish his last play, was a dominating influence on some of us – a prenatal influence, I might say:

I was about to enter a circle in which Ibsen's influence was marked. One of the plays produced by the Irish Literary Theatre which was the precursor of the Irish National Theatre was Edward Martyn's *The Heather Field*, and I remember reading a criticism of it – I did not see it – in which it was said that the play should be translated into Danish or Norse or whatever language Ibsen wrote in, and have it produced in Scandinavia. The first time I met George Moore was after an amateur production of *A Doll's House*. I spoke to him about it and I remember George exclaiming, 'Shakespeare, Sophocles – what are they to this man?' But the most genuine of the votaries of the great Scandinavian was my contemporary, James Joyce. He learned Danish – or whatever the language was – to read Ibsen, and he was able to write the first review in English of Ibsen's last play, *When We Dead Awaken*.[2] I remember a walk with James Joyce along the South Circular Road when he repeated to me in the original a lyric of Ibsen's about water lilies. When I spoke to him of George Moore's superlatives, young Joyce, with that unruffled criticial intelligence that seemed to have been always his said of *A Doll's House*, 'Of course it will remain interesting as a post-card written by Ibsen will be interesting.' To him Ibsen's great play was *Hedda Gabler*; he acted in it in an amateur production. Joyce's real tribute was the letter he wrote him on Ibsen's seventieth birthday – 'I had shown', this young man wrote, 'what, as it seemed to me, was your highest excellence – your lofty, impersonal power. . . . How your wilful resolution to wrest the secret from life gave me heart, and how in your absolute indifference to public canons of art, friends and shibboleths, you walked in the light of your inner heroism.'[3]

But even now I have not got round to telling you how I, with such little attachment to the theatre as it was in Dublin, came to write what purported to be a play. Well, for a few years before this time, when I was still a youngster, Yeats, Edward Martyn and others, founded an Irish Literary Theatre. The scheme was to have plays written by Irish writers produced in Dublin by London actors once a year. The Irish Literary Theatre gave productions that, I think, went over three years. I was able to be at the last of these productions – *Diarmuid and Grania* written by W. B. Yeats and George Moore. Written by two such diverse minds, the play could not have been a good one. It was followed by a play in Irish – the first play in Irish to be given in a theatre, An Craoibhin's Aoibhinn's play,[4] with An Craoibhin himself in the part of the poet Hanrahan. . . . Looking back I perceive that, between the production of *The Countess Cathleen* and the production of *Diarmuid and Grania* a new force had arisen in Ireland. The force was contained in the Gaelic League that, quite suddenly, had become very significant. I suppose that a new generation that had turned from the barren disputes of Parnellites[5] and anti-Parnellites had now arrived. The Gaiety Theatre was crowded with young men and women from the Gaelic League branches – the gallery, anyway. They sang national songs in the intervals. (In those days there was always someone in the gallery who could sing and sing very well and his songs would be taken up by others.) After that production the Irish Literary Theatre came to an end, but there was a feeling than an Irish theatre would come into existence.

And now I am getting back to where I started from – a publication in the *Weekly Irish Independent*.

Now in those days there was a very stern and unbending wing to the revival, and that wing was Cumann na nGaedheal. The Cumann combined Fenianism with Gaelicism; its President was John O'Leary,[6] its moving spirit was Arthur Griffith. From Cumann na nGaedheal, Sinn Fein was to come. But Cumann na nGaedheal would not go into literary history if it did not have a women's auxiliary. That auxiliary was Inghinidhi na hÉireann, and when I mention Inghinidhe na hÉireann I am mentioning the mother of the Irish theatre.

Inghinidhe na hÉireann had an illustrious personage at its head – Maud Gonne. It had brought into its ranks many brilliant young women – but more than brilliant – illuminated by an idea and devoted in support of it. Its Executive Secretary was Mary Quinn who became the first actress of the National Theatre Society, one of its members was Mary Walker, another member was Sara Allgood. Without Inghinidhe na hÉireann I do not think an Irish theatre would have come into being.

And there was that sterling young Ulster woman, living in Belfast or Bangor, who was to write the first plays that Inghinidhe na hÉireann produced – Alice Milligan. Her pageant, *The Last Feast of the Fianna*, had been produced by the Irish Literary Theatre. She had, with Eithna Carberry,[7] edited the *Shan Van Vocht*. She wrote for the Cumann na nGaedheal festival a play, *The Deliverance of Red Hugh*. I could say a great deal about Alice Milligan who fortunately is still with us, but I will only mention her extraordinary disinterestedness and a sort of practicality, northern and womanly, that went with her vision and dream.

Left to themselves and influenced by the beginnings of the dramatic movement and having Miss Gonne to direct them, Inghinidhe na hÉireann began staging what was then in the mode – tableaux vivants. These were scenes from Moore's melodies – living pictures that were carried along by the music. 'Avenging and Bright Fall the Swift Sword of Erin' in which for a minute the audience would see an appealing Deirdre, a frowning king and stalwart young heroes who would stand for no betrayals. I was in an audience in some hall devoted to nationalism and Gaelicism when I saw the tableau of 'Silent O Moyle be the Roar of Thy Waters' and watched the enchantment of the children of Lir. My latent dramatic interest was stirred and I went home and started to write the play with whose publication my talk to you began.

And so I have got round to what the demon researcher wrote to me about, but in getting round to it I have suggested, I hope, the atmosphere that surrounded the beginning of the Irish theatre.

Having written *The Children of Lir*, I sent it to Inghinidhe na hÉireann. I held back from doing this for some time because I did not know the proper method of addressing the Secretary if I wrote her in my O'Growney Irish.[8] Of the Irish I knew I felt that any form of address would be too familiar. So I decided to write in English and begin my epistle, 'Dear Madam'.

It was Mary Quinn who initiated my dramatic career by presenting me to the two men to whom whatever success *The Deliverance of Red Hugh* had was due – Willie and Frank Fay. And here I want to sketch the characters of these two without whom the Irish theatre could never have come into existence, or, if it had come into existence, could never have developed into what we have today. You have seen their portraits in the Abbey vestibule – very lifelike portraits they are indeed. Except for their common interest in the theatre there was nothing to mark these two men as related. They were sons of a respectable Dublin family. Willie had broken loose and had gone about the Irish countryside with travelling shows and circuses. He was an artisan with the rationality, the intellectual equipment of a superior workman. Frank was the scholarly type. In their wage-earning capacity Frank belonged to a firm of auditors, Craig Gardner, while Willie was an electric fitter who had learned the theory while he was putting up wires in the rebuilt Theatre Royal. Except that they were both undersized in appearance they had little resemblance to each other. Frank, with his open face and open eyes

– Willie wore glasses – was much less of the world than his brother. Trim in get-up he gave the impression of a man in whom a sense of measure was strong; he was much less of a mixer than Willie, more of a solitary. Now and again he showed the crankiness of a student who sometimes found the work-aday world distasteful. On these occasions he would remain apart, smile while his eyes glittered, and remark, 'I've got the hump, my boy, that's all'. What a character for a Browning poem was Frank Fay, and what a pity Browning did not do a portrait of him for his 'Men and Women'! But Browning did do a portrait of Frank Fay in advance: it is of the Grammarian in 'A Grammarian's Funeral'. That passionate devotee to language who settled Hoti's business and for ever fixed the place of the enclitic De was Frank Fay in a previous incarnation.

This is an occasion when it is proper to pay a tribute to Frank Fay. Several years ago, with Dudley Digges, I went to hear a lecture in New York by James Cousins who had been with us in the early days of the National Theatre Society. As we listened to words that were given with an unusual, with an admirable enunciation, Dudley Digges said to me: 'Where in Dublin is there a monument to Frank Fay?' How many whose beautiful speaking has been praised owed that accomplishment to Frank Fay – Dudley Digges, Mary Walker, Sarah Allgood and others. How often did a band of us come home from a Sunday walk in the hills or along the streets after a rehearsal, repeating verse in the way that Frank Fay would have us repeat it, giving value to all the vowels:

> Her flag is folding and unfolding, and in its fold
> Her Raven flutters; rob him of his prey,
> Or be his prey, I follow the white birds.

But it was only in a combination that Frank Fay was theatrically successful, and it was with his brother Willie that the combination was made. Frank was the elder of the two brothers, but when I was with them I did not realise that. Willie was looked up to as the head of everything, and by no one was this precedence more insisted on than by Frank. Indeed a great deal of the personal prestige which permitted Willie to be boss was continuously and voluntarily supplied by Frank. 'You'll have to see the brother about that, my boy', he would say, referring one to an authority that could not be gainsaid. Or, 'I may tell you that the brother wouldn't like that at all', he would say as if informing one that there was no use in going against acknowledged infallibility. It was this continuous enhancement of prestige, together with a bit of showmanship on his own part – for after all he was a showman – that enabled Willie Fay to stabilise a group of Dubliners long enough to give a base for a national theatre. But it was not always smooth going. Sometimes the bitterness that was signified by the glitter in Frank's eyes would be discharged even at 'the brother'. I remember a rehearsal in the Coffee Palace, a rehearsal of AE [George Russell]'s *Deirdre*, at which the two flew at each other. The company hid behind sets and properties. There was a line in the play that said, 'I foresee that the Red Branch will go down in a sea of blood.' When we got clear of the encounter I heard AE say, 'I foresee that the National Theatre Society will go down in a sea of fists.'

At the time when I made my debut, Willie and Frank Fay, with young Dudley Digges and young P. J. Kelly were still the Fays' Comedy Combination. They played old-fashioned farces. When I was taken into the company they were rehearsing a farce called *His Last Legs*.[9] But already the national movement had impinged on the Fays' Comedy Combination. Willie Fay had produced Alice Milligan's *The Deliverance of Red Hugh* and Frank Fay had given the players instruction in speech. And now the Irish Literary Theatre had come to its end. The work should be carried on, and it was the Fays' Comedy Combination that undertook to do just that.

Willie was the centre of the Fays' Comedy Combination. He was much less nationalistic than Frank, and might have been content to go on playing comedy and farce. Willie wore glasses, and the eyes behind them could give shrewd and reckoning glances; there was something in the face that suggested a man who had no bad opinion of himself; it was quick-tempered and controlled, and could be complacent when he reclined with a briar pipe in his mouth. Willie saw himself as a master-mind. When the company, at that time formed into the National Theatre Society, made its first visit to London one of the actresses became sick after the long train journey. The company was anxious about the way she did her part. She did it very well. When relief was expressed to Willie Fay he took the pipe out of his mouth and said, 'I sat where I could bring influence on her.' That was Willie Fay: nothing could go wrong if he made up his mind to keep it right.

It might seem from what I have told you that this early effort was spasmodic, that it could hardly result in the creation of an important or enduring body of work. At some point there would have to be a core of purpose. Well, that core was supplied by W. B. Yeats who, as he has told us, wanted to get into his verse 'a more manful energy'[10] and knew that the way to tap that manful energy was to put himself into the theatre, and by Lady Gregory who, although she wrote excellent comedies for the theatre, had for her main purpose to help Yeats to realise himself as a great dramatic poet.

We were in the middle of rehearsing AE's *Deirdre* when Yeats appeared amongst us with the offer of his *Kathleen Ni Houlihan* which he had just written. But who were we? Were we the Fays' Comedy Combination? We were rehearsing *His Last Legs* alternatively with *Deirdre* but on the innovating side we were yet nameless. And where were we rehearsing? In the Coffee Palace which was some place near the Custom House. The Coffee Palace was a philanthropic institution dedicated to the idea that if Dublin working men gave up their draughts of Guinness and took to coffee there would be better and happier men and women. There was an attempt to throw a glamour round coffee. Hence 'Palace'. And there was also an attempt to give the converts to coffee some uplifting kind of entertainment – lectures and inoffensive plays. The Fays had put on comedies under this dispensation, and so we had the Coffee Palace for rehearsals of *Deirdre*.

With the rehearsal of *Deirdre* in the Coffee Palace the national theatre had its real beginning. Two groups coalesced, forming a nucleus: there were the professional people, Willie Fay, Frank Fay, young Dudley Digges, young P. J. Kelly, and there were the political ideologists – Mary Quinn, Mary Walker, and to them were added the poet AE and with him one or two disciples from his Hermetic Society and myself as an apprentice dramatist. It was Frank Fay who had discovered *Deirdre*, and, since the speeches were just in his line, decided to give a production of it. In Standish O'Grady's *All Ireland Review* this play was being published, an act an issue, and the third act had not yet appeared and had not yet been written when the play was put into rehearsal. AE rarely went to the theatre, but he had gone to see *Diarmuid and Grania* and was shocked to see the way the heroic characters were treated in that play. He was roused to write a different kind of heroic play as a protest, and that was the play we were rehearsing. When *His Last Legs* was disposed of we went to the rehearsing of it in earnest, and by that time we had *Kathleen Ni Houlihan* to rehearse, too. And then we had W. B. Yeats for a leader.

The poets gave consciousness to the group in those early days. Everyone dealt in poetry either at first or at second hand. Frank Fay was in his element declaiming and instructing in declamation. He revelled in the poetry of Yeats. Rehearsing with him was a memorable training in vocalisation and verse-delivery.

After a long period of rehearsal in which we apprentices learned a great deal, *Deirdre* and *Kathleen Ni Houlihan* were put on in a hall[11] belonging to the Carmelite Fathers in Clarendon Street, a hall in which the Fays had put on comedies. We were all very exalted when it came to the production. Maud Gonne was to play the old Woman in *Kathleen Ni Houlihan*. Willie Fay had decided to produce *Deirdre* behind gauze veils and we all thought that this was a remarkable innovation. The hall was packed; I remember; the audience, too, had come with an exaltion that reached the stage. There were great moments in the production – certainly Maud Gonne's exit in *Kathleen Ni Houlihan*; certainly the dignity and pathos of Dudley Digges both in *Kathleen Ni Houlihan* and *Deirdre*; certainly the words said by Mary Walker in her vibrating voice that was like bird calls on a still day. Certainly Mary Quinn's Deirdre, Frank Fay's speeches as Concobar, Willie Fay's acting as the man of the house in *Kathleen Ni Houlihan* must have made memorable impressions. But there were other parts of that production that stay in my memory. I remember AE standing up to repeat his magical chant as Cathbad the Druid, a chant that had really the effect of an incantation. Dudley Digges as Naisi in *Deirdre*, spoke to Mary Quinn as Deirdre, telling her of the heroic companionship he had left when they went into exile. He said, 'There was one there, a small, dark man whom some thought to be a god in exile', and then he named Cuchullain. I was conscious that a thrill went through the audience. It was the first time the epic hero was named in an Irish theatre. At the end of the performances there was a feeling amongst us all – and that included the audience – that something momentous had been reached.

Each of the authors was called before the curtain. AE went on and delivered one of the noblest addresses I have ever listened to. He looked magnificent in his height and with his fine beard. He spoke about the meaning of that tragic story in which the beautiful and the faithful are destroyed by treachery. And he said 'Better to perish through an excess of noble trust than to live through the vigilance of suspicion.'

The time that the society got itself a habitation is important, and I shall speak of that. The habitation was a hall beside a grocery shop in Camden Street, a hall, as a critic who was induced to come to a performance said, not wide enough to swing a cat in, well, not a good-sized cat. There we built a platform, hammered together benches, rehearsed the play that Yeats wrote for the society, *The King's Threshold*. It was at this period that Sara Allgood joined the society.

I remember it as a happy, active time. We enjoyed each other's company, for the bulk of us were young and trusting. Young apprentice poets like Seumas O'Sullivan, James Cousins, George Roberts and myself had a place where we could read and discuss our verse. We had the inspiration of having W. B. Yeats and AE come amongst us and had an occasional visit from George Moore. But here we were to be sharply reminded that now we were an organisation and had to submit ourselves to controls. One of our society, P. J. Kelly,[12] was haled up for trial. He belonged to the original company and had passed from playing in *His Last Legs* to playing in *Deirdre* and *Kathleen Ni Houlihan*. Considering himself as free as before the society was formed he played in an outside production without asking permission of the society. Willie Fay was stern and demanded his expulsion from the society. P. J. Kelly was drummed out. I remember his leaving through the door that went out into Camden Street and seeing the tense faces of his colleagues, the unbending look of Willie Fay, and realising that a change had come in the spirit of the society.

But although we were now an organisation each of us still had personal authority. We recognised Willie Fay as an executive and W. B. Yeats had great influence on us. But when it came to selecting a play the society as a whole body voted. A play was offered and it had the approval of Willie Fay. It was by James Cousins whose short plays *The Racing Lug* and *The Sleep of the King* had been already performed by the society. The play was a comedy and had the sort of situations that the Willie Fay of *His Last Legs* was used to. But Yeats vetoed the production; he would withdraw from the society if the selection of plays was not vested in a small reading committee. The committee would then recommend its selection to the society as a whole.

With the election of a reading committee a further step was taken in the making of our loose society into an organisation. And it was now that the influence of one who had a great share in shaping the society was to be felt. That one was Lady Gregory. We had produced a one-act comedy of hers, *Twenty-Five*, but now we were to witness the growth of her influence in another capacity.

On the reading committee that was formed there was placed W. B. Yeats, AE, Lady Gregory, Fred Ryan, myself, with Arthur Griffith and Maud Gonne as representatives of the nationalist interest. When our first meeting was about to be held the question was raised as to where we should hold it. 'It will be warmer at Lady Gregory's hotel', said W. B. Yeats. 'But it will be cooler here', said AE indicating our draughty hall. We chose to be warm and went to Lady Gregory's hotel.

Hers was the Nassau, which is no longer in existence, and she had a drawing-room there, looking out on the street. With our meetings in that room, either as a committee to select plays or as a body to have the selected plays read, the centre of the National Theatre Society shifted. That centre was no longer the hall where rehearsals were held. It was in Lady Gregory's apartment.

It was from this time that Lady Gregory's influence came to be a dominating one. Her main interest was in W. B. Yeats' dramatic career. She had not shared the life of an important diplomat, Sir William Gregory,[13] for nothing. Her own diplomacy now became effective in the Theatre Society. It was she who estimated the forces, who countered the dissident elements, who precipitated the situations. But because her diplomacy combined resolution with an apparent artlessness, and preparation with flattery of address, it was annoying to those who could see through a millstone. She created a hegemony in the National Theatre Society, W. B. Yeats' and her own. It was through this hegemony that the Abbey Theatre was created.

I have forgotten whether it was at this time or a little before it that a crisis arose in which a youthful and unsure person, myself, was the centre. I had written a little propagandist play, *The Saxon Shillin'* for Cumann na nGaedheal. It was published in the *United Irishman* and was thought very well of by that separatist society. I will say here that after its publication I was in a room where the head of Dublin Castle, Sir Anthony MacDonald, was. He had granite-like features, a grave demeanour, and was addicted to an eyeglass. Putting up his eyeglass he looked at me steadily. 'And so this is Mr Colum,' he said, 'who has shaken the foundations of the British Empire in Ireland with his anti-recruiting play.' Well, a time came when Cumann na nGaedheal that still had connection with the National Theatre Society, requested Willie Fay to put on *The Saxon Shillin'*. Willie Fay declined on the ground that the main situation could not be staged effectively.[14] But there were those in the society who thought that his refusal to have anything to do with the production came from the fact that he did not want to have the garrison deployed against the hopeful theatre enterprise. There was a great row in which this person – at least in the eyes of Arthur Griffith, Maud Gonne and Mary Quinn – played a very weak part. The consequence was that Arthur Griffith and Maud Gonne withdrew from the society. And so the link between the theatre and Cumann na nGaedheal was broken.

But a more important crisis arose with the acceptance of a one-act play which W. B. Yeats brought to us as we were hammering benches together in the hall in Camden Street. This was *The Shadow of the Glen* by John M. Synge. It was accepted for production against the protests of Dudley Digges and Mary Quinn who thought that it was a play that let the Irish country people down – in those days the cult of the peasant was very strong. They resigned from the society and we lost two of our best players.

In casting it, the part of Nora was given to the beautiful Mary Walker and the part of the tramp to W. G. Fay. The enthusiastic John Butler Yeats attended a rehearsal and wrote an article for the *United Irishman* welcoming the play as a satire on the arranged marriage, the marriage for money, which the Dublin intellectuals looked on with very morose eyes. But the editor and readers of the *United Irishman*, aware that the Theatre Society had slipped from the straight and narrow path of nationalism were prepared by JB's well-intentioned article to find in *The Shadow of the Glen* an anti-peasant manifesto.[15] Who was J. M. Synge? Well, he was a landowner or he was connected with landowners, and his was a landowner's view of the peasantry. It was the Big House against the Cabin. And when it was talked of, as it was before production, there were people who were prepared to be very fierce about that issue. Well, *The Shadow of the Glen* was produced in the Molesworth Hall before a scanty and shivering audience, for the hall was cold and the season was winter. I remember that Synge stayed at the back, beside the entrance. He was a very nervous man, and I noticed with surprise that he was shaking during the performance. At the curtain there was a call for author. Synge walked up the middle of the hall to take the call. As he did there was a hiss, a single hiss, from a woman in the audience. It was a signal, not for a demonstration, but for some signs of unrest among the audience. It was prophetic of the Dublin audience's reception of Synge's future plays, *The Well of the Saints* and *The Playboy of the Western World*.

Then came the first visit to London which was rapturously acclaimed by the London critics. They brought my first three-act play, *Broken Soil* over. I should mention that Yeats did not favour the production of this immature play in London but the membership of the society insisted on doing it.

In the next stage of the history of the theatre there was a great deal of unrest. New players had come into the group, including Arthur Sinclair and J. M. Kerrigan. They were kept on the outside by the original society who had put their work into it so far as well as a little money, as much as moderately paid working people, as we all at the time were, could afford. These newcomers, good actors as they were acknowledged to be, were given no votes in the conduct of the theatre. Then there was a feeling amongst the old members that the nationalist idea, out of which they conceived the theatre had grown, was being shelved. There was another visit to London with Synge's, Yeats', Lady Gregory's plays, and my own play, *The Land*, more mature than the first play of mine that was given on the first visit. Before that came Miss Horniman's gift of a theatre for the society.

But with that gift went the demand that the general control of play production and policy should be renounced by the National Theatre Society and all power placed in the hands of a directorate which would be made up of W. G. Fay, W. B. Yeats, Lady Gregory and J. M. Synge. The debates on this issue went on and on. The extreme nationalists were against giving power to the directorate because they thought it meant cutting the theatre off from its nationalist origins. Others, like Fred Ryan, were opposed to the change because it was against the democratic spirit we had so far. But Yeats, whose influence was now paramount, and who was fond of using the slogan, 'The tools to him who can use them' was determined to create the directorate. There were debates in public and private; there were many changes of sides. And on the flank some of us felt harassed by Miss Horniman who had come over to Dublin and annoyed some of us by her repeated declarations that the Gaelic League was out for her blood. And the national theatre was not composed of the homogeneous elements as it had been. There were the newcomers who had no votes and so had no interest in preserving the democratic spirit that some of us talked about. The time came when we were asked to vote on what some of us thought to be our own extinction. There was a secession. With the exception of the Fays and Sara Allgood, the best known of the old members went out of the National Theatre Society.

What happened after that is history that I am sure you all know and that I need not enlarge on. My conclusion will be a comment . . . Plutarch lied: the great thing cannot be altogether the creation of the one great man. When Willie Fay wrote about the foundation of the theatre, when Lady Gregory wrote about it, they were on the side of Plutarch, the side of the historian who is there to tell us that the great man, the hero, does everything. The theatre was the creation of a man – in one case, Willie Fay with his brother, in the other W. B. Yeats. But let us be more discriminating than Plutarch. There are certain imponderables working through minor men and women that instigate great men to give form and scope to what the others are reaching towards. Without these imponderables, without the fermenting but unkeyed-up minds surrounding the great man, no dominating work is ever achieved. The fermenting minds, the man who can give them focus, were present in the moment that created a national theatre for Ireland. My recollection assures me that behind the writers and players was a national feeling that manifested itself through the young men and women belonging to the politico-cultural clubs in the Dublin of the time; it was they who gave the project spirit and the breath of life. And W. B. Yeats, himself a man of the nationalist clubs and societies, knew the worth of that national feeling even though he wanted to raise it to another level.

NOTES

Padraic Colum (1881–1972), poet, playwright, biographer, novelist, short story writer, essayist, folklorist and writer of children's stories. He became a member of the Irish National Theatre Society, was an original Abbey charter signer, and wrote three of the Abbey's earliest plays: *The Land* (1905), *The Fiddler's House* (1907) and *Thomas Muskerry* (1910). He was an intimate friend of the giants of modern literature in Ireland, England, France and America. See Zack Bowen, *Padraic Colum* (Carbondale, Illinois: Southern Illinois University Press, 1970); Alan Denson, 'Padraic Colum: An Appreciation with a Checklist of His Publications', *Dublin Magazine*, 6 (Spring 1967) 50–67; and Padraic Colum, *The Road Round Ireland* (New York: Macmillan, 1926).

1. Both plays by Dion Boucicault (?1820–90).

2. James A. Joyce, 'Ibsen's New Drama', *Fortnightly Review* (London), n.s. 67 (1 Apr 1900) 575–90.

3. Letter to Ibsen dated March 1901, reprt in *Letters of James Joyce*, ed. Stuart Gilbert (London: Faber & Faber, 1957) pp. 51–2.

4. *Casadh an tSugáin* [*The Twisting of the Rope*]. 'An Craoibhin Aoibhinn' [The Sweet Little Branch] was the pen name of Douglas Hyde.

5. Followers of the political leader Charles Stewart Parnell (1846–91).

6. John O'Leary (1830–1907), Fenian.

7. Pen name of Anna MacManus (1866–1911), writer. Her writings did much to stimulate the early Sinn Fein movement. With Alice Milligan she founded the *Shan Van Vocht* in 1896.

8. The Irish taught by Father Eugene O'Growney (1863–99), a leading figure in the Irish language revival movement.

9. A farce by W. B. Bernard.

10. '. . . to me drama . . . has been the search for more of manful energy, more of cheerful acceptance of whatever arise out of the logic of events, and for clean outline, instead of those outlines of lyric poetry that are blessed with desire and vague regret' (Yeats' Preface to *Poems, 1899–1905*).

11. St Teresa's Hall.

12. See P. J. Kelly's recollections, p. 48.

13. In 1880, Lady Gregory married Sir William Gregory, a widower whose estate at Coole Park, Gort, was not far from that of her father, Dudley Persse. Sir William died in 1892.

14. At a general meeting of the Irish National Theatre Society on 15 Feb 1903, W. G. Fay refused to produce *The Saxon Shillin'*, a propagandist play against enlistment of Irishmen in the British army, ostensibly on the grounds of a weak ending. Colum, however, later declared that Fay did not wish to incur the hostility of the 'garrison'. *The Saxon Shillin'* was published in *Lost Plays of the Irish Renaissance*, ed. Robert Hogan and James Kilroy (Newark, Delaware: Proscenium Press, 1970).

15. See John B. Yeats, 'Ireland Out of the Dock', *United Irishman* (Dublin), 10 October 1903, p. 2; and 'The Irish National Theatre Society', ibid., 31 Oct 1903, p. 7.

Some Account of the Early Days of the INTS*

FRANK FAY

When Coquelin[1] came to Dublin to play *Cyrano de Bergerac* for the first time in Ireland, a friend of mind asked me to write a criticism[2] of that great actor's performance for a newspaper which did a great deal to arouse Ireland – tired of political squabbles that followed the fall of Parnell – to national self-consciousness again. For this paper, the *United Irishman*, I wrote a number of articles on theatrical topics,[3] amongst others on the Irish Literary Theatre which Mr Yeats, Mr Edward

*Manuscript lecture in the National Library of Ireland.

Martyn, Mr George Moore and Lady Gregory had founded with the object of producing plays which they thought good dramatic literature, but which the regular theatrical manager had no reason for producing. What disturbed me about the Irish Literary Theatre was the fact that its plays – the work of Irish writers – were played by English actors who naturally were not a bit like what they were intended for. They were excellent actors, but they destroyed whatever Irish atmosphere happened to be in the plays in which they acted. My comments on the work of the Irish Literary Theatre led to my acquaintance with its leading spirit Mr Yeats; it also led to my being asked to assist in staging some tableaux of Irish historical subjects by a society of ladies – the Daughters of Erin – founded by, I think, Miss Maud Gonne. In this work I had the assistance of my brother who had spent some seven years on the regular stage, playing in all sorts and conditions of plays. These tableaux having proved very successful, the Daughters of Erin decided on giving a similar entertainment later on in the same year (1901), with the addition of a play or two. The production of these plays was put into my brother's hands, and to act them he had the assistance of an amateur company which he had organised before he went on the regular stage, and which had continued to play in Dublin during the years he spent in the theatrical profession. On his leaving the professional stage and settling down in Dublin, he continued to play at the head of this amateur company as an amusement. Three members of that company are now in New York, one with Mr Sothern,[4] and one – Mr Digges – has been playing with us in *The Rising of the Moon*.[5] In the plays referred to above, which he produced for the Daughters of Erin, the chief members of his own amateur company were supplemented by members of the Daughters of Erin Society and of an associated literary society. At the performances of these plays, Mr Yeats was present and said to the writer one evening at the fall of the curtain, 'I like the grave acting of your company.' The mystic poet and painter George Russell [AE] also saw these plays, and entrusted my brother with the production of his three-act play *Deirdre*. Mr Yeats, a little later, gave us his *Kathleen Ni Houlihan* for production, and both plays were produced in April 1902 at St Teresa's Hall, Clarendon Street, Dublin for three nights to large audiences, many being turned away each night. The company by which these two plays were acted, consisted of my brother, myself, Mr Digges, Mrs Digges, Mr P. J. Kelly (now with Mr Sothern in this city) and some others, principally young poets and writers. Both plays were rehearsed by my brother, W. G. Fay; the scenery was painted by him and by AE, and the dresses were designed for *Deirdre* by AE and made in Dublin by lady friends of his. After the performance of *Deirdre* and *Kathleen Ni Houlihan*, those who had been associated in the acting of them, thinking it would be a pity to let the work drop, subscribed among themselves and rented a little hall in Camden Street where they stored the little scenery and properties they had accumulated and rehearsed under my brother's direction some other plays, amongst them Mr Yeats' farce *The Pot of Broth*, which, with *Deirdre* and *Kathleen Ni Houlihan*, formed the programme of the first Samhain festival organised by Cumann na nGaedeal, a Dublin political body. Curiously the three original actors of *The Pot of Broth* are now in New York – W. G. Fay, P. J. Kelly and Mrs Digges (Mary Quinn). After the Samhain festival, the company which till then had been known as 'W. G. Fay's Irish National Dramatic Company', changed its title to the Irish National Theatre Society. The desire of its members was that AE, who had given us our first Irish play, should be our President; but, at his suggestion, I proposed Mr Yeats who was and is still President of the Irish National Theatre Society. The title, if I remember rightly, was suggested by me, because at that time I was greatly excited by an article which William Archer wrote in the *Morning Leader*, a London daily paper, describing how Ole Bull, the great Norwegian violinist, had formed the Norwegian national theatre out of a few young men and women who had answered an advertisement inserted by him in a Bergen newspaper asking Norwegians who wanted to make a profession of acting, singing, etc. to communicate with him. The story of how the amateur actor André Antoine (now director of the Odeon, Paris) formed the Théâtre Libre out of an amateur company of which he was a member also interested me deeply, and my brother and myself discussed the possibility of doing similar work in Ireland. Until Ole Bull founded a Norwegian national theatre, his countrymen had thought 'Norwegian', which I understand is practically a dialect of Danish, unfit to be spoken on the stage. In the same way we thought it was time to make the Irish accent and idiom, in speaking English, a vehicle for expression of Irish character on the stage and not for the sole purpose of provoking laughter. That we succeeded we have had plenty of opportunity of knowing. Mr A. B. Walkley the critic of the London *Times* was especially enthusiastic about the diction of the company on one occasion of its first visit to London, which came about in this way. Mr Stephen Gwynn, MP was present at the Samhain festival plays, already referred to, and was so impressed by the possibilities of what he saw that he wrote a long article in the *Fortnightly Review*, entitled 'An Uncommercial Theatre', in the year 1903, and backed up his opinion by bringing the company to London for a matinee and evening performance, which were given at Queen's Gate Hall, Kensington. All the London critics were present and were very enthusiastic over both plays and players; and the audience before which we played included Mr J. M. Barrie and Mr Henry James. The plays acted on that occasion were Mr Yeats' *The Hour-Glass* and Lady Gregory's first play *Twenty-Five*, *Kathleen Ni Houlihan*, *The Pot of Broth*, and a two-act satire on Dublin municipal life, *The Laying of the Foundations*, by Fred Ryan, our then Secretary, now a writer on an Egyptian nationalist paper at Cairo. This first London visit was difficult to arrange. We were all, at that time, at business in the day – typists, electricians, bookkeepers, shop assistants, etc. We had all to arrange to get away for the day at a time of the year when business was in full swing. We arrived in London early in the morning, had breakfast, some of us went to bed for an hour or two, and were wakened up just when we were beginning to enjoy our sleep, and hurried over to the hall to play for the first time in our lives before a picked London audience and before all the dramatic critics! I should not like to endure the strain I felt while waiting for my cue to go on to stage as the Fool in *The Hour-Glass*, again. But we were all on our mettle, and the plays went without a hitch. After the performance we returned to our hotel, had dinner and returned again for the evening performance. Twenty minutes before the curtain rose we got news that one of our principal actresses was too ill to go on, which I need not say filled us with consternation! But one of the other ladies volunteered to play the part, and Mr Gwynn announced this from the stage. Fortunately, however, the actress who had been taken ill recovered in time to appear, and the evening performance also passed off without a hitch. At the close of the performance I did not know whether I was in my head or my heels. We returned to Dublin next morning. The chief strain of the experiment, of course, rested on my brother, who was responsible not only for the stage management and acting of us all, but had the most exacting parts to play. Of his acting in *The Pot of Broth*, William Archer wrote: 'Of individual performers, one, Mr W. G. Fay, showed extraordinary accomplishment in the part of the Beggarman in *The Pot of Broth*. This was a perfect piece of acting – perfect no less in its sobriety than in its humour.'[6] In training the actors, my brother, from the start, was compelled to depart from the kind of acting and stage management required by the plays he had played in on the regular stage. What are known as Irish dramas, for instance, are played too rapidly to be true to Irish life, which is leisurely. Again, the plays which are now being written in Ireland have a dialogue so lifelike that it would be ruined if made in the least theatrical in its delivery. In ordinary English plays, at any rate, people do not talk on the stage as they do in the street or in a room, whereas our dialogue allows us to talk exactly as Irish peasants talk in a cottage or on the road or in the fields. On the regular English stage, dialogue has to be made interesting; the talk of the Irish peasant is as a rule wonderfully interesting, and often even unconsciously poetic. Of course education, by making the younger generation talk 'good English', would soon put an end to this gift of vivid speech, but it will take some time to accomplish that excellent object. Depending so much on dialogue, my brother from the first suppressed all but absolutely essential movement. The critic of the great provincial English paper,[7] which in things theatrical has a higher standard than even the London press thus described what my brother had got out of us. 'These Irish actors' wrote this critic, 'have contrived to reach back past most of the futilities that have grown upon the ordinary theatre, and to get a fresh, clear hold on their craft in its elements. They know how to let things alone; how to stand still when nothing is to be done in the way of enhanced artistic effect by moving; how to save up voice and gesture for rare passages of real poignancy; how to fade into the background when attention has to be concentrated on a single other character.'[8] Mr Walkley, the critic of the London *Times*, also spoke of our methods with approval[9] and I am proud to think that some of the New York critics are of the same opinion. I notice, for instance, in the *Globe* of 3 March in a criticism of *A Doll's House* the following: 'in the case of these Russian players, as in that of the Irish players, we note that when they have anything to say on the stage they say it sitting facing each other or standing in natural attitudes. They do not "cross" at the semi-colons to lend "action" to the play, thereby giving a serious conversation the appearance of a minuet.' I have in Ireland a newspaper cutting containing an interview with Mr Kyrle Bellew[10] in which he protests against incessant movement on the stage, and I noticed in *The Warrens of Virginia*,[11] so beautifully and so sincerely played by Mr Keenan and his comrades, that movement was reduced to a minimum, and that the play was played, as we have always tried to play our plays, as a real thing, the audience being treated as onlookers, and not directly appealed to.

The formation of a company to act plays by Irish authors set many people to work at writing plays. Mr Yeats, Lady Gregory, Mr Synge, Mr Colum, Mr Boyle, Mr Fitzmaurice and many others have written for it, and doubtless the fire which has been kindled will be kept alight, for Ireland, where discontent reigns and the passions are loose, is full of unworked dramatic material.

Three years ago a friend of Mr Yeats' gave him the Abbey Theatre, and six months' playing in it proved that certain members of the company, who up to that time had worked solely for the joy of the thing, would have to devote themselves exclusively to the work; and these – my brother and myself among the number – consequently left their places of business. New plays had to be given frequently, necessitating daily rehearsal which could not be given by people engaged in other occupations, and frequent performances had to be given to develop the acting powers of the company. The Irish National Theatre Society used to play only twice a month, but when they went to the Abbey Theatre they used to play a week in each month. When the principal members of the company gave themselves up exclusively to acting, performances were given every Saturday during the season, say from October until the middle of May, and a new play was produced each month and was always played for a week, so that a good deal of work was got through. My brother had to rehearse every one of these new plays, create the action, choose the dresses, often paint the scenery, and, until quite recently, look after the business side of the Abbey Theatre as well. Last season the company played thrice a week.

The company has played four times in London, first at the Queen's Gate Hall, next at the Royalty Theatre, then at St George's Hall, and in last June at the Great Queen Street Theatre, now Kingsway Theatre. It has played twice in Manchester, at the Midland Theatre; thrice in Glasgow (twice at the King's Theatre and once at the Royalty); twice at the Lyceum Theatre, Edinburgh; and at the principal theatres of Aberdeen, Newcastle-on-Tyne, Hull and Cardiff. It has also visited Leeds and Liverpool, and has played twice at Oxford and Cambridge. In Ireland, outside of Dublin, it has played at the theatres in Wexford, Waterford, Cork, Galway; and at Dundalk, Loughrea and Longford.

Most of the plays in the company's repertoire are peasant plays, that is plays dealing with peasant life. They are dressed exactly as in real life, the dresses being specially made by the tailors employed by the peasantry, and the properties are absolutely correct. The actors have most of them peasant blood, if they are not the children of peasants, and instinctively talk, move and act as peasants would, and are familiar with the habits of the country folk. It has been a common complaint that too many peasant plays are produced; but authors will only write what interests them; and (at any rate in Ireland) it is among the working classes and the peasantry that you find the real live Irish. The better classes imitate, as well as they can, which is not saying much, the English accent and manner, and one of the reasons why the Abbey Theatre has seen so little of them is that its ideal is Irish life and theirs is English. They do not want to see peasants, dressed in rough frieze coats, talking what they call 'bad English', wearing their hats while their women folk are in the kitchen, and occasionally speaking with biblical frankness. All that is to them 'common', a thing to be abhorred. Other people complained that the Abbey Theatre should have gone farther afield for its plays than Ireland. But my brother and myself at any rate set out to provide a company of Irish actors to interpret the work of native dramatists. There were already plenty of actors to do the other class of play. England has Shakespeare, France has Molière, Germany has Goethe and Schiller, Denmark has Holberg, Norway has Ibsen. Ireland has not yet a dramatist to come near any of these; when she has, it will be time enough to bring to her national theatre the flowers of foreign fields.

NOTES

Frank J. Fay (1870–1931), first voice coach and first fine actor of the Abbey Theatre; elder brother of W. G. Fay. On 6 Feb 1908, *The Irish Independent* carried an announcement that the Fays had been engaged by Charles Frohman to appear in some of their more successful parts in the United States and that they were to sail for New York immediately. This lecture, which may stand as a summary of the Fays' work for a national theatre, was read to an Irish audience in New York in 1908, after the Fays had left the Abbey Theatre.

1. Ernest Alexandre Honoré Coquelin (1848–1909), French author and actor.
2. Frank J. Fay, 'M Coquelin in Dublin', *United Irishman* (Dublin), 2 (1 July 1899) 1.
3. Frank J. Fay's dramatic criticism has been collected in *Towards a National Theatre*, ed. Robert Hogan (Dublin: Dolmen Press, 1970).
4. Edward Hugh Sothern (1859–1933), Anglo-American actor and manager who became leading man of Frohman's Lyceum company.
5. *The Rising of the Moon* was presented at the Savoy Theatre, New York on 24 Feb 1908.
6. William Archer, 'Irish Plays', *World* (London), 12 May 1903, 784–5.
7. The paper was the *Manchester Guardian*; and the critic was C. E. Montague (1867–1928), who was dramatic critic to this paper from 1890 to 1925.
8. C. E. M[ontague], 'Gaiety Theatre: The Irish Plays', *Manchester Guardian*, 18 Feb 1909, p. 4.
9. [A. B. Walkley], 'The Irish National Theatre', *Times Literary Supplement* (London), 8 May 1903, p. 146.
10. Harold Kyrle Bellew (1855–1911), English actor.
11. By the American playwright William C. de Mille (1878–1955).

Looking Back on the Abbey*

MAY CRAIG

The school excursion, in the lovely summer of 1906, was to Killiney. In charge of us was Father Eugene McCarthy, of St Michael's and John's (our parish church), and I was looking after the younger girls. I was nine years old at the time, but tall for my age. (The nuns used to call me Daddy-long-legs.)

There were songs and dances and games, and I recited *The Wreck of the Hesperus*. The thought of wanting to go on the stage never entered my mind, even though I always looked forward with excitement to those evenings when my mother would bring myself and my sister to the opera or to Shakespeare, or to the annual pantomime.

* *Evening Press* (Dublin), 12 Mar 1960, p. 11.

None of us knew that Father McCarthy was a great friend of William Fay until that evening in January 1907, when he called to ask if he might bring me to the Abbey Theatre to see Mr Fay, who was producing a play there.

It appeared that Mr Fay had told Father McCarthy he had not enough girls in the company for the parts which the play required. My mother gave permission, and so I went to the Abbey.

When I arrived, the company had just finished rehearsing the first act of *The Playboy of the Western World*. I was introduced to Mr Willie Fay, who told me that I would be required for the second act. He then brought me to the greenroom. Most of the company were there.

I saw a man with sad eyes, a dark face and a little beard. He was telling a very beautiful young girl, who was making coffee for the company, how they made coffee in Paris. The man was Synge; the beautiful young girl was Maire O'Neill.

After a while, I met Frank Fay (Willie's brother), who was playing Shawn Keogh, and Brigit O'Dempsey (Willie's wife), who was playing Sara Tansey. I was then introduced to Synge.

He asked me if I could say the lines: 'And I brought you a little laying pullet – boiled and all she is – was crushed at the fall of night by the curate's car.'

I noticed he said the words in a curious way, breaking them up like this: 'And I brought you . . . a little laying pullet. Boiled and all . . . she is . . . was crushed . . . at the fall of night . . . by the curate's car.'

I said the lines as well as I could. Then Brigit O'Dempsey, listening to me, said to Synge that she was a professional actress and was getting little enough for what she was doing, and that Honor Blake's lines should be divided between Sara Tansey, which she was playing, and Susan Brady, played by Alice O'Sullivan.

And that is how it was. The lines were divided between the two actresses. I had nothing to say as Honor Blake in that first production of *The Playboy*.[1]

I used to carry on the pullet and when the line came Brigit O'Dempsey would put her arm around my shoulder and lead me forward to Christy.

Otherwise, I used to romp around with the other two, giggling and laughing, and giving the impression that I had just 'come over the river lepping the stones'.

Looking back, I can see that Synge, who was insistent that his lines should be spoken in a certain way, was all the time stressing the importance of rhythm. He also wanted the girls to be simple village girls.

Maire O'Neill as Pegeen Mike was very beautiful. She was also exceedingly kind. She was a great actress, even a little greater, perhaps, than her sister, Sara Allgood, who played the Widow Quin. Offstage, in those days, Maire wore glasses. You could see that Synge was very much in love with her.[2]

I used to see him as he has been drawn by J. B. Yeats (the poet's father) in that pencil sketch 'Synge at Rehearsal' leaning forward and looking up adoringly at Maire.

The first night of the play there was a little hissing at the mention of the word 'shift'. In the third act, when Pegeen attempts to burn Christy with a lighted sod, there was a loud uproar which continued until the end of the play.

After the curtain had fallen there was a meeting of the players in the greenroom. Lady Gregory and Synge were there. There was a discussion as to whether or not the play should be continued. The majority agreed that the play should not be taken off. Yeats was away at the time. Lady Gregory said that she had sent for him and that he would arrive the following day.

I found it very exciting, but I hardly knew at the time what it was all about. Nor did I think then that in the years to come I would be in the middle of another theatre riot, in O'Casey's *The Plough and the Stars*.

The next night the row started in the first act and it increased as the play went on. It was impossible to hear a word the players said. Yeats in a pale grey suit, his glasses ribboned, his tie flowing, and his long black hair greying, harangued the audience, saying that there were people who had come to hear the play and people who had come deliberately to prevent them from hearing it.

He said that the theatre was bound by no rules. Its purpose was to help young authors and young players, and it would continue to do so in spite of unruly interruption. He told the players to save their voices and to do nothing more than to shape the words with their lips. The rioting grew worse. By this time the police were in and fights were taking place in the stalls and the pit.

Lady Gregory had asked her nephew, Hugh Lane, to bring over some boys from Trinity with him. This only made matters worse. More fights started. The players did what Yeats told them; but at one point I heard Arthur Sinclair, who played Michael James, using words (about the audience) that were never written by Synge!

Night after night the rioting went on – boos, shouts, whistles, tin trumpets, rhythmic hand-clapping, fights, arrests. But the play went on, too, and continued for a further week. People came from all over Dublin simply to see what the row was about. I found it all strange and exciting. Looking back on it now, *The Playboy* row[3] was much bigger and certainly much more noisy than the row over *The Plough*.

There was the difference, too, that the first was on moral grounds, the second on political ones. The fact that I had nothing to say, as Honor Blake, hardly mattered; for after the opening night, it was not possible to hear what any of the players said. When my sister called for me to bring me home on the last night I little thought that I would ever see the Abbey again.

I did, though. I returned there in October 1916, to appear as Raina in Shaw's *Arms and the Man*, with Fred O'Donovan, Maureen Delany, Louis O'Connor and Kathleen Murphy. In the meantime, I had done quite an amount of acting (mostly in Boucicault melodrama) with F. J. McCormick at the Workmen's Club in York Street and at St Francis Xavier's Hall with such fine actors as Paul Farrell and Peter Nolan.

I have been in the Abbey Theatre ever since. It is sad to think that I am the only one left of that band of players who appeared in the first production of *The Playboy of the Western World*.

NOTES

May Craig (*ca* 1889–1972), actress who joined the Abbey company in 1916 and remained with it all her life.

1. This casts an interesting light on the final draft of the text. The lines quoted here by May Craig are credited in the text to Nelly McLaughlin, while Honor Blake has lines about 'a little cut of cake' (besides six other lines prior to this moment.) According to alterations made in the copy registered by the Lord Chamberlain's Office on 27 Apr 1907, Nelly's speeches were given to Honor Blake in the first production. It now seems that it was the *actress* Brigit O'Dempsey rather than the character Sarah Tansey who influenced Synge's final revisions.

2. For a note on Maire O'Neill and her recollections of Synge see p. 81.

3. The objections against the play were made on religious, moral and patriotic grounds. On religious grounds, the audience objected that the play's references to God, to the Catholic Church, and to the marriage sacrament were blasphemous and profane. On moral grounds, the audience objected that the play's attitude to parricide was equivocal and morally indefensible. The third line of attack was that the play was unpatriotic and likely to reflect discredit on Ireland.

Synge and the Early Days of the Abbey*

MAIRE O'NEILL

Maire O'Neill, she for whom John Millington Synge wrote specially his greatest plays, *The Playboy of the Western World* and *Deirdre of the Sorrows*, is in her fifties now, but when I met her recently I found that her voice is still as fresh, velvety and musical as when first she crossed the footlights of the Abbey in the exciting springtime of Yeats, Lady Gregory, the Fay brothers and Synge himself. It was a brave group of young men and women – none of them older than twenty-five and none of them trained in the art of the theatre, but all of them united with one burning ambition – to have their own literary playhouse.

Sara Allgood is the famous sister of Maire O'Neill, and, though they have had no immediate ancestor on the stage, there is in the family tree of four generations ago the name of Mary Haynes, well-known to the Dublin theatre of her day.

'There were four brothers and four sisters in my family of Allgood', Maire told me. 'One brother is in the Civil Service in Dublin, one became a religious in an Irish monastery, and the other two were killed in the 1914–18 War. One of my sisters is here in London, one in Dublin, and of course Sara has settled down in Hollywood.'

'Why did you change your name?' I asked.

'Oh, I wanted to be different to Sara, of course, who kept the family name of Allgood. You know the dreams and ambitions of a young actress: she wants to be independent and different from everyone. I wanted to be different from Sara, and to be on my own, to make my own fame and name, so I chose to be Maire O'Neill. . . . And here I am.'

I was anxious to speak about Synge, but Miss O'Neill's words on her quondam sweetheart were few but significant.

'What is there I cannot say about John? To me he was everything, in his work and personality. Today he still remains the same for me. I have had no reason to change my opinion. Just as the rest of the world hasn't

*Extracted from *Irish Press* (Dublin), 21 Apr 1949, p. 4.

changed its opinion either. The history of the stage has made him immortal. He was one of the first of the Abbey Theatre writers. That is one of his greatness. But perhaps his greatness to me is wound up with the fact that for me he wrote his most famous plays, *The Playboy of the Western World* and *Deirdre of the Sorrows*, when I was only eighteen.'

Before they could marry, John Millington Synge died at the very young age of thirty-nine. It took Maire O'Neill a long time to get over that blow, so that she did not marry till she came across to England in 1911 and met John Mair [*sic*].[1]

Their son, John, became a writer, and his best book *The Fourth Forger* dealing with the John Ireland forgeries of Shakespeare's works is still sought after especially in literary and dramatic circles. The son, John, died in a plane crash in 1942. The daughter, Pegeen, worked in publicity for Rank for two years, but gave it up in favour of lyric-writing.

I manoeuvred the conversation back to our main topic, and Maire O'Neill continued:

'I left the Abbey in 1911 and came to London with the Company. We filled the theatres with *The Playboy* for two years. In New York in 1913 we played to crowded houses for six months in Lennox Robinson's *Whiteheaded Boy* [*sic*].[2] Then we went south to Australia and stayed there for six months doing Sean O'Casey's *Juno and the Paycock*. Incidentally, I was the first to televise *Juno* in this country.[3] Since those early days I've paid another visit to America, in between playing all over Great Britain and doing films. One great actor who has since become famous in films, Claude Rinas, was with me in Carl Capek's *The Insect Play*.'

NOTES

'Maire O'Neill' was the stage name of Molly Allgood (1887–1952), who joined the Abbey Theatre in 1905 and became one of its leading actresses. For her, Synge created two of his most famous characters and wrote some of his most moving poetry. In 1906 he quickly fell under her spell. In the Ireland of eighty years ago, however, the difference between them could hardly have been greater. He was fifteen years older, but his education and his class background provided a much more formidable barrier. For a long time he was unwilling to tell his mother or his family about her. Virtually everything about the relationship seems discordant, though: Molly's gaiety and Synge's intensity; her flirtatiousness and his fastidiousness; her vitality and his ill-health. Synge and Molly became secretly engaged, but the wedding was postponed when he became seriously ill. See *Letters to Molly: John Millington Synge to Maire O'Neill 1906—1909*, ed. Ann Saddlemeyer (Cambridge, Massachusetts: Harvard University Press, 1971); Elizabeth Coxhead, 'Sally and Molly (Sara Allgood and Maire O'Neill)', in *Daughters of Erin* (London: Secker & Warburg, 1965) pp. 167–224; and 'Maire O'Neill', *Irish Times* (Dublin), 3 Nov 1952, p. 4.

1. George Herbert Mair, drama critic on the *Manchester Guardian*, who seems to have been responsible for suggesting that C. P. Scott should act as arbitrator between the Abbey directors and Miss Horniman when they were having their final quarrel. Mair died on 3 Jan 1926. Six months later Maire O'Neill married Arthur Sinclair, the Abbey actor.

2. The reference cannot be correct as *The Whiteheaded Boy* had its première at the Abbey Theatre on 13 Dec 1916.

3. Maire O'Neill had no competitor but her sister Sara Allgood when it came to playing O'Casey parts, to which she constantly returned.

The Abbey Theatre*

PEADAR KEARNEY

Entering from Marlborough Street, and viewing the tastefully decorated and furnished vestibule of the Abbey Theatre, one finds it hard to realise that here, less than thirty years ago, stood the City Morgue, as drab and as gruesome a chamber as could be found in any capital in Europe.

Divided from the morgue by a single wall was the Mechanics' Theatre, one-time Mecca of all who aspired to democratic culture and progress, equipped with what were in those days the most popular reading-rooms and library in the city.

Thither our fathers brought us on a Sunday morning and pointed out elderly men once prominent in stormy times long past; now, perhaps quietly browsing through the columns of forgotten periodicals, where once their names loomed large . . . they, too, also forgotten.

But the dawn of the new century saw the wheels of progress quickening in their revolutions, and such things as mechanics' institutes and quiet elderly men had to take themselves off into the shades and make way for a mighty change in the lives and conditions of men, which was an improvement perhaps – perhaps not. Be it so.

The Mechanics' Institute, in the auspicious hall of which Mitchel, Meagher, Doheny and the rest debated the pros and cons of revolution away back in 1848,[1] had deteriorated step by step, finding an inglorious finale as the twopenny rendezvous of the submerged tenth where, amid the reek of cheap tobacco and ribald jokes, a lady in tawdry tinsel pathetically appealed to her grimy and not very attentive audience to join in the chorus. And in the next apartment, on slabs of stone, lay the

---

*Seamus de Burca, *The Soldier's Song: The Story of Peadar Kearney* (Dublin: P. J. Bourke, 1958) pp. 34–9. These recollections were written in 1935.

waifs and strays of life, garnered from river and laneway, who had 'ceased from troubling', forgotten by all save God.

Yet amid such grim and uninspiring surroundings was launched the most widely discussed and probably the most successful theatre experiment of modern times.

Taking over of the Mechanics' Theatre wherein to evolve a national dramatic renaissance seemed at the time to be something akin to the valiant knight who went forth tilting at windmills. Many men and women have given their genius, their time and their scanty means to make the Abbey what it is today; but when the history of the theatre comes to be written, the names of Frank and Willie Fay will head the roll of honour.

These two men, with barely the means to live, but amply endowed with practical enthusiasm, brought the infant experiment through debt and danger and the stress of circumstances; contending against cynical indifference and unreasoning opposition, succeeding, ere severing their connections, in steering the fragile craft through its initial storms and anchoring it safe and sound in the harbour which gave every hope of future success and prosperity.

They were ably assisted to an extent undreamt of by Abbey admirers – by Seaghan Barlow, whose craftsmanship and inventive genius, called forth by the difficulties to be surmounted, were a revelation even to those who knew him intimately for years before. A quarter of a century has elapsed and Seaghan is still on the muster roll of the Abbey. *Saoghal fada cuige!*[2]

Let those who are familiar with the Abbey Theatre today try to realise it as it was for a considerable time after its inception. Where the splendid Marlborough Street entrance now leads into the stalls, the morgue still functioned; inside, an auditorium dreary and undecorated; a stage lacking in every essential, scanty dressing-room accommodation; no greenroom, scene dock or paint loft. Willie Fay making shift to paint a cloth one side of the stage, or up aloft in the improvised flies. Seaghan Barlow in the cramped space under the stage making papier-mâché shields and jabbing liquid bronze on the points of wooden spears, with which in an hour or so the heroes of the Fianna would strut the boards.

In the forenoon a group of young men and women would be found on the stage, while out in the artificial twilight of the house the dim figure of Frank Fay would be seen, seated, book in hand, while his clear, melodious voice would be heard as he toiled patiently through the daily grind of voice-production and elocution.

Patience! If ever a human being had succeeded in acquiring that virtue it was Frank Fay. Clever as most of his pupils must have been, nevertheless they owe their position today to the painstaking labours of their first teacher.

Out of what sort of material did Fay build his company? The stage has always had a peculiar fascination for people with money to burn – people who will gladly pay even for the privilege of 'walking on', and who need not bother whether 'the ghost walks' or not. The Abbey had its share of such people who, apart from their worldly wealth, if they showed any ability got their chance in common with many others who were obsessed with the idea that they were born to shine in the theatrical firmament.

The fully attested results are illuminating. Not one of those who achieved lasting fame as Abbey Players but was of the working-class. Sara Allgood, Maire O'Neill, Maire Nic Shiubhlaigh, Arthur Sinclair, J. M. Kerrigan, Joe O'Rourke, Sydney Morgan, Fred O'Donovan and others of the original company left workshops and desks, risking their means of livelihood for what at the time appeared to be a forlorn hope. And the circumstances in which they made their initial effort needed the most indomitable determination to see it through.

It was a pet joke of Willie Fay to count the audience and volunteer the information that 'the ghost may walk this week', and the vigorous hand-clapping of an individual in an empty house would often cause the players to miss their cues.

In spite of many rebuffs and disappointments the movement progressed, a regular audience being built up, the players improving day by day, and the splendid repertoire of plays accumulating from unexpected sources. But in Ireland a cause never seems to succeed until it meets with palpable opposition, because in Ireland apathy kills and opposition supplies the necessary incentive for ultimate success.

For the Abbey Theatre the first definite clash came when Arthur Griffith, in the columns of the *United Irishman*, made a fierce attack on Synge's *In the Shadow of the Glen*. The origin of the attack was, and still is, obscure; but it seems to point more to a personal issue between Griffith and W. B. Yeats – who had been a contributor to Griffith's paper – than to anything else.[3] But at that time Griffith was very popular and, through the *United Irishman*, wielded an immense influence over the growing number of young nationalists who in most things were prepared to accept his verdict as final.

Anyhow, the controversy that raged round the *Shadow of the Glen* started a prejudice against the Abbey which came to a head when semi-organised attacks were launched against Synge's famous comedy, *The Playboy of the Western World* when it was first produced there in 1907 (St Stephen's Day).[4] Riots broke out in the theatre, and pandemonium reigned supreme whilst the unfortunate actors mouthed their lines.

On the second night of the play W. B. Yeats strode on to the stage a proud, defiant, commanding figure. He was greeted by prolonged cat-calls and derisive jeers from a howling mob lost to all sense of reason and balance; Mitchel's 'bellowing slaves and genteel dastards'

incarnate, foaming at the mouth in manufactured impotent rage – the
Gaelic League well represented in suits of Donegal tweed. Yeats literally
stared the obstreperous audience out of countenance, hypnotised them
into hushed silence, that was like a sudden calm in a tempest, a flash of
lightning preceding thunder.

'I have never been taught to bend the knee', said the poet–dramatist, a
lock of hair falling over the broad forehead, the shoulders thrown back,
the strong chin jutting forward, the pugnacious mouth, the proud defiant
eye. 'I have never been taught to bend the knee and, please God, I never
shall. As long as there are people who want to see this play, they will see it
in spite of all opposition.'

Nine-tenths of the young men who thronged the Abbey Theatre for the
first time in their lives to raise a shindy – a pastime dearly loved by all
healthy young men – eventually became loyal and regular supporters of
the Theatre. *The Playboy* is now universally recognised as a masterpiece.

Such was the necessary opposition which, combined with the
opportune financial support from Miss Horniman, definitely established
the Abbey on a secure basis and started it forth on its career towards
world-wide fame.

NOTES

Peadar Kearney [Peadar O Cearnaigh] (1883–1942), songwriter, nationalist
and uncle of Brendan Behan. In 1907 he wrote the words of 'A Soldier's Song',
the Irish National Anthem. He was connected with the Abbey Theatre as an
odd-job man and small-part actor.

1. The hall, where John Mitchel (1815–75), Thomas Francis Meagher
(1823–67) and Michael Doheny (1805–63) debated revolution in 1848, was the
Music Hall, which stood on the site of the present Metropolitan Hall on the side
of the street opposite to the Abbey.

2. Long life to him!

3. See the review of the play, *United Irishman* (Dublin), 17 Oct 1903, p. 1; and
W. B. Yeats, 'The Irish National Theatre and Three Sorts of Ingorance', ibid.,
24 Oct 1903, p. 2.

4. The play was first produced on 26 Jan 1907.

The National Theatre*

SARA ALLGOOD

The editor of the *Weekly Freeman* has asked me to contribute to his St Patrick's Day Number something about my associations with our national theatre, and I do so with pleasure, trusting that my narrative will interest many in our work.

To commence at the beginning, there is a little hall in Camden Street – for, I suppose, it is still here – it is at the back of a shop, and one goes into it by a door between two shops. When I knew it, in the spring of 1903, one had sometimes to push aside a tub of butter or a box of eggs before one could pass the threshold. It was here that I first met the group of players and playwrights whose work led to the foundation of the Abbey Theatre. I remember that the hall was very cold and very small; if full to the door, I doubt if it would have held more than forty people. The roof was leaky, for it was a wet night, and I had to move from the place where I was standing, because drops of rain fell upon me and made a puddle at my feet. When I joined the company, the hall was only used for purposes of rehearsal, but I hear from others that there were no dressing-rooms, and that the company had to dress behind screens which were put on the stage for the purpose. The hall had been a dream, and after one or two performances an impossible dream. I had known Mr W. G. Fay when he and his brother played farces at the Coffee Palace,[1] though I had never played for him, and it was he who brought me to Camden Street, and gave me a part in a revival of Lady Gregory's first play *Twenty-Five* and in the first performance of Mr Yeats' *The King's Threshold*. A little before this I had seen the company setting out on their first London visit, and felt very sorrowful at being left behind, but when somebody at the end of *Twenty-Five* handed me a basket of flowers I felt that all my ambition had been satisfied. What more could one ask from life? My admirer was very kind, for the part was very small. After that I played one or two small parts in new plays – Brigid in Mr Colum's *Broken Soil*, Kathleen in *Riders to the Sea* and the mother, Mrs Gillane, in *Kathleen Ni Houlihan*.

It was in Lady Gregory's play, *Spreading the News*, that I achieved my first success.[2] This play was first produced in December 1904, at the opening of the Abbey Theatre. While the rehearsals were going on, the Mechanics' Institute was being turned into the Abbey Theatre, very

*Extracted from the *Weekly Freeman* (Dublin), 20 Mar 1909, p. 11.

timidly, for I thought that something would happen, but what, I did not know if I were found there, I went down day after day to see if the work went rapidly. I made excuses to get away from my place of business for ten minutes or for half an hour. I pretended that I had some important message to deliver, but it was only to see if the Abbey stage was beginning to show itself in its new shape among the scaffolding and broken masonry.

At last the theatre was ready, and we had our final rehearsals in it a few days before the opening.[3] Till the performance and the applause I had no idea that I had got anything, but a little part like those I had played before. I am afraid if I had dared I would have asked for the part of the deaf applewoman, because she is on the stage all the time. How finely W. G. Fay played[4] that night. Frank Fay was not, I think, as fine in *On Baile's Strand*[5] that night as he was a few months before in Mr Yeats' *The King's Threshold*.[6] He was our elocution teacher and voice-producer, and if my voice is expressive I attribute all to his teaching. After that there were disputes. What were they all about? They were very intricate, and a year ago I remember seeing at the Abbey a girl from the University of Chicago; she had a notebook and pencil, and she was asking questions of everyone she met. She had chosen the Irish dramatic movement as a thesis for her university degree, and she was deeply interested in that split. When her thesis is published we will all understand why we quarrelled. Some were so angry that they seceded, and one of them in doing so left behind her for my legacy the part of *Kathleen Ni Houlihan*. I had wanted it for years. I got it; that is all I intend to remember about the dispute. There had been many Kathleens; everyone had played it in their own way. Miss Maud Gonne's performance (the original Kathleen) I cannot clearly remember, as I was very young at the time. One of the other players who had taken the part before me had, I thought, been most struck with the supernatural element in the character. She gave us Kathleen as Ireland, immortal, spiritual, divine, if you will, but Ireland in sorrow, struggling without hope.

Perhaps our sorrows are more spiritual than our joys. I had a different conception. I did not wish to make my audience feel that 'Kathleen' called that young man to a hopeless sacrifice. When I stand at the door rechanting,

> They shall be remembered forever
> They shall be alive forever,
> They shall be speaking forever,
> The people shall hear them forever

I call into my thoughts all those who have died for Ireland. I say to myself then death was victory. Ireland, too, will be victorious. I fill myself with joy. 'Dervorgilla',[7] that is the sorrow of Ireland, but 'Kathleen' looks into the future.

It is scarcely possible to omit from these memories some references to *The Playboy*, the most stirring and memorable event so far in my theatrical career. The Widow Quinn was scarcely a part to my liking, but an actress cannot always choose and pick her part, but must loyally do her best with the character allotted to her. It must be said that Mr Synge makes this comparatively easy, for all his characters are boldly and definitely outlined. In many plays the characterisation is vague and flabby, and out of a mass of dialogue, the moulding and vitalising is wholly left to the creative instincts of the players. Between these two kinds of dramatists, there is all the difference to the actors, between getting into a sack and into a close-fitting costume. All Mr Synge's conceptions spring, like Minerva, fully developed from his head. I had already played Molly Byrne in *The Well of the Saints*, and Maurya in *Riders to the Sea*, a part very precious to me, in which an eminent Manchester critic[8] was kind enough to describe my impersonation as the finest old woman study on the English stage. I will never forget, if I were to live as old as Maurya herself, that historic night when the curtain rose for the first production of *The Playboy*. Naturally we were all in a state of trepidation. Mr Synge's former works had been so bitterly assailed,[9] that we wondered how this play, his masterpiece, over which he had laboured so long, would be received. The play had been carefully rehearsed, and its production excited great expectations. The theatre was crowded that night, and many were turned away. Never did a band of Irish actors face a more cultured and representative Irish audience. Judges, barristers, solicitors, clergymen, artists, musicians and literary men filled the stalls. Gaelic Leaguers, Sinn Feiners, university students – the pick of the freshest intellect of the city crowded the balconies and the basements. The first act went splendidly amid laughter and applause, and curtain after curtain were taken. The second act followed, and was loudly applauded. Just in the middle of the third act, following a speech, which one of the actors had been instructed to cut out, the storm burst, and the house broke up in disorder.[10] For a week the theatre was turned into a pandemonium. It is not necessary here to recount the deplorable scenes that followed. The actors were the chief sufferers. For three or four nights the play was faithfully performed, but not a syllable was heard across the footlights. Rumours were prevalent that the stage would be rushed and the company maltreated. A force of sturdy policemen was placed in the precincts of the stage to guard against this, but nevertheless our nerves were shaken, and after the fearful strain of a week of turmoil, threatenings and maledictions, we were left in a state of total collapse. One incident occurs to me, which has not been recorded, in which I played an impromptu part. On Saturday – the evening of the last performance – just before the public was admitted, I found the theatre crowded with police. They were ranged all around the walls and up the centre of the pit benches. Acting on an impulse I rushed on the stage, and passionately informed them that unless they left the theatre I would not play that night. Moved by the vehemence of my attack they looked uneasily at each other, but of course they could only follow their instructions. I did not carry out the threat, for it would only have made matters worse, and I had no desire to make the position of the directors more painful and complicated than it was at the time. The story of *The Playboy* went out to the end of the earth, and I have read accounts of it in newspapers from Korea, Australia, South Africa, Canada, the United States, India, etc. It will go down the ages as one of the toughest fights in theatrical history, and posterity will not forget the little band of players, who, through eight performances, never deserted their posts, but unflinchingly faced the music, and played their parts through din and terrors of a great public upheaval.[11]

The editor asks me to talk of all my parts, but they are very numerous, for we have a large repertoire now at the Abbey that I have played in. I think our audiences at the Abbey like me in *Riders to the Sea*, next after *Kathleen Ni Houlihan*, but I will admit to you that I would like a long part with plenty of fine clothes, in which it would not be necessary to make up 100 years old.[12] Instead of talking about all these parts you will let me say, will you not, that it is pleasant playing at the Abbey, where we have nearly all known each other for years, and can take pleasure in one another's success. We are confident that some day our movement will take its place in the intellectual history of Ireland, and through the slights and blights of its early stages it will yet emerge as an honoured possession and a glory of our native land. It will perhaps then be said of us, that we did a 'good deed in a naughty world'; although I fancy nowadays that there are many who think, that our deeds were very naughty in an exceptionally good world.

NOTES

Sarah Allgood (1883–1950), actress who had her first big success in Lady Gregory's *Spreading the News* on the opening night of the Abbey Theatre, 27 December 1904. After many successful American tours, she settled in Hollywood in 1940. Her 'Memories' are in the Berg Collection, New York Public Library. See Micheál MacLiammóir, 'Some Talented Women', *Bell* (Dublin), 8 (May 1944) 117–27; I[vor] B[rown], 'The Allgood Sisters', *Drama* (London), no. 77 (Summer 1965), 45–7; and 'The Story of the Irish Players', *Sunday Record–Herald* (Chicago), 4 Feb 1912, part 7, p. 1.

1. The Coffee Palace Hall, 6 Townsend Street, had been the home of the Ormond Dramatic Society.

2. As Mrs Fallon.

3. On 27 Dec 1904.

4. He played the part of Bartley Fallon.

5. Frank Fay played Cuchulain in W. B. Yeats' *On Baile's Strand*.

6. He played Seanchan (Chief Poet of Ireland).

7. Whose tragic love for Dermot McMurrough led to the Norman invasion of Ireland in 1169. Lady Gregory's play, *Dervorgilla*, was staged at the Abbey Theatre on 31 Oct 1907.

8. C. E. Montague. See his review of the play, 'Gaiety Theatre', *Manchester Guardian*, 18 Feb 1909, p. 4.

9. *The Shadow of the Glen* had displeased Synge's fellow countrymen because the fickleness of the wife might be construed to be an attack on Irish women; it will be remembered that Maud Gonne and Dudley Digges had walked out of the Molesworth Hall on the first night of this play. *The Well of the Saints* had annoyed them because there was something cynical in the idea that the old beggar and his wife could love each other when they were blind, but hated each other when they miraculously recovered their sight.

10. Cf. 'The first-night audience, already made uneasy by the disturbing rumours circulating about the play, erupted at the word "shifts", the line being made even more explosive by Willie Fay's substitution of "Mayo girls" for Christy's "drift of chosen females standing in their shifts"' (Ann Saddlemyer, Introduction to *J. M. Synge, Plays II* (London: Oxford University Press, 1968) p. xxi).

11. See James Kilroy, *The 'Playboy' Riots* (Dublin: Dolmen Press, 1971).

12. In 1915 Sara Allgood accepted the lead in *Peg O' My Heart*, a slight and amateurish comedy which was wildly successful and in 1916 toured Australia and New Zealand with it. Her playing of Juno in 1924 on the first night of O'Casey's *Juno and the Paycock* is part of Irish theatrical history. She gave another unforgettable performance in London in 1926 as Bessie Burgess in O'Casey's *The Plough and the Stars*.

Recollections of the Abbey Theatre*

SEAGHAN BARLOW

In 1902 I was a member of a club that met in a hall at the back of Walker's newsagent's shop at No. 18 High Street. There I made the

*Lennox Robinson, *Ireland's Abbey Theatre: A History 1899–1951* (London: Sidgwick & Jackson, 1951) pp. 69–76. Editor's title.

acquaintance of the Walkers, and through them I met W. G. Fay, whose Comedy Combination Company was about this time giving their final performance of *His Lost Legs* [*sic*]¹ at the old Coffee Palace Hall, in Townsend Street. One night in the Walkers' house, conversation turned on the new dramatic movement and the need for an Irish theatre. As I knew nothing about it I was merely a listener.

Soon after this, a meeting took place in the hall attached to Walker's shop, and at this meeting the National Dramatic Society was founded. As far as I can remember, the two Fays, Mr Yeats and Lady Gregory were present at this meeting. Later on, Frank Walker took me up to No. 34 Camden Street, where rehearsals, etc. were carried on. It was a ramshackle old hall, at the back of a butcher's shop, and you had to dodge past the carcase of a dead sheep to get in through the hall door. I saw Mr W. G. Fay, Maire Nic Shuiblaigh and some others there.

I went to St Teresa's Hall, Clarendon Street, to see the first production of *Deirdre* by AE [George Russell], and *Kathleen Ni Houlihan* by W. B. Yeats.

Later on, at supper in the Walkers' house, I met W. G. Fay, and talk came round to the chance of finding a suitable hall to play in. The old Mechanics' Theatre was mentioned, but it had been condemned and closed by the Corporation and the cost of putting it in repair would be too big. So the Molesworth Hall had to be hired until Miss Horniman appeared.

I was often in the Walkers' house at this time, and saw a good deal of the work that was done behind the scenes by Mrs Walker, who, assisted by Mrs Martin, made most of the costumes used at that time; they were nearly all made of hessian, as that was the cheapest and most serviceable material for costumes such as were used in *The Hour-Glass*, *The Shadowy Waters*, etc. In some cases, indeed, hessian was even used for costumes in peasant plays.

The names of Yeats, Lady Gregory and Synge were little known to the general public at that time, and the receipts at the Molesworth Hall were scarcely enough to cover the expense of hiring the hall and carting the scenery, etc. back and forward. For this reason, the utmost economy was necessary in the production of plays. Scenery, costumes, properties, etc. had to be provided at the lowest possible cost, and this condition remained for a long time even after the Abbey Theatre had opened, as Miss Horniman paid only the lighting expenses.

About a month or so before the theatre was due to open, I went down to what had been the Mechanics' Theatre (I think it was a Saturday afternoon). The builders' men had knocked off work, but I found my way in somehow, and found W. G. Fay and Fred Bryers (the scenic artist) working on the stage, painting scenery that had been made for the opening. As I volunteered to make myself useful, I was at once handed a brush, and left to paint a door while they went out to tea. Later on Fay told me about other things that needed doing. There were a number of large shields and spears to be made for *On Baile's Strand*, as well as a couple of benches, etc. So I began to turn up at the theatre every evening after my day's work was over, to put in another few hours' work, using mostly scrap timber left behind by the builders.

I had, of course, no knowledge of stage-craft at all at this time, and it was Willie Fay who first taught me, but I soon picked it up, and in fact I was soon able to suggest improved methods of doing certain things.

The shields had to be made of papier-mâché, about which I knew nothing, but Mr Fay showed me how to make moulds according to his designs, and, when I had the moulds made, to fill them in with the paper. This was a longish job, owing to the numbers of layers of paper I had to fill in, and they took a long time to dry when filled, but we got them all done in time.

In the first twelve months or so the Abbey Company only played for seven nights at the beginning of each month, beginning on Saturday night and running to the following Saturday night, the week always ending with a stage party, the refreshments provided being tea, claret-cup, Gort cake and sandwiches. On one occasion I was pressed into service as cook. Lady Gregory came to me with a basket of eggs and asked me to boil them hard. I did not know how long one had to boil eggs to make them hard, but to make sure I boiled them for about ten minutes, and when sliced they were hard enough. Another job I got was slicing lemons into a large jug to make claret-cup. These parties were very enjoyable affairs and the Gort cake was great stuff, provided you were careful about the raisin stones. Lady Gregory never forgot to show appreciation of any effort, even when it was not successful. In fact, she was, at times, so lavish in praise that one was inclined to suspect her sincerity.

In the early days of the theatre there were no rooms beyond the stage on the Custom House side, and all work had to be done either on or underneath the stage. The builders had put in a narrow wooden bridge across the back of the stage to facilitate painting of cloths, but this bridge had been put so high that one could not paint more than the upper six feet of backcloth from it, and the lower half had to be painted on the stage, rolling up the cloth to reach the centre. Willie Fay had asked me if I could lower this bridge so that about two-thirds of the cloth could be done from it, and I had done so, and while I was finishing the job at the fly-rail, he happened to be standing right underneath when I accidentally dropped a hammer and the handle struck him by a glancing blow on the head (had it struck him fairly he would have been seriously injured), but he was not much hurt, and merely asked if I was trying to kill him!

Some time later, however, he got his own back by sending me down to take the cap off one of the stage plugs, and then pressing his fingers down on the contacts while I was below, which gave me a severe shock.

After the Fays left, Mr Yeats was for a while quite despondent about the future of the theatre, and actually discussed with his sister the possibility of finding a job for me. Lady Gregory, however, was more optimistic, and after some discussion it was arranged to carry on, with Sara Allgood as coach and producer, under the direction of Lady Gregory and Yeats and (in the case of his own plays) J. M. Synge, Joseph O'Rourke stage manager, and myself as carpenter and scene-painter. Robert Gregory had gone to Paris for his art studies, and the directors had decided to produce *The Well of the Saints* in the autumn with a proper setting; it had already been done, but only with such scenery as we could at the time afford. Mr Synge went to London to get designs by Mr Ricketts.[2] When he returned they were handed over to me, and I felt a bit nervous when I saw what I was expected to do. But Mr Ricketts had sent very clear and definite instructions about the painting and I had plenty of time, so I did my best, and when the sets were finished Lady Gregory was so pleased with them that she wrote to Robert in Paris about them, and on his return some months later the first thing he did was to call at the Abbey to see the scenery I had painted. She also wrote to tell the Fays in America about it.

After this I was trusted to carry out designs by all sorts of people, and was left to my own devices. Robert Gregory had designed settings for his mother's play *The Image*, and when I had the scenery made and ready for painting he came up to Dublin to do it, I assisting him; when we were about half-way through the work, it happened that Tramore races were on, and when he came in that day he was not dressed for work. He said, 'Seaghan, you can do stones better than me, I'm going to Tramore races!' and off he went. But next day (or the day after) Lady Gregory came up to the paint-room, as I was working on the wings which showed the tops of windswept trees. After watching me for a minute or so, she said, 'Give me the brush, Seaghan.' I handed her the brush I was using and she then showed me how the strokes I had been making should be drawn upwards, and not downwards, as I had been making them. She asked me, had I taken any drawing lessons, and I told her I had not, only the ordinary school sort. She said, 'You ought to.' But my wages at the time did not run to drawing lessons, so I had to do without. Frank Fay and I had many arguments as to who should have the stage, as he would come along with a pupil to coach when I would be engaged in rather noisy work, and I had no other place to work. The result was usually a hot argument. On one occasion, after one of these, Willie Fay said to me, 'Tell him you'll sack him, Seaghan, if he's not careful!'

We could not afford at that time to spend much on scenery, and many of our settings consisted of curtains made of hessian and dyed in the theatre. This dyeing was a messy job when dealing with large quantities of hessian. I remember we got a large galvanised bath and dipped the hessian in it, and from that into another full of water, then draining each piece as best we could, and finally hanging them up to dry. We had clothes-lines all over the place; but it worked.

The builders had put in two great beams, on each side of the stage, stretching from back to front, and carrying wing grooves. These beams prevented us from using cloths wider than twenty-one feet, and I had suggested their removal, and was engaged on the job the morning Miss Violet Darragh arrived.[3]

I was sitting astride the beam, removing bolts and dropping them on the stage as I did so, but taking care, of course, that they would not strike anyone passing below. Just as I dropped one, however, Miss Darragh passed underneath, and looked up at me she said, 'Oh, I suppose *I* don't matter!' Mr Yeats, coming fast after her, called up to me, 'Seaghan, save them for the orchestra!'

On one occasion I was working in the paint-room, when Lady Gregory came in to speak to me about something. I had been smoking my pipe, and I at once left it down on the table to answer her, but she said, 'Go on smoking your pipe, Seaghan, I like to see a man smoking.'

Shortly after this she was returning to Gort for the Christmas, and before she left she came into the theatre and handed me a large bar of tobacco, saying, 'There's a smoke for Christmas, Seaghan', and told me that if it was not what I liked, I could change it for my favourite brand at the shop.

Mr Yeats had a habit of interrupting actors in the middle of a speech, which was rather trying. On one occasion, after several of these interruptions, Frank Fay lost his temper and asked him how he expected him to deliver his line properly, when he did not know what he was talking about!

On another occasion, when Mr Wright had been making experiments with an arc-lamp, to get an effect Mr Yeats wanted, and had tried one medium after another in vain, suddenly Mr Yeats called up from the stalls, 'That's it, Wright, that's it; what is that ?' 'Oh, it's the bloody gelatine gone on fire!' said Dossie.

At another rehearsal, he wanted the shadow of a cat thrown on to a pillar at the side of the stage. We had cut cardboard silhouettes and tried holding them in various positions in front of the lamp, but without success, then Dossie tried a new adjustment of the lamp itself. As he stood in front of the lamp Mr Yeats called up, 'That's not bad, Wright.' It was the back of Dossie's head!

All of us on the staff were very sorry when the Fays left, and on the night W. G. Fay and his wife were leaving for England, I went down to the boat to say goodbye. Mrs Martin was there also, and Jack Keegan; I cannot remember if Tommy Allgood was there.

Jack Keegan was the boy who used to look after the boiler, and do props, etc.; and in later years he became a very useful property-man. He was killed in France in 1916. Tommy Allgood is now in a Cistercian monastery. While the Fays were still at the Abbey, I think about 1906, Mr Yeats brought Mr Ben Iden Payne to the Theatre,[4] and he remained for about six months, but he was not popular with the players. While Mr Payne was at the Abbey, he produced Maeterlinck's *Interior*,[5] and, I think, Yeats' *The Shadowy Waters*.[6]

About the beginning of 1909, Mr Norreys Connell (Conal O'Riordan)[7] came to the Abbey as manager and producer, and he was one of the most courteous and considerate men I have ever met, always cheerful, and painstaking at rehearsals, polite to everyone; although he could be sarcastic when necessary.

He remained at the Abbey for about eight months, during which time he produced two of his own plays, *An Imaginary Conversation* and *Time*.[8] While we were on a visit to Cork, he wrote a letter of advice to the players, to be read by Mr Henderson,[9] who was the Secretary at that time, and the reading was very unfavourably received by the members of the company. Soon after Mr Norreys Connell left the Abbey.

NOTES

Seaghan Barlow had a long record of service at the Abbey Theatre as master carpenter, scenic painter, impromptu designer, a student of Greek and an occasional actor, a veritable dragon in guarding his stock of scenery. Lennox Robinson rightly described him as 'sullen over his cocoa and his Greek, he states he can do nothing. An hour later, everything is done to perfection' (*Ireland's Abbey Theatre*, p. 66). Barlow died in July 1972.

1. *His Last Legs*, by W. B. Bernard.
2. Charles Ricketts (1866–1931), British painter, sculptor, art critic and stage-set designer.
3. In 1907, Violet Darragh crossed the Irish Sea to play Deirdre in Yeats' play of that name. Her salary was much larger than that of the older ladies in the company and there was naturally much jealousy, and after *Deirdre* she did not appear again.
4. Iden Payne joined the Abbey Company as producer in Mar 1907.
5. *Interior* was presented at the Abbey Theatre on 16 Mar 1907.
6. Iden Payne did not produce *The Shadowy Waters*, which had been performed on 8 Dec 1906, before Payne arrived.

7. Conal O'Riordan (1874–1948), novelist and playwright. In 1909 he became managing director of the Abbey Theatre.

8. *An Imaginary Conversation* opened at the Abbey Theatre on 27 May 1909; and *Time*, on 1 Apr 1909.

9. W. A. Henderson, the manager.

Recollections of the Abbey Theatre*

UDOLPHUS WRIGHT

Soon after I became articled to a firm of electrical engineers, I was told one day after knocking about the firm's shop to go to a large building at eight o'clock in the morning and there I would meet the foreman. The building happened to be the Eye and Ear Hospital, Adelaide Road. I arrived in due course at the appointed hour and asked where I would find the electrical foreman. A sixty feet perpendicular ladder was pointed out to me, and I was told if I went up that I would find him on the top floor, which I managed to do with fear and trembling. I then found the foreman who happened to be W. G. Fay. From the start we got on very well together, during the continuance of that particular contract and many others. It was not long before we got talking of other things besides electrical work, and – after he had listened to some of my stories of stealing out at night down the country (in the small town of Carrick-on-Suir) to see dramatic shows, the stage being the side of a caravan let down and the auditorium a canvas tent – he asked me would I like to come round and see a rehearsal of some plays which were about to be presented at the Molesworth Hall. Of course I jumped at the opportunity. The rehearsal room in those days was the Camden Hall. There I met the members of the company.

Strange to say, I just cannot remember what the first rehearsal I saw was – I think it was Lady Gregory's *Twenty-Five*. All the people were very nice to me, and for the first production in the Molesworth Hall I just made myself generally useful on the stage. During these rehearsals there were a great many people came in and sat round the gas stove until long after I had to leave to get home. They were AE [George Russell], the Rt Hon. W. F. Bailey – of course W. B. Yeats, George Moore, Edward Martyn, and James Joyce on a few occasions. I then remember W. G. telling me that I was to be a pupil in *The King's Threshold*, and that I had

*Lennox Robinson, *Ireland's Abbey Theatre: A History 1899–1951* (London: Sidgwick & Jackson, 1951) pp. 76–7. Editor's title.

been elected a member of the Irish National Literary Society unanimously. Soon after that we were introduced to a tall stately lady, whom I always thought rather austere, and that was Miss A. E. F. Horniman. She had come over in connection with the dressing of *The King's Threshold*, and immediately took our measurements for the costumes, a few of which are still to be found in our wardrobe. It was not very long after this that we were told Miss Horniman was going to build us a theatre, and from then on till the Abbey was opened, we saw quite a great deal of her. Though she was, as I said, not very approachable to the members of the company – at least so it seemed to me – I only saw her lose her temper once during a rehearsal of one of Yeats' plays, for which she had also made the costumes; which did not seem to please Mr Yeats too well, and during the rehearsal his mind seemed to be wandering from the play, and in those days he always carried a black stick which at this time he was swinging to and fro, so much that it got on Miss Horniman's nerves – so much that she exclaimed, 'For goodness sake, Willie! stop swinging that stick, or leave the rehearsal!'

NOTE

Udolphus (Dossie) Wright had been with the Abbey Theatre from the beginning until the 1950s serving as a small-part player, sometimes as a manager, at others as stage manager, occasionally as play director, more often as chief electrician.

Irish National Drama*

W. B. YEATS

'The side of our work with which we have achieved our greatest successes,' said Mr Yeats to our representative, 'is undoubtedly the peasant comedy and tragedy. We have placed upon the stage for the first time the real Irish life as opposed to the traditional. The dialect of Lever and of Lover[1] was a composite thing, and displayed a very limited understanding of the peasant mind. The proper understanding of the peasant mind only arose with an understanding of Gaelic.

'These peasant plays', he continued, 'are not primarily studies of

---

* Extracted from 'Irish National Drama: Five Years of Progress. Mr W. B. Yeats Interviewed', *Cambridge Daily News*, 25 May 1910, p. 2.

peasant life. Synge's plays, for instance, contain a philosophy of life just as truly as do the lyrics of Shelley. They express the ideas of the man in the symbolism of the peasant world he had studied so deeply and knew so well. His was not photographic art; it was symbolic. He used the Irish peasant as a means of expression, just as the painter uses the colours on his palette. His plays are the complete expression of his own soul.

'Lady Gregory's comedy is equally personal, but in a different manner. Both writers studied their symbols profoundly. Lady Gregory, I believe, wrote down over 200,000 words of peasant speech before she wrote a line of her dialogue. Synge, of course, lived in the cottages of the people as one of themselves.

'That part of our movement represented by Lady Gregory, Synge and myself, is individualistic. We aim at expressing ourselves, they in dialect, myself in verse. But there is a new movement arising that is representative of the social life and the economic conditions of Ireland. We have just produced in Dublin, for instance, and we shall stage it in London, a play by Padraic Colum, in which one sees what one often sees in Ireland, a man whose whole life is a struggle to get free from his duty to his family. The hero, Thomas Muskerry, a workhouse master, is a sort of King Lear of the workhouse. Then we have *Harvest*, by S. L. Robinson, a powerful play, in which is shown the struggle of the farming classes to bring up their children in the professions, thereby ruining their farms. We have produced another play which is a study of the moral conditions left behind by the Agrarian war, the fear of public opinion and the like – *The White Feather*, by Wray [sic].[2] These men are the historians of their times in a way that we are not.

'It is, of course, the poetical drama in which I am most interested, though until lately we have been unable to to do very much in that direction because we have concentrated on our peasant work. *Deirdre* has lately been played in Dublin, however, and I am now going back with excitement to this work – and with scenery that will give me real pleasure. Mr Gordon Craig, after years of study, has at last created a method for the staying of poetical drama which suggests everything and represents nothing.'

Asked for some description of this creation, Mr Yeats said that the invention was Mr Craig's patent, of which he had secured the Irish rights, and he could not enter into detail. 'One sees upon the stage', said Mr Yeats, 'a vast Cyclopean place, where one can have the light and shade of Nature for the first time upon the stage. At last one escapes from all the meretriciousness, from the bad landscape painting, from the stage lighting which throws a shadow which in no way agrees with the painted shadow. At last we shall have a stage where there is solemnity and beauty, and where for all that, the verse is free to suggest what picture it will without having to compete with some second-rate painter.'

Up to the present, Mr Yeats explained, they had worked on the lines he explained to the interviewer five years ago, when he criticised customary stage methods with great severity. They worked by suggestion rather than by representation. An inside scene they presented as faithfully as their purse permitted. There it was possible to attain realism. But a landscape painted in the ordinary stage manner, he contended, must always be meretricious and vulgar. 'The moment an actor stands near to your painted forest or your mountain, you perceive he is standing against a flat surface.' Far better, he argued, to suggest a scene upon a canvas, whose vertical flatness one accepts and uses, as the decorator of pottery accepts the roundness of a bowl or jug or the flatness of a plate.[3]

A woodland scene might be represented, he explained, by a recurring pattern, or painted like old religious pictures upon a gold background. Or there was the comparative realism of the Japanese print. This kind of decoration not only gave them a scenic art – which would be true art because peculiar to the stage – but it would give the imagination liberty, and without returning to the bareness of the Elizabethan stage. 'Mr Robert Gregory (Lady Gregory's son) has designed some beautiful scenes for us on those lines', added Mr Yeats.

In conclusion, Mr Yeats expressed himself as more than satisfied with the success the movement had achieved.

Mr Yeats was recognised by many people at the Theatre last night. His striking personality, so splendidly revealed by Mr Strang in his delicate drawing of the poet that now hangs in the Fitzwilliam Museum, attracted a number of students familiar with his Celtic poetry and anxious for an introduction to the famous author.

NOTES

William Butler Yeats (1865–1939), a foremost poet of the English-speaking world, dramatist, co-founder of the Abbey Theatre, member of the Irish Free State Senate, and winner of the 1923 Nobel Prize for literature. He gave this interview in Cambridge, England, during the visit of the Irish National Theatre Company, which he accompanied.

1. Charles James Lever (1806–72) and Samuel Lover (1797–1868), popular novelists.

2. *The White Feather*, by R. J. Ray [Robert Brophy], had its first production at the Abbey Theatre on 16 Sept 1909.

3. Cf. 'Samhain: 1904', in *Explorations* (London: Macmillan, 1962) pp. 177–9.

Aim of Irish Players*

FRED O'DONOVAN

The Irish Players now appearing in New York started as an amateur organisation in Dublin. Lady Gregory and William Butler Yeats, the poet and playwright, were even then interested in it. When an Englishwoman, Miss Horniman, gave the Players a large sum of money they became a professional company.

'All of the members of the original company were recruited from the Dublin business and university circles,' said Fred O'Donovan, one of the leading players of the company, in his dressing-room at Maxine Elliott's Theater, 'but when it became a matter of giving up their business and becoming professionals most of them went back to their regular occupations. Arthur Sinclair and Miss Sara Allgood are the only original members of the company left.'

'What was the original idea of the Players while it was still an amateur organisation?' Mr O'Donovan was asked.

'Those persons who felt that a literary renaissance in Ireland was inevitable believed that the movement would include the drama as well as the literary arts. They felt that the romantic Irish dramas of Dion Boucicault[1] were not a truthful reflection of Irish life and character. They reflected the sentimental Irishman as the English and those who wrote for English consumption liked to imagine him.

'The Irish Players wanted to put on the stage the real Irishman of today – to reveal real Irish conditions and real Irish character. Now, to reach the real Irish character, the poets and dramatists had to deal with the life of the peasantry, those who lived close to the soil and obtained their subsistence from it. The upper classes are veneered with English thought and manners, hence few of the plays which the Irish Players have presented deal with life in the cities – with business and social circles.'

'Do the Players restrict themselves to Irish drama entirely?'

'When they first took out a licence there was opposition from the other theatres in Dublin, which thought there were already more theatres than the city would support, and it was necessary to designate in the licence what sort of plays they intended to produce, and to quiet the opposition the Irish Players limited themselves to plays of Irish life, with an

*World (New York), 26 Nov 1911, p. 6.

occasional translation. Under the latest licence the field has been broadened to include some of the English classics. On our return to Dublin we will probably put on some of Shakespeare's plays and the comedies of Sheridan and Goldsmith, though the main object of the organisation, which is to encourage native Irish playwrights and to produce plays which truthfully portray Irish life and character, will not be laid aside.'

'Whom do you consider the greatest dramatist who has been brought out by this movement?' Mr O'Donovan was asked.

'In Ireland that distinction is accorded to the late J. M. Synge. His plays are closer to the soil than those of most of the other Irish writers and he has come the nearest of anyone to translating into English the thought, the idioms and the sentence structure of the Gaels in Western Ireland. His *The Playboy of the Western World* has come to be regarded in Ireland as the greatest achievement of the Irish dramatic movement in spite of the angry opposition which first met the play in Dublin.'

'You find Mr Synge's dramas true to Irish character?'

'Absolutely – allowing him the dramatist's licence of selecting an exceptional case. He reveals the spirit of Irish character, and of course character in Ireland is just as varied as in any other country.'

'In their acting the Irish Players seem to seek to be as natural and lifelike as possible. Is it their contention that there should be no exaggeration on the stage?'

'We seek first of all to act truthfully', replied Mr O'Donovan. 'Simplicity and naturalness of acting are but a means to obtain that end.'

'But can you act on the stage absolutely naturally and truthfully without making the acting seem pale and colourless? The stage itself is artificial and unnatural. The light is artificial, the scenery is a mockery and the passions unassumed. Under those conditions wouldn't absolutely truthful acting fail to convince the audience that it was true to human nature?'

'There must of course be selection of and emphasis in acting to make the essentials stand out with sufficient boldness to carry the dramatist's thought into the mind of the audience, but we seek to use as little exaggeration as possible. There is a great danger to the actor in exaggerating.'

'What is that danger?'

'The danger that, having begun to exaggerate, he will unintentionally heighten his exaggeration, for effect or for applause, until the essential truthfulness of his portrayal becomes lost. That is why we seek to be as simple and truthful as possible in all the plays which we present. We want it to be genuine. Even the props which we use are, as far as possible, the genuine article. Old sugan[2] chairs are required in one of the plays and they are the real things – over 100 years old. That genuineness of the physical accessories we strive to carry into the actions, thoughts and emotions of the characters portrayed.'

'Is it one of the tenets of the Irish Players to use as little scenery as possible?'

'Not necessarily. We seek simplicity and truthfulness in our scenery, as well as in the acting and the selecting of props. We have experimented with the scenery effects devised by Gordon Craig,[3] the son of Miss Ellen Terry,[4] whom many people regard as a crank. His style of stage scenery is adapted to representing grandeur and sublimity – great heights and far distances. His scenes are painted a neutral colour and the warmth of colour of nature is obtained by the means of gradations of lighting effect. In our plays of native Irish life such scenery effects would not do at all, because they tend away from the mood of naturalness. Gordon Craig's ideas were utilised with excellent effect, however, in one[5] of William Butler Yeats' little symbolic plays, and we shall probably make use of his ideas in some of our revivals of classic or foreign plays.'

NOTES

Fred O'Donovan (?–1952) joined the Abbey company in 1908 and played the lead in *The Playboy of the Western World* on its first American tour. James Joyce thought O'Donovan's interpretation of Christy Mahon was truer to what Synge intended than W. G. Fay's original interpretation. O'Donovan was a romantic style of actor, noted for his Robert Emmet in Lennox Robinson's *The Dreamers* (Abbey, 2 Feb 1915). He became manager in 1916, until February 1919 when he left the Abbey.

In 1911, the Abbey Theatre Company, known as the Irish Players, made their first American tour, which was so successful that they were obliged to remain in the United States from Sept 1911 to Mar 1912. The tour opened in Boston on 23 Sept.

1. Dion Boucicault (?1820–90), playwright and actor. Starting in the theatre in England as an actor, he then began to write plays and had a great success with a comedy, *London Assurance* (1841). He had the 'trick of the theatre', and is credited with about 150 plays, including adaptations. He excelled particularly in parts requiring pathos, and was accused of creating the 'Stage Irishman'.

2. Variant form of 'suggan' (Anglo-Irish), straw rope.

3. Gordon Craig (1872–1966), English actor, stage designer and producer. Through Yeats' interest in his work, Craig made a set of screens for the Abbey in 1910. See James W. Flannery, 'W. B. Yeats, Gordon Craig and the Visual Arts of the Theatre', in *Yeats and the Theatre*, ed. Robert O'Driscoll and Lorna Reynolds (London: Macmillan, 1975), pp. 82–108.

4. Ellen Terry (1847–1928), English actress.

5. *The Hour-Glass*, first produced by the Irish National Theatre Society at the Molesworth Hall on 14 Mar 1903. It is to the revival (and revision) of 12 Jan 1911 that O'Donovan refers here, since it marked the debut of Craig's screens at

the Abbey. Incidentally, it may be noted that this use predates the use of Craig screens in the famous *Hamlet* at the Moscow Art Theatre (Dec 1911).

Lady Gregory and the Abbey Theatre*

JOHN QUINN

I was away from New York when the Abbey Theatre company of Dublin first came here, and I did not see them play until the end of their first week. In writing to a friend to explain who they were and what they had accomplished, I pointed out the perfect naturalness of their acting, the simplicity of their methods, their freedom from all distracting theatricalism and 'stage business', their little resort to gesture, the beautiful rhythm of their speech, the absence of extensive and elaborate scenery and stage-settings, and the delightful suggestion of spontaneity given by their apparently deliberate throwing away of technical accomplishments in the strict sense of the word. I said that too many theatres have costly scenery and expensive properties to cover the poverty of art in the play or the players, just as poor paintings are sold by dealers in big glaring gold frames; and had the same refined quality, not always apparent at the first glance, that old Chinese paintings are seen to have when placed alongside of modern paintings by western artists.

As I observed the fine craftsmanship of the actors, without a single false note, each seeming to get into the very skin of the part that he impersonated, my thoughts went back some eight or nine years to what were the beginnings of this whole enterprise.

Yeats, Hyde and I used to sit up every night until one or two in the morning, talking, it seems to me, about everything and everybody under the sky of Ireland, but chiefly about the theatre of which Yeats' mind was full. These were wonderful nights, long nights filled with good talk, Yeats full of plans for the development of the theatre. The mornings were devoted to work, the afternoons to out-of-doors, and the evenings to the reading of scenarios for plays, the reading of short plays in English by Lady Gregory and in Irish by Hyde. Lady Gregory and Hyde read out to us from time to time their translations of Irish songs and ballads, in the

* Extracted from *Outlook* (New York), 99 (16 Dec 1911) 916–19.

beautiful English of her books and of Hyde's *Love Songs of Connacht*. Yeats and Lady Gregory made a scenario of a play and Hyde spent three afternoons 'putting the Irish on it'. She has written how one morning she went for a long drive to the sea, leaving Hyde with a bundle of blank paper before him. When she returned in the evening, Dr Hyde had finished the play and was out shooting wild duck. This play was *The Lost Saint*.[1] Dr Hyde put the hymn in the play into Irish rhyme the next day while he was watching for wild duck beside the marsh. He read out the play to us in the evening, translating it back into English as he went along, and Lady Gregory has written how 'we were all left with a feeling as if some beautiful white blossom had suddenly fallen at our feet'.

At that time I was more interested in Yeats' writing and lyrical poetry and in Hyde's Gaelic revival than I was in Yeats' plans for an Irish theatre. Yeats was more interested in the poetry that moves masses of people in a theatre and in the drama than in what suffices to make up a book of lyric poetry that might lie on a lady's or gentleman's drawing-room table. I told Hyde and Yeats that that reminded me of Montaigne's[2] saying that he had deliberately put indecencies into his essays because he hated the idea of those essays lying on women's tables.

Lady Gregory was then at work on her two great books, *Cuchulain of Muirthemne* and *Gods and Fighting Men*. In these two books she brought together for the first time and retold in the language of the people of the country about her, in the unspoiled Elizabeth English of her own neighbourhood, the great legends of Ireland. She did for the old Irish sagas what Malory did for the Knights of the Round Table, and fairly won the right to be known as the Irish Malory.

Another night I first heard the name of John M. Synge. Yeats told us how he had come upon Synge at a small hotel in Paris and persuaded him to come to Ireland, and of the wonderful book that he had written on the Aran Islands. Yeats and Lady Gregory had tried to have it published. I myself offered to pay the expense of making plates for it, but Yeats said that he wanted the book taken on its merits, even if Synge had to wait some years for a publisher.[3]

Synge's debt to Yeats has not, I think, been fully appreciated. It was Yeats who persuaded him to drop the attempt to rival Arthur Symons as an interpreter of continental literature to England, and to go back to Ireland and live among the people and write of the life that he knew best.

When Synge was writing his plays, poems and essays he came often to Coole. Other guests there were George Russell, the poet and writer, Douglas Hyde, 'John Eglinton',[4] the brothers Fay, George Moore and Bernard Shaw, and Lady Gregory's home really became a centre of the literary life of Ireland of the last ten years.

From this great old house, almost covered by creeping vines, with the most beautiful garden I ever saw, the house in which were stored up so many memories of statesmen, soldiers, authors, artists and other distinguished people, with its great library, its pictures, statutes and souvenirs gathered from many lands, nestling in the soft climate of the West of Ireland, under the gray skies and surrounded by the brilliant greens and rich browns of West of Ireland landscape, or bathed in the purple glow of the air as the sun declined, I carried away two vivid impressions: first, the realisation of a unique literary friendship between the chatelaine and the poet Yeats; and, second, of the gentleness and energy of this woman, the stored-up richness of whose mind in the next eight or nine years was to pour forth essays, stories, farces, historical plays, and tragedies, and translations from Molière and Sudermann, and who has, at the cost of infinite time and pains, proved herself to be, with Yeats, the directing genius of the new Irish drama.

The next year in Dublin I saw a rehearsal of *The Shadow of the Glen* and other plays in a little hall.[5] The actors were young men and women who worked in the daytime, none of them at that time drawing any pay from the theatre. I must admit that I then supposed that this venture would go the way of its innumerable predecessors – endure for a few weeks and then vanish. But I was mistaken. I undervalued the tremendous energy, perseverance and courage of its leaders, Lady Gregory, W. B. Yeats, and John M. Synge; for it has all through required great patience, and not merely courage but audacity in the face of detraction, false friends, discouragement and croakings of disaster meeting them from all sides. At no time during these years did either Lady Gregory or Yeats receive a penny of money or a penny of profit from their work for this theatre. Douglas Hyde once told me that, apart from his lyric poetry, Yeats' greatest gift to Ireland was the drama. I should add that another gift of Yeats to Ireland was the introduction to the Irish drama of Lady Gregory and John M. Synge.

Ireland now has what it did not have when I first went there – two art centres that all Irishmen may be proud of, the Abbey Theatre and the Municipal Gallery of Modern Painting. Some little time ago Bernard Shaw, writing of Dublin, said that he had returned there and had found it just as sleepy as of old, with the same old flies still crawling over the same old cakes in the windows, except for two things, the Modern Art Gallery and the Abbey Theatre, which were the things showing an influx of new life.

In Dublin that year I spent several long evenings with Synge. He told me of his wanderings in Europe and of his fondness for the people of the West of Ireland and of the Aran Islands. Synge, like Yeats, was much interested in the problem of style, but in a different way. He knew the language of the Wicklow peasant and of the West of Ireland fisherman and of the Aran and Blasket Islanders. Synge came to his style in the same way that Lady Gregory came to hers, by his knowledge of and sympathy with the people who speak Elizabethan English in the West of Ireland, the English of King James' Bible. When Synge's *The Playboy* was first produced in Dublin, it was hooted for a few nights by a few organised 'patriots' who tried in vain to disprove the reputation that Irishmen are supposed to have of possessing a keen sense of humour. Synge was surprised, but not hurt or even annoyed, at the outburst. He was too much of an artist not to know that some people hate all beauty and that others attack strange beauty that they do not at the first sight understand. His chief fear seemed to be lest the outcry against *The Playboy* might hurt the theatre or endanger the cause of his friends.

The first night that *The Playboy of the Western World* was given in New York it was preceded by *The Gaol Gate*,[6] which is a mournful play; and when the merry row over *The Playboy* was at its height, I recalled the words of the Irish chieftain in Chesterton's 'Ballad of the White Horse':

> His harp was carved and cunning,
>   His sword was prompt and sharp,
> And he was gay when he held the sword,
>   Sad when he held the harp.

> For the great Gaels of Ireland
>   Are the men that God made mad,
> For all their wars are merry,
>   And all their songs are sad.

This little company of Irish players and their directors have answered the question that is being so often asked in London and New York – how to make the theatres a success and yet give nothing that is not good art. They had done this, it seems to me, by courage in keeping to the road they have chosen, by nationality in keeping to the narrow limits to which they bound themselves – 'works by Irish writers or on Irish subjects' – and by the deliberate simplicity of staging, by which expense is kept down and they are not driven to put on plays for the sake of profit only.

What lesson can America get from this example?[7]

NOTES

John Quinn (1870–1924), American lawyer and patron of the arts. He had been a supporter of the Irish renaissance before the Abbey Theatre was even a name.

When the newspaper growlings against *The Playboy of the Western World* were mounting in New York ahead of the Irish Players, a welcome sight when Lady Gregory arrived there was her old friend John Quinn. See 'On the Death of John Quinn in New York', *Irish Book Lover*, 14 (Sept–Oct 1924) 122; *Complete Catalogue of the Library of John Quinn*, 2 vols (New York: Anderson Galleries, 1924); B. L. Reid, *The Man from New York: John Quinn and His Friends* (New York: Oxford University Press, 1968); and Daniel Murphy, 'The Letters of Lady Gregory to John Quinn', Ph.D. dissertation, Columbia University, 1961.

1. *An Naomh ar Iarraidh* was printed in *Samhain*, no. 2 (Oct 1902) pp. 14–18, with Lady Gregory's translation, *The Lost Saint*. The latter was reprinted in her *Poets and Dreamers*; see the Coole edition (Gerrards Cross: Colin Smythe, 1974) pp. 160–4.

2. Michel de Montaigne (1533–92), French author of the *Essays*, which established a new literary form.

3. Synge's book, *The Aran Islands*, was eventually published in London by Elkin Matthews, and in Dublin by Maunsel, in 1907.

4. John Eglinton was the pseudonym of William Kirkpatrick Magee (1868–1961), essayist and poet.

5. In Camden Street. Quinn's biographer, B. L. Reid, is in error in declaring that Quinn did not see the Players until Oct 1904. It is quite clear from Yeats' *Letters* that Quinn saw Frank Fay in rehearsal at the Camden Street Theatre in 1902. See Christopher Murray, 'Three Sketches by Jack B. Yeats of the Camden Street Theatre, 1902', *Prompts* (Dublin), no. 4 (Nov 1982) 3–7.

6. *The Playboy of the Western World* and *The Gaol Gate* were presented in New York for the first time at the Maxine Elliott's Theater on 25 Nov 1911.

7. The Abbey Theatre had its influence on the 'little theatres' movement in America.

The Shanachie Casts a Spell*

WALTER STARKIE

Ever since my exciting experience in 1907 at the riotous first performance of Synge's *The Playboy of the Western World* I had felt attracted towards the ramshackle old Abbey Theatre on the banks of the Liffey, and in the vacations I never failed every week to take my accustomed seat in the second row which had been reserved for me by my friend, Jack Larchet,[1] the conductor of the Abbey orchestra. Between the acts he would invite me round to the greenroom where I met the members of the company. During the Christmas holidays in 1909 he told me that they

Scholars and Gypsies: An Autobiography (London: John Murray, 1963) pp. 82–5.

were producing for the first time Synge's unfinished posthumous tragedy, *Deirdre of the Sorrows*, on 13 January 1910. 'Mind you keep that night free, Walter', he said. 'Molly Allgood,[2] to whom Synge was later engaged, will be playing the part of Deirdre.'

Jack later gave me a moving description of the death of Synge in the previous year. His last year had been a desperate struggle, for the doctors had diagnosed a cancerous disease and had operated; they had seen that there was no hope, but he kept working away feverishly at *Deirdre of the Sorrows*, and had reached the third act. Molly Allgood had strange premonitions of Synge's death: some years previously when the Abbey company were on tour in England she and Synge were sitting in a tea-shop and as she was looking at him the flesh suddenly seemed to fall from his face and all she saw was a skull. Just before the operation, and at a time when she felt confident that he would be cured, she dreamed that she saw him in a coffin being lowered into the grave and a strange sort of cross laid on the coffin. 'He died', Jack Larchet added, 'on 24 March, 1909. In the early morning he said to the nurse: "it is no use fighting death any longer", and he turned over and died.'

Looking back I can remember no play that produced so deep an impression upon me as *Deirdre of the Sorrows*. I still see clearly in my mind's eye the wild young princess gathering up her rich robes and jewels, and I hear her voice saying prophetically: 'I will dress like Emer in Dundealgan, or Maeve in her house in Connaught. If Conchubar'll make me a queen, I'll have the right of a queen who is a master . . . I will not be a child or plaything; I'll put on my robes that are the richest, for I will not be brought down to Emain as Chuchulain brings his horse to the yoke, or Conall Cearnach puts his shield upon his arm; and maybe from this day I will turn the men of Ireland like a wind blowing on the heath.'

To a youth from an English public school accustomed to plod through a Greek tragedy word by word in class and learn by heart passages from Shakespeare, *Deirdre of the Sorrows* was a revelation: it seemed as if some new kind of drama combining the qualities of the *Agamemnon* of Aeschylus and *Antony and Cleopatra* had been conjured up before me by the ghost of the departed dramatist whom I had seen three years before, a forlorn figure, sitting alone while pandemonium raged around him. The fascination of *Deirdre* has lasted all my life, and I have only to turn the pages of the printed play to recapture instantly the emotion I felt that night. The theme which sprang from ancient Irish folklore had become for every Irish man and woman what the legend of Helen of Troy was for the Greeks, and Deirdre's beauty has inspired the Gaelic poets for centuries. Deirdre is the prophecy that gave her her name, the meaning of which is *Alarm*; but Synge, who was treating the character of Deirdre alone, replaced the original theme of the folk legend by the more dramatic one of the horror of old age and the decay of love, and Deirdre says to Naisi: 'Isn't it a small thing is foretold about the ruin of ourselves, Naisi, when all men have age coming and great ruin in the end.'

Synge was haunted by the fear about his forthcoming marriage to Molly Allgood. He felt that he was too old for her, and in his last play he writes the tragedy of a young girl betrothed to an old man and in love with a young one. Deirdre too constantly reminds us that Synge's reveries over his own approaching death had already gripped him when he wrote the lines: 'Death should be a poor, untidy thing, though it's a queen that dies.' Even his obsessions in this play with 'the filth of the grave' spurred him on to write and emphasise the vitality, the wilfulness and wild beauty of the heroine which appears in the farewell scene where Deirdre says, 'Go to your brothers. For seven years you have been kindly, but the hardness of death has come between us.' The open grave in the last act of the play was a grim reminder of the playwright's frantic race to dramatise the tragic end of his heroine before death came for him likewise.

There was a poignancy in the acting of Molly Allgood that night which I have never felt in any subsequent performance I have seen: a ghostly quality, as though the slight brown-eyed girl, with her pale face the embodiment of tragedy, still lingered under the hypnotic spell of the dead author, and she moved about the stage as in a trance, and her voice had the ring of uncontrollable pathos when she murmured: 'I have put away sorrow like a shoe that is worn out and muddy, for it is I have had a life that will be envied by great companies. It was not by a low birth I made Kings uneasy, and they sitting in the halls of Emain.'

On my return to the Abbey Theatre in 1912 I heard from Joe Kerrigan,[3] one of the principal actors of the company, the story of their odyssey in the United States during their 1911 tour, when *The Playboy* excited riotous scenes in the theatre, especially in New York and Philadelphia. In the latter city the trouble become more serious, with the result that the whole cast of *The Playboy* were arrested for performing 'immoral or indecent plays'. Joe Kerrigan, who had been playing the part of Shoneen Keogh, gave me a graphic account of the scene in the court before the magistrate. The first witness for the prosecution, a publican, said that he had sat out the play until Shoneen's 'coat of a Christian man' was left in Michael James' hands. Then he made a disturbance and was ejected from the theatre. 'I found', he declared, 'as much indecency in that conversation as would demoralise a monastery.' His brother, a priest, however, endured the play to the end, and found that Synge had committed every one of the sins mentioned in the act. 'We actors', said Joe Kerrigan, 'were all raging from the start, but when that priest started to attack my – that is to say Shoneen Keogh's – character, I got so mad, Walter, that I bawled out "Oh my God!" The magistrate then said: "If that man interrupts the Court again, turn him out", forgetting that he was speaking of a prisoner in the dock! I declare to God the whole of us burst out laughing.'

'What did Lady Gregory say to all this, Joe?'

'She sat amongst us, looking like a queen. She placed all her trust in our lawyer, John Quinn,[4] who was a tower of strength. You should have seen her face during the cross-examination of the witness when Mr Quinn asked the witness if anything immoral took place on the stage, and the latter replied: "not while the curtain was up"! She smiled when the same witness, the publican, stated that "a theatre was no place for a sense of humour"! We won the day hands down, Walter, for the Director of Public Safety, when he was called, said that he and his wife had enjoyed the play immensely and had seen nothing to shock anybody.'

The attacks against the Abbey Theatre continued in Dublin and Kerrigan told me that Yeats was urged by many prominent men in the city to throw over Synge. 'We like your work,' they said, 'and we like the plays of Lady Gregory, Padraic Colum and Boyle,[5] and the Abbey Theatre looks like prospering after the lean years. Why insist on forcing on the Dublin public what they detest? We condemn Synge because his is not like the Ireland we know.'

In spite of all the attacks and hostility W. B. Yeats never budged. He knew that Synge had given to Ireland the best plays she had ever seen, and he and Lady Gregory were resolved that the theatre would not yield to the mob. They received, however, very little support from their fellow workers in the theatre, and Boyle and Colum, two of the most popular of the Irish dramatists, seceded in sympathy with the protests against *The Playboy*. But Yeats and Lady Gregory were heroically adamant, though the company for months played to empty seats. Within a couple of years, however, after *The Playboy* had been welcomed enthusiastically in London and in the United States, it was produced in Dublin without causing a ripple in the audience. Thus Yeats by his courageous championing of Synge rendered a noble service to dramatic art, but after the death of Synge he became so irritated with the endless procession of second-raters clamouring about the wrongs of Ireland that on one occasion, when he could stand it no longer, he cried: 'When a country produces a man of genius he never is what it wants or believes it wants: he is always unlike the idea of itself. In the eighteenth century Scotland believed itself religious, moral, and gloomy, and its national poet, Robert Burns, came not to speak of these things but to speak of lust and drink and drunken gaiety. Ireland since "the Young Irelanders"[6] has given itself up to apologetics, there is no longer an impartial imagination delighting in what is naturally exciting. Synge was the rushing up of the buried fire, an explosion of all that had been denied or refused, a furious impartiality, an indifferent turbulent sorrow. His work like that of Burns was to say all the people did not want to have said.'[7]

NOTES

Walter Starkie (1894–1976), autobiographer, critic and translator. He was professor of language and literature at Trinity College, Dublin and a director of the Abbey Theatre from 1926 to 1943. During the Second World War he was British Council representative in Madrid. He spent many of his last years in Los Angeles, where he was professor in residence at the University of California. His article, 'Ireland Today', *Quarterley Review* (London), 271 (Oct 1938) 343–60, also deals with the Abbey Theatre.

1. John F. Larchet (1884–1967), who was director of music at the Abbey Theatre for nearly thirty years.
2. Maire O'Neill; for a note on her and her recollections, see p. 81.
3. For a note on Joe M. Kerrigan and his recollections, see p. 133.
4. For a note on John Quinn and his recollections, see p. 104.
5. William Boyle (1853–1923).
6. 'Young Ireland' was the name given to the revolutionary party in Ireland, including W. Smith O'Brien, Gavan Duffy, Thomas Osborne Davis and Thomas Davies. Their propaganda and actions led to several state trials for sedition and treason. See J. C. Beckett, *The Making of Modern Ireland 1603–1923* (London: Faber, 1966) p. 334.
7. 'The Death of Synge', *Autobiographies* (London: Macmillan, 1961) p. 520.

Abbey Theatre Co.: Departure for America*

LADY GREGORY

Queenstown,[1] *Thursday*

In response to what has proved a genuinely enthusiastic invitation the famous Abbey Theatre Players, accompanied by Lady A. Gregory, whose enthusiasm in the up-building of the national theatre is boundless, left Queenstown today by the White Star steamer *Majestic* for New York. The company which left here consists of the following: Miss Sara Allgood, Miss Mona Bierne, Mr M. J. Dolan, Miss Kathleen Drago, Mr H. E. Hutchinson, Mr J. M. Kerrigan, Miss Eithne Magee,

* Cork Examiner, 20 Dec 1912, p. 6 (interview).

Mr Nugent Monck, Mr Sydney Morgan, Miss Eileen O'Doherty, Mr Frederick O'Donovan, Mrs Frederick O'Donovan, Mr J. A. O'Rourke, Mr Arthur Sinclair, Mr Udolphus Wright.

On their arrival at Queenstown last night, the company proceeded to the Queen's Hotel, where they remained overnight. The arrangements connected with their embarkation were made by Messrs James Scott & Co., agents of the White Star Line, who at Queenstown and on board the *Majestic*, devoted attention to the comfort of Lady Gregory and the company, for which suitable acknowledgement was made.

Before leaving, your correspondent met Lady Gregory at the Queen's Hotel, and there listened to the gifted authoress detail her impressions of the work to which she has rendered such priceless service, while she also referred to the tour, in which Lady Gregory takes a deep interest as the youngest member of the distinguished company of players whom she accompanies, and of whom she is naturally proud, as the players are, of the connection with Lady Gregory, whose desire is to achieve even still greater things for the brilliant Irish company so closely associated with her name.

In the course of the interview, Lady Gregory said she is looking forward to a great success in America, where they did very well last year.[2] They had many friends in America, all of whom were anxious to welcome them back. They were taking with them on this tour a great deal of new work. *The Playboy* would always be in their repertoire. Some of the new work is by Cork authors, including *Patriots*, by Lennox Robinson, which was a very great success, and deals with the present political conditions, and represents a dying away of the old physical-force movement in favour of more practical work. It is a simple, candid production, and shows how things have worked out in Ireland. They are also taking with them T. C. Murray's powerful play, *Maurice Harte*, which was a big success in London and Dublin. It was during its production in London that Mrs Asquith asked to be introduced to the author, which Lady Gregory had pleasure in complying with.

Lady Gregory likes America very much, and has many personal friends there whom she will be glad to see again. In her wanderings there before she met many of her tenants' children who went out from Ireland, and was glad to find them, all doing well.

Amongst other plays they are taking with them are *Family Failing*, by Boyle, which is a northern play, and deals with the Protestants of Belfast; the two-act comedy, *Damer's Gold*, by Lady Gregory herself, will be amongst the number. The Abbey Theatre will be carried on by the No. 2 company in their absence.

Their American contract lasts to 1 May, and they will be back for the Oxford Eights week, which they were specially booked for, and where they have had big success in the past.

Their second company visited several Irish cities and towns in the present year, including Belfast, Galway, Longford, Doneraile, etc., and did very well in all.

Considering the high quality of the players, they are glad to have them appear before large audiences, though, of course, the Irish productions in Dublin and the country interested them most. They got more money, too, by going to America, for until the Abbey Theatre is enlarged their receipts would continue small. Before enlarging the Abbey they hoped to devote their efforts and resources to having continuous plays. At present they play only half the week. Later, they will have more players, and with sufficient rehearsals they would do much more work. Their venture had opened up a new profession in Ireland, both for dramatists and players and its success was beyond question.

With the advent of Home Rule,[3] Lady Gregory says she believes the imaginative stir that will be caused by a National Parliament in College Green will greatly help every intellectual or imaginative movement. Everyone will be interested in the building of the nation, and she believes this national theatre a very important stone in that building.

Mr Roosevelt wrote an article, added Lady Gregory, some time ago, in the *Outlook*,[4] saying how much the Irish national theatre and dramatic movement had added to the dignity of Ireland. They heard of the same in foreign countries – France, Germany and Italy – and the question asked by those interested in drama is not, what is the English theatre doing, but how is the Irish theatre doing, as they find it the most interesting expression of national dramatic art to be found in any country.

At Kingsbridge[5] yesterday, they got a most enthusiastic and encouraging farewell, and were assured of an equally enthusiastic reception home. To the American people Lady Gregory wished to say, before leaving Queenstown, that the company looked forward with great delight and pleasure to the appreciative audiences and the kindliness and friendship of the American people, and not even the raging gale blowing now at Queenstown on their departure by the *Majestic* can quite depress their spirits. They open at Chicago on 30 December, with *Kathleen Ni Houlihan*, *Maurice Harte* and *Spreading the News*, and in the second half of the week in Chicago their plays would include *Mixed Marriage*, by a Belfast author,[6] which was very successful in Chicago before, so that all Ireland will be well represented in the productions.

Lady Gregory will remain with the company throughout the tour.

Miss Allgood, like her associates, looks forward to a thoroughly successful tour in the United States. Speaking of the parts, she thought the part of the Mother in *Maurice Harte*, and next to that, the *Patriots* and *Mixed Marriage*, suited her best.

On arrival on board the *Majestic*, Lady Gregory and the company were specially introduced to Captain Haddock and the officers, and their comfort on board carefully provided for.

Australia has sent an invitation to the Abbey Company for an extended tour in that country.

NOTES

In Dec 1912, the Abbey Theatre Company made its second American tour, which lasted until May 1913.

1. Cobh, County Cork.

2. The Abbey Theatre made its first American tour in Sept 1911. On the Abbey American tour see Adele M. Dalsimer, 'Players in the Western World', *Eire–Ireland*, 16 (Winter 1981) 75–93.

3. On 11 Apr 1912 Prime Minister Asquith introduced the Home Rule Bill into the British House of Commons. The third reading was not carried until Jan 1913, but because of the violent opposition of the Ulster Unionists the Home Rule Bill was never enacted.

4. Theodore Roosevelt, 'The Irish Theatre', *Outlook* (New York), (16 Dec 1911) 915–16.

5. A major Dublin railway station, now Heuston Station.

6. St John Ervine. *Mixed Marriage* was first staged at the Abbey on 30 Jan 1911.

The School of Acting at the Abbey Theatre*

NUGENT MONCK

Having turned to him as a greyhound does a hare I asked him what he thought of the Abbey School of Acting? He at once became enthusiastic. There are, according to him, sixty-five members at least of the new school, all energetic and sincere, but not all geniuses. I suggest that maybe he had forgotten that he was working on virgin clay. He replied yes, but incidentally remarked that there are many kinds of clay, some of which are plastic; there are others which are not. With regard to the Abbey School, he mentioned that he had found that the Irish School had wonderful adaptability. In England there were student actors wanting to know the why and the wherefore of every intonation and of every gesture.

* Evening Telegraph (Dublin), 20 January 1912, p. 5. Interviewed by J. P. M.

In Ireland it was different; the pupils he had met, immediately in most cases after the smallest hint fell absolutely into the parts, the acting might be good or bad, but it was natural, which was its great feature.

Then I suggested, 'You had nothing to do with their training, Mr Monck?' All I could get as an answer was, 'I occasionally suggested new movements.' To those who have seen the School of Acting, comment on Mr Monck's remark is superfluous.

I asked him did he find any difficulty in training the School for the mystery plays and the up-to-date Abbey plays. He answered, 'To a great extent no.' They had a good idea from the far side of the footlights (of which we will deal later on) of the ordinary Abbey plays; in the morality and mystery plays, according to Mr Monck, and the Dublin public will agree with him, training was wanting. In this he said that their appreciation of the parts, whether from natural talent or from training, was wonderful.

He was getting so enthusiastic on the players that I had to side-track him by asking how he came across the 'Abbey' first. He confessed that he staged *King Argimenes*[1] for them at the Court Theatre, London, in last year. I awkwardly enough then asked: 'Then you have been in the past a producer as well as an actor?' I got as a reply, 'I am principally a producer; my acting you can judge for yourself.' I next got him to talk of the Morality and Mystery plays. He had produced several. Mr Poel[2] practically started the movement with *Everyman*, but our (as we may now call him because he has Irish relations) Mr Monck promptly followed with the three Chester plays. He then produced in Norwich[3] and London *The Plays of Paradise*, and in London *The Song of Songs*, which were an artistic and also a financial success. He was now getting tired, and I was getting interested, so I stated that I did not believe in the revival of the Mystery plays.

As I expected, I had the sticking point and I stuck to it. His point was that at present in scenery and dress we overburden the play itself and the actors; it is absolutely necessary to go back to early times in order to counteract this growing tendency. He does not want the pre-Elizabethan drama without any adjuncts in the way of scenery to be the predominant feature on our stage. But as the pre-Raphaelite school went back to nature, he wants us to go back to the foundation of drama, and then as the pendulum always swings and then stops, we shall arrive at a happy medium. He was again getting anxious and tired (probably of me), so I said I did not agree with his system of lighting the stage. He promptly defended it. In this world as at present constituted, our lighting comes from on high, except when in the gloaming we sit over a fire. Mr Monck, who is practical, even though poetical, ignores the gloaming, and wants the light from on high. He instanced as a proof of his theory the success of the lighting in Lady Gregory's new play, *McDaragh's Wife*.[4] There you had an interior dim and dark, but there was a brilliant burst of sunshine coming through the open door at the back of the stage. He said such an effect could not be produced by footlights. I had seen *McDaragh's Wife*, and had admired the setting, so I could not disagree.

NOTES

During the Abbey Players' absence in America, Yeats brought over the Englishman Nugent Monck (1878–1958) to train a second company to take over the theatre while the main body of the players was on tour; this would make it possible to maintain a permanent touring policy upon which the economics of the theatre depended. As a disciple of William Poel, Monck was a principal pioneer of the revival of medieval drama in England. According to Yeats, Monck possessed 'an organising genius', 'a gift for awakening devotion' and 'a curious influence on the character of those about him'. It was Yeats' hope that a new company trained by Monck would create an audience for a poetic and visually more artistic form of theatre. Monck went with the Abbey Company to America in 1913 and returned to Norwich in 1914.

1. *King Argimenes and the Unknown Warrior*, by Lord Dunsany, was produced for the first time at the Abbey Theatre on 26 Jan 1911. It was produced by Lennox Robinson.

2. William Poel (1852–1934), English actor and theatrical manager known for reviving old plays.

3. Monck later founded the Maddermarket Theatre in Norwich.

4. *McDaragh's Wife* opened at the Abbey Theatre on 11 Jan 1912. The title of the play was later changed to *McDonough's Wife*.

The Abbey Theatre: Is It on the Decline?*

BRINSLEY MacNAMARA

Today the first and last of the No. 1 Company's performances for the season take place at the Abbey Theatre. May we not take this circumstance as being indicative of the end? The Abbey Theatre is at present in a state of collapse that has arisen out of inability to proceed beyond a point of achievement, which in itself is not of tremendous

* Irish Independent (Dublin), 9 May 1913, p. 4.

magnitude. For some considerable time it has been very successfully killing itself. Money is an excellent thing, but a national theatre is something larger. The Abbey has most miserably failed to raise itself to the dignity of a national theatre. The only material upon which such a proud institution might be built has fallen to the level of a touring company. Its extensive touring now includes 'the smalls' in England, 'the smalls' in America, and last week the second company toured 'the smalls' in Ireland.

Causes of Decadence

Meanwhile few new plays are being produced, and the splendid enthusiasm which brought forth the movement is being allowed to die. No new playwright, and we all know that most of the Abbey playwrights are not marvels of dramatic genius, is given the chance to arise. Those who were lucky enough to gain a place in the first repertoire are being most surely played to death. The work of the players is degenerating, and the once exalted name of the Irish National Theatre has been vulgarised by vulgar associations. Two years ago it was alive. It had done something, and it promised something greater. Today it is anaemic and doddering. We have not far to seek the causes of its decadence. Among the very first we may number the wearying and wholly unjustified repetition of certain plays. You cannot go on producing *The Rising of the Moon* and *The Workhouse Ward* to the end of time. All the world is bound to see them at least once, and for most of the world a repetition must be very boring.

Synge and 'The Playboy'

To have produced one dramatist of world proportions is the Abbey's proudest boast, but surely J. M. Synge would have arisen without the help of the 'Abbey' or of Mr Yeats, much as the latter covers himself with glory for having 'found' him. To be convinced that Synge was bigger than the Abbey we have only to consider that since his death the better side of the Abbey has been on the decline. The plays of his day had promise; the post-Synge plays promise nothing but this end.

Whatever may be said for or against *The Playboy*, the fact that it has been brought down to the level of a common freak show should turn every sincere person against it, and make him 'feel a kind of pity'[1] for the great soul of Synge. In London it is the drawing card each season at the Court Theatre. Now in *The Playboy* Synge meant to express the magnificent wildness of our national temperament as viewed through the wildness that was in his own. At the Court Theatre the great British mind sees only what it can see, and giggles in vulgar laughter at the most splendid passages.

Produced in a Cheap Way

In America the average man went to see it for the same reason that he would go to see any kind of freak show, that is, to have it to say he was there.

The Playboy is not a cheap play, nor is it intended to ridicule the Irish character, but in England and America it is produced in a cheap way and under circumstances which make the thing it represents ridiculous. It is a fact that when the American managers of the Abbey Company's tour wanted to clear their losses on a play like *Damer's Gold*, *The Playboy* was always dragged out by the heels and put up as a cockshot. Last year the Irish American was foolish enough to pay for the privilege of throwing things at it, but the exercise of a little common sense has killed it more effectively than any deluge of exploded eggs.

The Hypnotism of Mr Yeats

Your typical Abbey dramatist is hedged in on the one side by the achievement of Ibsen, and on the other by the hypnotic power of Mr Yeats. The great Irish play can never be written until we get away from both these tyrannies. Had Synge lived he would have written the great Irish play. There can be no question about that. Yet he had not liking for the 'joyless and pallid words'[2] of Ibsen. And in 'Synge and the Ireland of his Time' [in *J. M. Synge and the Ireland of his Time* (Churchtown, Dundrum: Caula Press, 1911)] Mr Yeats very magnanimously admits that he never knew what Synge thought of his (Yeats') own work. The truth is, that he stood quite apart from the mind of Mr Yeats, and so he shall live in literature.

Today, if one attempts to criticise Mr Yeats, the little dramatists lift their hands in holy horror, and say, 'Oh Mr Yeats is a great personality, we owe everything to Mr Yeats!' Mr Yeats may be a large personality, but why? Because the men who surround him are very small. They have abased themselves in his sight.

The Abbey Convention

The selection of an Abbey play is a secret and marvellous process. It has never been rightly known how it is done. Who the selectors are, goodness alone knows. Some say the directors, others the manager, and the cynical will tell you that the stage carpenter has a hand in it, and so the story goes. This we do know, however, that the selection must be a very easy job, as each succeeding Abbey play is merely an inferior copy of the poor play that preceded it. The whole mistake of Abbey playwriting lies in the fact that it is limited by a formula. Formulas of any kind are destructive of genius or even superior ability, and when a man must get a certain number of 'blasts' and 'bloodys' into a certain space, the evolution of his theme is bound to suffer.

Subdivision of Irish Life

Then there is also the peculiar subdivision of Irish life for dramatic purposes, which is even more absurd. Thus we are asked to believe that all the idiotic and 'moony' peasants of the world are to be found in the barony of Kiltartan. Cork is the only county where the real foul-mouth Irish peasant still dwells in all his indiluted and 'bloody' strength. Hence Cork has produced only 'realistic' dramatists. The Midlands can produce only the depressing drama of the land, and small ambitions [fossilised].[3] It is only in Kerry, Mayo, or the western islands that there is any imaginative wildness. We may expect nothing from Belfast but the play of second-hand sociological ideas, and Dublin – Dublin with all its splendid humanity – has no dramatic life at all. Mr Yeats is quite satisfied with this geographical distribution of dramatic materials, and as the Abbey at present poses as a school of realism a play by a Corkman must stand a better chance of production than a play by a man from any other part. Now as one Cork play must, in terms of the convention, be very like any other Cork play, we get results like those of the last Cork play, *Broken Faith*,[4] which seemed to be a conglomeration of scraps from every Cork play that had ever been written.

The Abbey's Need

The Abbey is exhausted. It needs new life, the high old life of enthusiasm and idealism which is ever new. The halo has fallen from about the head of Mr Yeats. His gesture has lost its eloquence. He has put on the garment of the commonplace and dwells amongst the successful business men of his time. A new inspiration is needed, an idea of a national theatre, retaining all that was best in the decaying form, and developing organically from that form, so that it may attain to something which the Abbey never was and never could be, a free theatre working along independent lines, and apart from the colossal egotism of two individuals.

NOTES

Brinsley MacNamara [John Weldon] (1890–1963), novelist, short story writer and playwright. He joined the Abbey Theatre company as an actor in 1910 and toured America with it. Between 1919 and 1945, he had nine plays produced at the Abbey, the best-known of which are *The Glorious Uncertainty* (1923) and *Look at the Heffernans!* (1926). MacNamara was never truly a man of the theatre, however, despite a lifelong association with the Abbey, for which he served briefly in 1935 on the Board of directors. See Andrew E. Malone, 'Brinsley MacNamara: An Appreciation', *Dublin Magazine*, July 1929, pp. 46–56; 'Revelations by a Director of the Theatre', *Irish Independent* (Dublin), 29 Aug 1935, p. 7; 'Resignation of Abbey Director,' *Irish Independent* (Dublin), 4 Sept 1935, p. 9; Brinsley MacNamara, *Abbey Plays 1899–1948, Including the Productions of the Irish Literary Theatre* (Dublin: At the Sign of the Three Candles, [1949]); Michael McDonnell, 'Brinsley MacNamara: A Checklist', *Journal of Irish Literature*, 4 (May 1975) 79–88; and Christopher Murray, 'Brinsley MacNamara', in *Modern British Dramatists, 1900–1945*, part 2, ed. Stanley Weintraub (Detroit: Gale Research Co., 1982) pp. 3–8.

1. Christy Mahon says to Pegeen Mike in Act Three of *The Playboy of the Western World*: 'It's little you'll think if my love's a poacher's, or an earl's itself, when you'll feel my two hands stretched around you, and I squeezing kisses on your puckered lips, till I'd feel a kind of pity for the Lord God is all ages sitting lonesome in His golden chair.'

2. In his Preface to *The Playboy of the Western World* Synge wrote: 'One has, on one side, Mallarmé and Huysmans producing this literature; and on the other Ibsen and Zola dealing with the reality of life in joyless and pallid words.'

3. MacNamara was himself from the Midlands, and was about to expose their pusillanimity in his controversial novel, *The Valley of the Squinting Windows* (Dublin and London: Maunsel, 1918).

4. *Broken Faith*, by S. R. Day and G. D. Cummins, was first produced at the Abbey Theatre on 24 Apr 1913.

Memory of the Abbey Theatre*

L. A. G. STRONG

I had also discovered the Abbey Theatre. Vi[1] and I frequently talked broad Dublin, and he one day told me that I should go to the Abbey, where I would hear it spoken to perfection.[2] The first programme I saw there consisted of *The Rising of the Moon* by Lady Gregory, and J. M. Synge's *The Playboy of the Western World*. Synge was dead, but once, when I was very small, I had caught a glimpse of him outside the house where he stayed with his relatives in Glenageary. He wore a broad-brimmed hat, which for some reason caught my attention, and I stared at it until I

* *Green Memory* (London: Methuen, 1961) pp. 144–6. Editor's title.

became aware that the dark, saturnine face beneath it, with its heavy brows and dark moustache, had softened into a smile of amusement.

The chief parts in Lady Gregory's play were taken by Sidney Morgan, to whom Ivor Brown paid noble tribute when he died – 'Let us now praise second players' – and J. M. Kerrigan, whom I take to be the finest character actor the Abbey produced. I saw him in many parts, and always had to look at the programme to find out which was he. *The Playboy*, a revival against which the Dublin press protested – 'that foul travesty of Irish life' – had Fred O'Donovan in the title part. His was a very different reading from Willie Fay's, more romantic, more in key with the vigorous good looks which George Moore approved, than with the small, satirical and weazened Fay. Eithne Magee was the Pegeen, a lovely girl, who brought to the part grace, impetuosity and passion. It was a joy to meet her many years afterwards, when I was judging at a festival, and many is the argument we have had over this and that point, including the text of the play and the emendations which were made to avoid trouble in America.

I managed in three summers to see almost all the stalwarts of the Abbey company. Through the theatre too I came to know a little about the writers whom Yeats had gathered round him. The first book by a contemporary poet I bought out of my pocket money was Seumas O'Sullivan's *Poems*, to which I was directed, most improbably, by a review of James Douglas in the *Star*. From O'Sullivan, for whose work I keep an inordinate affection, I came to Joseph Campbell's *Irishry*, and Padraic Colum's *Wild Earth*. I had a copy of *The Playboy* in the beautiful little half-crown edition published by Maunsel, and the first guinea I ever earned I laid out on completing the set.

A great deal has been written about the acting at the Abbey and some of the praise has been exaggerated, naturally enough, because of the contrast between this intimate and direct style of acting, learned in a small theatre, and the style which had become conventional in London. Still, these players gave performances of an extraordinary quality. No actors I have ever seen gave the same illusion of real life. Again and again a character on the stage seemed to have wandered up there from among the audience. When, a little later, I saw a performance of St John Ervine's *John Ferguson* at Hammersmith, with a cast including actors of the capacity of Miles Malleson and Herbert Marshall, J. M. Kerrigan, playing the part of Jimmy Caesar, seemed like the one real man in a company of actors. I do not claim that this was necessarily a virtue from the producer's point of view, but it was a quality of the Abbey playing.

NOTES '

L. A. G. Strong (1896–1958), man of letters. His other writings include *Dublin Days* (Oxford: Blackwell, 1921) and *Personal Remarks* (London: Peter Nevill, 1953).
    1. Strong's cousin.
    2. Strong was deeply interested in dialects, and used to gather dialect material wherever he went.

My Early Days with the Abbey*

LENNOX ROBINSON

One Sunday early in 1909 I got a letter from Mr W. B. Yeats stating vaguely that he and Lady Gregory were considering certain new arrangements in the Abbey Theatre and could I come to Dublin and meet them?

Within half an hour I was prostrated by a physical complaint which an access of nerves always inflicts on me, but I travelled to Dublin next day and on Tuesday afternoon went to the Nassau Hotel to meet him and Lady Gregory. Mr Yeats was late for the appointment and she entertained me by telling me how he had just put *The Green Helmet*[1] into rhymed verse and how lovely it was.

She seemed to me an old lady, but twenty years later she did not seem a day older. And he, when he came, seemed middle-aged; he was twice my age, that is to say he was forty-four.

He made a speech which he had obviously thought out. He said that the Norwegian theatre at Bergen, recognising Ibsen's genius, had attached him to that theatre at the age of twenty-three. A dramatist should know his instrument, and to make me a good dramatist I should work in a theatre. Had I any plans for myself, and prospects? I had none. Very well, I would be made manager and producer of plays at the Abbey Theatre and I would be paid £150 a year.

It was fantastical. I knew next to nothing of the theatre, I had a very poor education, I could not add up figures, I had once been a master at a preparatory school in England and had been dismissed at the first

*Lennox Robinson, Tom Robinson and Nora Dorman, *Three Homes* (London: Michael Joseph, 1938) pp. 223–33.

opportunity. But if Mr Yeats was crazy I was not and I accepted on the spot.

I hurried home, I bought a suit of clothes, and I am sure the four shirts and the warmer vests. I had only a few days for these things, for I was going to London for six weeks. I was to live in Mr Yeats' rooms; Bernard Shaw was helping, he was making me his secretary. It was as fantastical, as silver-spooney as that.

Being Mr Shaw's secretary was only a form of words. I had no duties, I never typed a letter for him, but as his 'secretary' I was admitted to all rehearsals and he and Mrs Shaw showed much kindness to a very awkward young man.

It was a magical six weeks. I lived alone in Mr Yeats' rooms in Woburn Buildings. Dark rooms lit by many candles, shelves and shelves of books. All the poetry and all the plays I had been wanting to read seemed to be there.

I watched and compared the methods of three producers: Boucicault, Shaw and Granville-Barker.[2] Boucicault[3] was sane and practical, perhaps not very inspired, but he seemed to evoke the best from his players. Mr Shaw thought more of his play than of his actors; his main idea seemed to be that everyone should speak very loudly and very slowly so that no word could be missed, even at the back of the gallery.

The result was a very slow performance, and after the first night a great deal had to be cut out of *Misalliance* – one of his most subtle and, curiously, little-played pieces.

But Mr Granville-Barker completely captured my imagination. For rehearsal he had devised a stage-cloth painted into squares a foot each way like a gigantic chessboard. And when you moved you veered three squares across – the bishop's move, or two to the right or to the left, or at very critical occasions you might even make the knight's move. But woe betide you if you landed on your wrong square. Every move was part of a pattern; so was every gesture, every speech.

During these happy weeks one thing troubled me. Lady Gregory's son, Robert, was a good boxer and she thought it would be an excellent thing if the future manager of the Abbey Theatre could be trained in that manly art and accomplished enough to throw out drunks and rowdies from the theatre. Therefore it was laid upon me to get lessons in boxing.

I dreaded the idea; six foot and several inches high, weighing less than ten stone, I could not see myself in a ring save prostrate in a corner. But my future position seemed to depend on it and so one of the players, big, handsome Charles Bryant, a boxer himself, was asked to recommend me a teacher.

He promised to do so but was very busy rehearsing and each week mercifully put it off till the next week, and I left London as ignorant of boxing as I am now. However, Lady Gregory never knew and I was able a few years later, in her presence, to remove several very disagreeable (and very big) men from a theatre in New York.[4]

After six weeks of watching and watching I had to come back to Dublin and face the Abbey company and instruct them in the art of acting. I had to face Sara Allgood and Maire O'Neill, Arthur Sinclair, Fred O'Donovan and J. M. Kerrigan – masters of their craft, and I so ignorant. Even Mr Yeats grew a little afraid for me, but he brightened when I told him of Granville-Barker's chessboard stage-cloth.

'Get one painted,' he said – 'that will terrify them. You will terrify them. You will have complete authority over them.'

So Seaghan Barlow, our stage carpenter, painted one and we rehearsed on it for a few weeks, but his paint did not dry and the lines quickly grew blurred and after a month the cloth disappeared.

I quickly landed the theatre into trouble. King Edward VII died early on a Saturday morning. We were to play a matinee, but ought we to? I knew that the other theatres in Dublin would close, but did the national Abbey Theatre take notice of the demise of an English king?

Mr Yeats was abroad, Lady Gregory in the West of Ireland. I wired to her in the middle of the morning asking for instructions.

The hours slipped by and there was no answer. My inclination was to play and the players agreed with me, and duly the curtain rose on Padraic Colum's *Thomas Muskerry*.[5] Before the matinee was over her reply came: 'Better close through courtesy.' But the mischief had been done. It would seem wavering not to play that night, so play we did.

Lady Gregory had written her answer while the telegraph boy waited. The message had left her house before midday and what happened to delay its dispatch we never could find out.

But the reverberation was very serious. Miss Horniman was still subsidising our theatre and would continue to do so until the end of the year. Sturdy Englishwoman that she was, she demanded my instant dismissal.

The directors refused and she stopped her subsidy, which meant a loss of £600. The directors pointed to her promise and said she could not break it. The case was submitted for arbitration to the *Manchester Guardian*, who decided in the directors' favour and she paid the money.

The directors, with a noble gesture, returned the money and the incident was closed, though I believe that to the end she referred to me as 'that Robinson'.

I was dreadfully conscious of having cost the theatre £600, but I was able to make some amends later when our secretary left and I did his work as well as my own. I was in the theatre by half-past nine each morning, answered letters and lodged the previous night's receipts, rehearsed from half-past eleven till two and generally rehearsed again at five o'clock, and was front-of-house man at night and counted and checked the money. I was getting to know my theatre from top to bottom.

The players fought among themselves incessantly. Perhaps from their early amateur days they had inherited a tradition of intriguing for parts, and there were endless jealousies. For several years two of our principal actors never spoke to each other. An actor on tour thought I had allotted to him a room unworthy of his fame: he took possession of the star dressing-room and – boxer or no boxer – I had to throw him out of it by force.

But on the whole I was on excellent terms with them; yet, after five years of constant production, of long tours in America and England, the theatre got on my nerves. I was itching to write but I had only found time to write one play, *Patriots*. Mother had not been so wrong when she said that she 'dreaded your literary work may be swamped by routine work', and in June 1914, I resigned.

NOTES

Lennox Robinson (1886–1958), playwright. From the staging of his first play in 1908 until his death, he was associated with the Abbey Theatre as writer, producer and director. In 1951 he published *Ireland's Abbey Theatre: A History 1899–1951* (London: Sidgwick & Jackson) a valuable contribution to the history he had helped to make. See Michael J. O'Neill, *Lennox Robinson* (New York: Twayne, 1964).

1. *The Green Helmet*, a play in ballad metre by W. B. Yeats (founded on *The Golden Helmet*), was presented for the first time at the Abbey Theatre on 10 Feb 1910.

2. Harley Granville-Barker (1877–1946), English playwright, actor, director and critic.

3. Dion the Younger (1859–1929), second son of the playwright; joined Charles Frohman at the Duke of York's Theatre as actor/producer in 1901 and remained there until 1915. He produced the original *Peter Pan* in Dec 1904.

4. Cf. 'The men near were calling to him to clear out, but they didn't help to evict them. It was Robinson who came at last and led him out like a lamb' (Lady Gregory, *Our Irish Theatre*, 3rd edn (Gerrards Cross: Colin Smythe, 1972) p. 119).

5. *Thomas Muskerry* was produced at the Abbey Theatre for the first time on 5 May 1910.

My First Visit to the Abbey*

AUSTIN CLARKE

The streets were bright with sunshine as I stole into the Abbey Theatre for the first time. I had hesitated so long at the corner, watching the last of the small crowd hurry to the Saturday matinee, that I was already several minutes late. In some vague way, I had heard of Irish drama and its traditions, for knowledge of outside affairs comes painfully and confusedly to a young student living in the shadow of examinations.

Scarcely had the programme seller taken my ticket at the door of the pit when she disappeared into what seemed complete darkness. I groped my way after her, full of alarm and bewilderment, for from the Stygian gloom came the most lamentable outcry that I had ever heard in my life.

As I grasped the back of a seat and sank down I could make out dimly on the stage two robed figures. When my eyes became accustomed to the gloom I saw that they were standing before an immense locked gate. At first, in my confusion, I thought that this must be some ancient tragedy and that these two shadowy figures were stricken souls in Hades.[1]

But gradually I realised that they were shawled women and that this unbashed hullabaloo was the famous *caoine*.[2] It seemed to me as if the dismal muse of Irish history were present, adding her own groans to those embarrassing cries. The shock of that sudden encounter with Irish tradition was so great that to this day I cannot remember what play followed *The Gaol Gate*,[3] by Lady Gregory. But the experience was so strange and exotic that I determined to return again.

In those years after World War I the literary tradition of the Abbey was not as yet in complete abeyance. The hilarity of farce was controlled, if not in kind, at any rate in time. The farces were shorter and were always preceded by a serious one-act play or a poetic play by Yeats; sometimes the order was reversed and farce was confined to the curtain-raiser.

Inordinate laughter is so complete an experience in itself that we rarely remember what brought those stitches to our sides, those contradictory tears to our eyes. Memory requires some violent jolt from the past to stir it into activity. So I remember best of all that moment in *A Minute's Wait*,[4] when an infuriated goat held up the one-way traffic of the West Clare Railway. Did a well-trained billy-goat really rush across the

Irish Digest (Dublin), 66 (Sept 1959) 77–9.

stage, scattering market-women, farmers and decrepit railway officials? Or was it only a scuffle in the wings which left that indelible moment of idiotic mirth in the mind?

But the plays of Yeats were a deeply imaginative experience, and as the poet put on his own plays as often as possible, the experience was a constant one. On such occasions the theatre was almost empty. There were a few people in the stalls, including Lady Gregory, and, just after the last gong had sounded, Yeats would appear, dramatically, at the top of the steps leading down into the auditorium.

Scarcely had the desultory clapping ceased, when Yeats would appear outside the stage curtain, a dim figure against the footlights. He swayed and waved rhythmically, telling humbly of his 'little play', how he had rewritten it, and what he had meant to convey in its lines. As the twenty or thirty people in the pit were more or less scattered, I was isolated usually in one of the back seats. On such occasions I felt like Ludwig of Bavaria, that eccentric monarch who sat alone in his own theatre. I enjoyed the poet's curtain-lecture, almost as if it were a special benefit performance for myself.

One night, however, my youthful and romantic illusions were suddenly shattered, and in a trice the Celtic Twilight was gone. As the poet appeared punctually outside the curtain, a dazzling light shone around him. It might have been the light of his later fame! I glanced up and saw that the brilliant shift of illumination came from the balcony.

A spotlight must have been clamped to the rail and switched on as the poet appeared.

But my conclusions may have been unjust, for in youth we do not understand the complexities of human motives. I did not realise at the time that poetic drama was slowly vanishing from the Abbey Theatre. It seems to me now that, consciously or not, the poet may have been making a last despairing gesture to call attention, not to his own picturesque person, but to the struggling cause of poetry on the stage.

The most exciting play which I saw in those early days at the Abbey Theatre was, ironically enough, not an Irish one, but a continental experiment in dramatic impressionism. It was *Hannele*,[5] by Gerhardt Hauptmann, a play in two scenes. When it first appeared in the 1890s, this small play caused a sensation. It infuriated critics in Paris as a sample of German infantilism, and was denounced as blasphemous in New York.

It depicts, with all the relentless compassion of Hauptmann, the delirium of a child rescued from drowning and brought to a workhouse hospital. Reality and hallucination mingled in the strange scenes; sacred and profane figures dissolved into one another. It was all a confused blur to me at the time, but I realised instinctively that the play was a poetic protest against the oppression of the young and that insidious sense of spiritual guilt which is instilled by custom into the adolescent mind. It was a first glimpse of analytical drama.

Another memorable experience was the production of *The Post Office*, by Rabindrinath Tagore. His play expressed religious intimations, not with that familiar emotionalism which dulls understanding, but in new images, cool, clear and surprising.[6]

I was fortunate in catching the last of that imaginative movement which inspired so many writers here, and in seeing all of Yeats' plays before they disappeared from the theatre he had founded. So I remember gratefully that sunlit Saturday when I stole into the Abbey Theatre for the first time and heard with astonishment the wailing women.

NOTES

Austin Clarke [Augustine Joseph] (1896–1974), poet, playwright and novelist. In 1940, he and Robert Farren founded the Dublin Verse-speaking Society which performed on radio and in the Abbey Theatre. In 1944, he founded with Farren the Lyric Theatre company which performed at the Abbey until the 1951 fire. At his death, he was generally considered the finest Irish poet of the generation after Yeats. His book *Twice Round the Black Church: Early Memories of Ireland and England* (London: Routledge & Kegan Paul, 1962) includes background to the Irish drama.

1. Hades (in Greek mythology), the pagan underworld, i.e., hell.

2. Lament. Cf. 'It is written in a lyrical prose, and has a "caoine" composed for it by Arthur Darley that was beautifully chanted by Miss O'Neill'. W. G. Fay and Catherine Carswell, *The Fays of the Abbey Theatre: An Autobiographical Record* (London: Rich & Cowan, 1935) p. 206.

3. *The Gaol Gate* had its première at the Abbey Theatre on 20 Oct 1906.

4. *A Minute's Wait*, a comedy in one act by Martin J. McHugh, opened at the Abbey Theatre on 27 Aug 1914.

5. *Hannele* was presented at the Abbey Theatre on 20 Feb 1913.

6. *The Post Office* was produced at the Abbey Theatre on 17 May 1913. It was in harness with Tagore's play that Padraig Pearse was invited to present his pupils of St Enda's College in a play in Irish, *An Rí* [*The King*], written by Pearse himself, in which the prophetic line occurs, 'Mochion an bás ma' s é ordaitear dhom' ['Welcome is death if it is appointed to me']. Prophetic, too, in the light of future events, was the title of Tagore's play – *The Post Office*.

Eileen Crowe Tells Her Story*

EILEEN CROWE

QUESTION. Your name has become indissolubly associated, Miss Crowe, with the great tradition of the Abbey Theatre. How did you first come to joint the company?

ANSWER. I was always crazy about the theatre – I used to attend plays at the Abbey Theatre most, but I went to the Gaiety Theatre, too – but I never thought that I myself would walk on a professional stage. In fact the idea entered my head for the first time when I saw a newspaper advertisement for the Abbey School of Acting.

Q. So you went round and entered yourself for the school?

A. Yes. Lennox Robinson and Arthur Shields still laugh at the girl who came to the audition and asked, when requested to do something, 'Will I do it with actions?' It was a play about Colmcille[1] which I had been doing at school, and I couldn't imagine myself reading it without 'actions'.

Q. And the actions were successful?

A. They must have been, for I was admitted to the school, where Michael Dolan had a class at the time. In one way I was particularly lucky to have joined at that time, as most of the first company were away in America (it was the period of *The Whiteheaded Boy* tour). So in six weeks' time I found myself playing leading parts in the Abbey, which was probably very bad for me. I think it is much better to start with small parts and learn your job that way. The other way round, you have to learn it backwards.

Q. What were your first parts?

A. The very first part I played was that of the Girl in Terence MacSwiney's *The Revolutionists* [*sic*].[2] The second was Sarah Curran in Lennox Robinson's *The Dreamers*.[3]

Q. Have you always been with the Abbey company?

A. Yes, except for six months when I toured in England and Northern Ireland in *Peg O' My Heart*.[4]

Q. What is your favourite part?

---

*Condensed from 'Questionnaires to Celebrities, No. 19: Eileen Crowe', *Commentary* (Dublin), 3 (Oct 1944), 3–18. Editor's title.

A. I think my very favourite part, which I played for only three days, was Mrs Borkman in Ibsen's *John Gabriel Borkman*. The play was put on to commemorate the fiftieth year since the death of its author, [*sic*][5] and was not scheduled for a run.

Q. So that explains its short run!

A. Yes. But, of course, remember that in those days no play was allowed to run for more than two weeks, however successful. The only exception was *Juno*, which ran for three weeks on its first production, but that was *most* exceptional. It could have run for twelve months at that time. Yeats was very definite about the two weeks' rule.

Q. What made them relax on this occasion?

A. Well, by Wednesday morning the theatre was booked out. Not a seat left for the remainder of the week. The theatre was besieged. They had to keep it on.

Q. Did it get tremendous notices on the first night?

A. Oh, terrific – terrific. *The Shadow of a Gunman* had more or less prepared people for *Juno*. The former had caused something of a sensation. One of my favourite parts is Minnie Powell in *The Shadow of a Gunman*. It is one of the few 'straight' parts which have any character in them. Most playwrights fall down on them. They are generally insipid. Probably for that reason I have always preferred character work.

Q. Did you come much into contact with O'Casey at the time?

A. Oh, yes. I was in the audience on the first night of *The Shadow of a Gunman*. I went round after the first act wildly enthusiastic, and found Sean O'Casey sitting in the greenroom very, very nervous. He was tremendously pleased when I told him how enthusiastic was the audience. I think it was a pity O'Casey ever left Dublin.

Q. You said you preferred character work. Do the characters come alive for you straight away? I mean, do you very quickly have a conception of how you will play them?

A. When a play is read, some characters come to life straight away, even to the clothes they are wearing. Some characters come to life during rehearsals. There are some characters I haven't been happy about until the dress rehearsal. At the last minute they suddenly seemed to become real people – to me, that is.

Q. Can you give a concrete example?

A. Well, take *Grogan and the Ferret*.[6] The moment that play was read, I saw the 'Ferret' just as I played her.

Q. That was one you saw in the round, even to the dress, straight away?

A. Yes. Seeing the character straight away doesn't always mean you play it straight away. You aim towards what is in your mind's eye and get it later on in rehearsals.

Q. Are you ever completely befogged, say, by a badly conceived character?

A. That happens very often. You just can't see a play. You very often simply have to create characters where the author hasn't supplied the material.

Q. I wonder if Dublin actors find difficulty in getting the accent and character of the western speech of Synge's characters?

A. There may be something in that, but Maureen Delany, who comes from Galway, also finds it hard to learn. The thing about Synge and Lady Gregory is that once you have learnt their lines you never forget them. Speaking of Irish accents, I remember that out in America, somewhere on the west coast, we were talking to an American in a hotel lobby, who, after listening intently to us for a long time, exclaimed: 'D'you know, I can understand you perfectly!'

Q. That, of course, was on one of the Abbey Theatre tours out in the United States. Any other experiences?

A. Most of our plays on that first Abbey tour were given in colleges, where the greater part of the students had never seen a play of any kind. They didn't quite get them in the way a Dublin audience would, but they were most appreciative. One of the most appreciative audiences we ever played to was in the college for coloured students in Tusgegee, Alabama, where they got every point in the two plays we did there, Lennox Robinson's *The Whiteheaded Boy* and *The Far-off Hills*. They have never gone better than they went there. The coloured students' faces merged with the blackness of the auditorium, and it was an extraordinary experience to see nothing but rows of white teeth in the darkness. Whenever a laugh line came, as when Pierce conquers Marian at the end of *The Far-off Hills*, they jumped in the air with delight. It was a great experience! We had a marvellous time in Hollywood, where we were fêted and made much of, but it is a very different matter for players who go there looking for work. Among the 'extras' acting in the picture we made of *The Plough and the Stars* were film people who had once been great stars.

Q. Was it the Abbey Theatre company who made the film?

A. No, just five of us: Barry Fitzgerald, Arthur Shields, Denis O'Dea, Peter and myself. We were brought over specially by RKO to make the film.[7] The director was John Ford.

Q. 'Peter and myself'! Who's Peter?

A. My husband, F. J. McCormick. His real name is Peter Judge.

Q. Then are his initials, F. J., also part of the pseudonym?

A. Yes. As a matter of fact, he doesn't even know what they stand for.[8]

NOTES

Eileen Crowe (1899–1978), actress.

1. St Colmcille (521–97), one of the three patron saints of Ireland.
2. *The Revolutionist* was produced at the Abbey Theatre for the first time on 24 Feb 1921.
3. *The Dreamers* was performed at the Abbey Theatre for the first time on 2 Feb 1915.
4. Since there is no record of any Abbey tour between 1914 and 1931, Eileen Crowe could mean the production at the Ambassador's Theatre, London, 1920–1. *Peg o' My Heart*, an Irish–American comedy by J. Hartley Manners, was presented for the first time at the Gaiety Theatre, Dublin, on 11 Oct 1915.
5. This play was presented on 3 Apr 1928 to commemorate the one hundredth anniversary of Ibsen's birth, not the fiftieth anniversary of his death. Ibsen was born in 1828 and died in 1906.
6. *Grogan and the Ferret*, by George Shiels, opened at the Abbey Theatre on 13 Nov 1933. Eileen Crowe played the part of Miss Hatty.
7. The film was shown for the first time in Jan 1937.
8. For Eileen Crowe's recollections of F. J. McCormick, see p. 179.

Great Days at the Abbey*

ARTHUR SHIELDS and J. M. KERRIGAN

Two actors who were with the Abbey company before the First World War live in Hollywood today: Arthur Shields (brother of Barry Fitzgerald) and J. M. Kerrigan. Both have vivid memories of the early years of the company. Arthur Shields recalls: 'The Method? I don't know whether you'd call it the Method or not, but we based our acting on observation of real characters we saw around us.

'I remember, about 1912, J. M. Kerrigan taking me out to Donnybrook to a public house. "Watch the barman now", he said. Then when we got back to the Abbey he made me give an impression of the barman, and criticised me where he thought I should improve it.'

When I questioned J. M. Kerrigan (who played in the first performance of *The Playboy of the Western World* in 1907)[1] about this, he said: 'Yes, we used to analyse the characters we played, pretty thoroughly. Often, we'd sit for hours in the greenroom, discussing the "other life" of the characters in our current play – that is, what those characters would do in situations besides those in which they were involved on the stage.'

Arthur Shields[2] believes that with F. J. McCormick (who played the part of Shell in Carol Reed's film *Odd Man Out*) the Abbey method reached its high point.

*Extracted from the *Irish Times* (Dublin), 19 Mar 1963, p. 8.

'His observation of the smallest detail in a character was uncanny. Of course a lot of his delicate touches went unnoticed. But it all contributed to the picture, d'ye see. He disappeared body and soul into a part. He talked in character in the wings before he went on the stage.'

He recalls an amusing instance of the lengths to which McCormick's realism took him. 'F. J. was inclined to be pious. But when he played the part of Seamus Shields in Sean O'Casey's *The Shadow of a Gunman*, I noticed that he used the Dublin expletive "Jasus" fairly frequently. I commented on this. He denied indignantly that he ever used the word on the stage. I was playing Donal Davoren, the poet in the play, and since I'd nothing better to do I wrote down in my note-book the number of times the word was used – thirty-three. F. J. was flabbergasted. Lost in the part.'

From its earliest years, the Abbey was influenced by realistic techniques. W. G. Fay (with Frank Fay the co-founder of the Actors Company) after seeing an Ibsen work wrote: 'Obviously, this sort of play demanded a new technique.' But Yeats was seeking a different sort of realism, the quality he had observed in the Irish storytellers, 'a restraint and delightful energy, perfect in its vivid simplicity'. He wanted to abolish 'the English idea that an actor, when not speaking, must always be moving his hands or feet, or jigging about somewhere in a corner'.

Kerrigan recalls: 'He told us he would like to put us in barrels. When the central character was speaking, perfect stillness from the rest of the cast was insisted on, and their attention was focused on him.'

'It was like putting a light on an actor' is how Shields recalls it.

Frank Fay was ideal for Yeats' purpose. He was a fanatical elocutionist. Though he left the company at an early stage, his influence remained. He taught the players 'to use words like a ball, to hit the back wall with them'. On tour, Shields recalls, the company went to each new theatre on the first morning to try it for pitch. They whispered across the auditorium until words billowed out from their well-trained diaphragms, like feathers borne on puffs of wind.

Yeats was not, Kerrigan thinks, a good guide as to how his own verse plays should be spoken. Synge was more perceptive. 'Say what's there, and if there's poetry in it, it will come out', he would tell the company.

The Abbey directors, Yeats, Synge and Lady Gregory, were bonny fighters. Riots were frequent in the theatre. Kerrigan remembers Synge on the stage as the bottles and garbage flew, during the first performance of *The Playboy of the Western World* in 1907. Synge pulled the curtain down to protect the actors.[3] But Frank Fay, who played Christy Mahon, pulled it up again. He believed in art for art's sake.

On tour in Boston,[4] when the missiles began to fly, Kerrigan heard a whisper. It was from Lady Gregory, who had crept on the stage behind a set. 'Reserve yourself, we're going to pull down the curtain and play it again'. And they did play it again, right through.

The introduction of a prostitute on the stage, in Sean O'Casey's *The Plough and the Stars*, provoked another riot in 1924 [*sic*].[5] 'God, Yeats was magnificent', Shields recalls. 'He came out in front of the curtain and faced the bottles and stones. Didn't give a damn. Stood there with his hands up, flaying hell out of them with his tongue.'

Yet in other ways Abbey audiences helped the actors. The pit, composed of students and working men, would rise to applaud Yeats' mighty lines. There was fine language close to the actors, in the ordinary speech of the Dublin people.

'May the wife that you find be the one that is best, and may you lead her to your bed of honour', an old woman said to Kerrigan after a performance she had enjoyed. Arthur Sinclair in the part of King James in *The White Cockade* created an impressive air of majesty. 'Tell me, sir, have any of your family royal blood in them?' a labourer asked in a public house after the play.

Maire O'Neill (sister of Sara Allgood) is remembered by both Shields and Kerrigan as the greatest actress they ever saw. 'She lifted you on a wave', said Shields, who played Christy Mahon to her Pegeen Mike in Australia, 'that carried you with her and brought you successfully to shore. Often she fought like a wildcat in the wings with you. But once she was on stage, only her art counted.'

The early theatrical tradition of Dublin may have had some influence on the Abbey, though Kerrigan is the only actor I know who has referred to this. 'Jimmy O'Brien at the Queen's, where the old melodrama was played, was a really great comic actor. Once, after Coquelin saw O'Brien act in Manchester, he put his arms round him and said: "*Cher maître*."'[6]

Kerrigan and Shields were paid five shillings a week at the Abbey in the years before World War I. But the life was exciting. Ireland was in the grip of a national revival. The Abbey Theatre was a power-house of ideas. After the Insurrection of 1916, Yeats was to write:

> Did any play of mine send out
> Certain men the English shot?[7]

Arthur Shields fought in the Insurrection in 1916 in James Connolly's Citizen Army; afterwards he was sent to prison. Today he recalls with a gleam in his quizzical blue eyes how even in non-political plays Yeats seemed to sense the presence of forces that were shaping the destiny of the nation.

'Dublin has again achieved the heroic', he told the audience after T. C. Murray's *The Pipe in the Fields*.[8] 'Tonight, as I listened to this play, I seemed to see a lonely figure standing amid our people again. Parnell.'[9]

NOTES

1. J. M. Kerrigan played the part of Jimmy Farrell (a small farmer) in *The Playboy of the Western World*. He had joined the Abbey Theatre in 1906. For more on him see W. A. Henderson, 'The Success of Mr Kerrigan', *Evening Herald* (Dublin), 26 Apr 1913, p. 6; and Liam O'Briain, 'Joe Kerrigan', *Irish Bookman* (Dublin), 2 (Oct–Nov 1947) 69–71.

2. On Shields see also Marion Fitzgerald, 'Arthur Shields Remembers', *Irish Digest* (Dublin), 82 (Dec 1964) 51–3, repr. in this book, pp. 156–8.

3. Cf. 'My friend, Mr Kerrigan, wrote to me later repudiating this statement. He said that "no missiles were thrown on the stage during the run of *The Playboy* at the Abbey"; that "Synge never appeared on the stage during the performance of the opening night, and the old Abbey audience were not in the habit of bringing empty bottles to the theatre", and finally he authorised me to say "I emphatically deny such statement was made or even suggested"' (C. P. Curran, *Under the Receding Wave* (Dublin: Gill & Macmillan, 1970) p. 107).

4. *The Playboy of the Western World* was presented at the Plymouth Theatre, Boston, on 13 Oct 1911.

5. *The Plough and the Stars* opened at the Abbey Theatre in 1926, not in 1924.

6. Dear master.

7. The Yeats lines are misquoted. They read:

> Did that play of mine send out
> Certain men the English shot?

The reference is to *Kathleen Ni Houlihan* (1902). The lines are from 'The Man and the Echo'.

8. *The Pipe in the Fields* was first staged at the Abbey Theatre on 3 Oct 1927.

9. Charles Stewart Parnell (1846–91), political leader.

The Coming of Age of the Abbey*

GEORGE W. RUSSELL

About a quarter of a century ago Ireland began to assert and practise its right to cultural independence, making it apparent to the world that it had a distinction, a spiritual personality of its own. That personality asserted itself in many directions. It began to drink at the fountain of its own youth, the almost forgotten fountain of Gaelic culture, and at the same time to be intensely modern, to create a literature which had

* *Irish Statesman* (Dublin), 5 (2 Jan 1926) 517–19.

enough of the universal in it to win recognition from lovers of literature in Europe and America. It was our literature more than our political activities which created outside Ireland a true image of our nationality, and brought about the recognition of a spiritual entity which should have a political body to act through. No single activity of that newly kindled Irish personality did so much to attract attention to Ireland as the Abbey Theatre, whose twenty-first birthday, its coming of age, was celebrated last Sunday by a special performance.[1] The swift upspringing of a dramatic literature and art in a soil that seemed sterile, has something mysterious about it. Thirty years ago there did not seem a people in Europe less visited by the creative fire. Then a girl of genius, Alice Milligan, began to have premonitions of a dramatic movement, and she wrote little plays to help the infant Gaelic League, and she went here and there, an elfish stage manager, with a bag crammed with fragments of tapestry to be used on the actors in order to create the illusion of the richly robed ancient Irish of romance. These activities excited a poet of the time to write lines full of an affectionate irony parodying one of her own lyrics and attribute them to Alice:

> At Samhain of Little Plays,
> As I was in an awful stew;
> There were not dresses half enough
> And I was wondering what to do;
> There came this thought into my mind –
> Why, cut the dresses right in two!

> At Samhain of Little Plays
> I pinned the actors up with care,
> And gave to each a leg, a sleeve,
> And whispered in their ears, 'Beware!
> My dears, for God and Ireland's sake,
> Remember, this side out with care!'

With Alice Milligan, with whom the brothers Fay were co-workers, were the infant beginnings of Irish dramatic art. But even earlier William Butler Yeats had been making essays in poetic drama. In his prodigal boyhood he wrote many strange beautiful poems in dramatic form, *The Island of Statues*, *The Equator of Wild Olives*, *Mosada*, *The Seeker* and a little Indian play[2] which alone has a place in his collected works. *The Countess Cathleen* and *The Land of Heart's Desire* were his first serious efforts to write poetical plays which might be staged. Mr Edward Martyn had caught the dramatic infection which was soon to become an epidemic, claiming almost every Irish writer. George Bernard Shaw was beginning, outside Ireland alas, the writing of plays which was finally to make him the most celebrated dramatist of his time. George Moore was deflected for a time from the novel, and has told the history of his brief fever for the land of his birth in that masterpiece of malicious frankness, *Ave, Salve, Vale*.[3]

At first the new Irish playwrights were unaware of the genius for acting latent in their countrymen. They brought over professionals from England. But all this was changed when the brothers Fay showed they were capable of training Irish actors to speak beautifully and act with subtlety. After a performance in St Teresa's Hall, at which the lovely *Kathleen Ni Houlihan* of Yeats was first staged, it was realised that Irish actors were a more fitting and an infinitely better vehicle for Irish dramatists to use than the English professionals. An Irish Theatre Society was formed. A little later, by the generosity of Miss Horniman, the Abbey Theatre was purchased and presented to Mr Yeats and his colleagues. At that time hosts of new dramatists were appearing, the most original of these, John Millington Synge, was soon to achieve an international reputation. We have only to mention the names of Lady Gregory, Padraic Colum, Lennox Robinson, Lord Dunsany, T. C. Murray, Oliver Gogarty, Brinsley MacNamara, Seumas O'Kelly, William Boyle, George Fitzmaurice, St John Ervine, who, with many other writers of talent, helped Mr Yeats to create the most varied dramatic literature of our time. In Munster, Daniel Corkery, and in Ulster, Rutherford Mayne, with their colleagues, participated in the overflowing vitality, and helped to make regional schools of drama of great merit. That the creative stream has not run dry is proved by the recent emergence of Sean O'Casey, whose *Juno and the Paycock*, a tragi-comic masterpiece, has excited as intense an interest in London as in Dublin. And what superb acting have we not had for many years. The brothers William and Frank Fay who were the creators of an Irish art in acting, and who fixed the tradition, Dudley Digges, Sara [Sally] Allgood, and her sister, Maire O'Neill, Maire (Mary) Walker, Arthur Sinclair, Fred O'Donovan, J. M. Kerrigan, Arthur Shields, Barry Fitzgerald, Sidney Morgan, Maureen Delany, Eileen Crowe and F. J. MacCormick [*sic*], a long list of names of past and present Abbey actors who delighted us, come up in memory. The foreigner could recognise in this amazing activity the evidence of a nationality which was creative and living, while the words or deeds of politicians made no such universal appeal. There is, we believe, not a country in Europe from Russia in the East, to Spain in the West, where some work of the new Irish dramatic school have not been translated and staged. We doubt if that genius has been recognised as fully in Ireland, where it was born, as it has been elsewhere. It has been our habit to grumble, to criticise, to accept as a matter of course brilliant writing and acting as if they were nothing, to cry out when venerable superstitions were smashed, as that of our having the finest peasantry in the world, when they really were one of the most incompetent in Europe. There was fresh observation instead of formulae, insight instead of superstition, realism and idealism wedded. The record of the Abbey Theatre will make a splendid page in the literary history of Ireland, and Senator Yeats, Lady Gregory and Lennox Robinson, who for so long have been its directors, may feel a justifiable pride over what has been accomplished.

While we say this in praise, frankly we wish, for the sake of the Abbey itself, that it shall continue to live in that exasperating atmosphere in which it grew up. Nothing can be worse for an intellectual movement than a chorus of approval. Universal approbation means that the people have come to be on its own level, and it is not ahead of them, and therefore it has ceased to belong to the aristocracy of intellect and character. If it ceases to produce plays which set the pit and galleries shouting, it will then be time for it to go into limbo. We need many cultural shocks, the intellect of Ireland has lain sleeping for so many centuries that a national theatre, if it is to play a great part, must probe every problem. It must not only try to rise to the heaven of the national imagination, but it must not be afraid to turn up the sub-soil, explore the depths and abysses. There are many gentle and futile souls who are shocked by realism. But there is no depth which cannot be sounded if the plummet is dropped from a height. We do not wish for the Abbey a career all quarrels and controversies, for that would be contrary to human nature, which must have plenty of jovial, lovable and desirable life to keep it sweet. But we hope it will never lose its ancient fearlessness about public opinion, or that its directors will ever come to hesitate about the production of a masterpiece lest it might for a time lose some popular favour. In the end, its audience will begin to love it for its daring, will prefer the work which shakes them out of their mould of mind to the work which echoes back to them their own surface emotions. It was by such cowardice the great drama of the Elizabethan age degenerated until there was no poetry, no imagination, no reality, only the despicable theatre which came to be known as the Theatre of Commerce. It may seem that our benediction on the Irish National Theatre is mixed, that we are praying for trouble as well as success. It is true, that is our wish, for we know that when the waters are not troubled there is no angel of healing. It is only the smug who want life to stand still and to wear its best covering and to hide not only its high beauty, but its sores. But at the moment, the Abbey has a deserved success, the state has given it recognition,[4] a minister[5] speaks at the celebration of its coming of age. We congratulate it, and hope that it will not be killed by all the kind things said about it.

NOTES

George William Russell (1867–1935), poet, painter, economist and editor. He was a pivotal figure in the Irish revival. His famous pen name, AE, was a shortening of an earlier pen name, Aeon, which utterly defeated a compositor. He was active in the Irish Literary Society and in the early stirrings of the theatre. In 1902, his drama on the legendary Deirdre was acclaimed as an evocation of Irish ideals. See AE, 'The Irish Literary Drama', *Daily Express* (Dublin), 28 Jan 1899, p. 2.

1. The Abbey Theatre celebrated its twenty-first birthday on 27 Dec 1925. See Andrew A. Malone, 'The Coming of Age of the Irish Drama', *Dublin Review*, 181 (July 1927) 101–14.

2. 'Anashuya and Vijaya', in *Collected Poems* (London: Macmillan, 1963) pp. 10–14. It was first published under the title 'Jealousy' in 1889. In a note in 1925 Yeats said that 'this little Indian dramatic scene was meant to be the first scene of a play about a man loved by two women, who had the one soul between them' (A. Norman Jeffares, *A Commentary on the Collected Poems of W. B. Yeats* (Stanford: Stanford University Press, 1968) p. 6).

3. This trilogy, *Hail and Farewell* (1911–14), gives a mordant account of Moore's ten years in Dublin with a candour and directness new to his time.

4. Eight hundred and fifty pounds was voted as an annual subsidy (in succeeding years the subsidy was increased), and so the Abbey Theatre became the first state-subsidised theatre in the English-speaking world.

5. Ernest Blythe (then Minister of Finance). See his recollections, pp. 161–71.

The Abbey in Those Days: A Memoir*

DENIS JOHNSTON

Just over fifty years ago I happened to be directing a rehearsal of our national theatre company in its first presentation of *King Lear*[1] when I was interrupted by a message from the box-office to the effect that a Mr Shakespeare wished to speak to me on the telephone.

As might be expected I was somewhat taken aback by a call at this time from such a source. So, suspending all operations on the stage, I hurried to the receiver in the front hall only to find that it was not, as feared, a stricture from another world on my treatment of the play, but an enquiry from a local photographer of the same name as to when it

---

* *The Writers: A Sense of Ireland*, ed. Andrew Carpenter and Peter Fallon (Dublin: O'Brien Press, 1980) pp. 67–70.

would be convenient for him to come and take some pictures of the production for publicity purposes.

Needles to say I was somewhat relieved at this discovery, and I listened attentively while he described how on a previous occasion both he and his equipment had been accommodated on a number of planks placed across the seatbacks in the parterre, from which elevation he and his valuable camera had been precipitated into the narrow space between the rows owing to the unexpected disintegration of the platform. He hoped that a disaster of this kind was not going to occur again. Nowadays in the reconstructed Abbey,[2] there are no such hazards in the taking of production pictures under proper auspices, but in the heyday of Mr Shakespeare there were peculiarities in the old building that affected not only photography but also the presentation of many of the plays themselves.

It is well known from many published works that the handsome, sober-looking grey building in Marlborough Street that came to be known as the Abbey Theatre had previously been a morgue, notwithstanding the fact that it bore on its parapet a carved inscription reading 'Savings Bank'[3] – surely a rather cynical expression, however it got there, to apply to a repository for broken bodies! What is not so widely known is that the operative part of the interior, as we came to know it, had nothing to do with a morgue, but for many years had been a centre for popular vaudeville, opening off Lower Abbey Street, and known as the Mechanics' Institute. It already had a small stage, and no doubt other facilities for the refreshment and entertainment of the mechanics of its day.

How this strange combination of buildings came to be amalgamated into the original Abbey Theatre by its most assiduous, non-paying member of the audience, the late Joseph Holloway, is a matter on which very little information is now available. All that is clear is that the morgue provided the principal entrance hall, the box-office, a tea and coffee bar, a repository for hats and coats, a short flight of stairs up to the theatre's gallery, and a few steps down to the stalls. Upstairs in this front building the offices were to be found, together with two of three extra dressing-rooms and possibly some lavatory accommodation, although personally I cannot remember ever having found any such convenience.[4]

The Mechanics' Institute provided the auditorium and its two principal peculiarities: firstly that it lay at a right angle to what was now its main entrance, unusual in a theatre, and secondly that the stage backed on to a public lane, which still runs down the blind side of the present building. This meant that no extension could ever be made to the depth of the playing area, which when combined with the absence of any facilities (apart from a narrow lighting bridge) for flying scenery, had a noticeable effect on the structure for most of the plays written for the theatre by the more experienced Abbey playwrights. An interesting academic thesis will no doubt be written some day attributing Yeats' adoption of the technique of the Noh Play to the difficulties raised by the birds required to be flying overhead in his *The Shadowy Waters*, while there was always a difficulty in the last act of *The Plough and the Stars* in shooting Bessie Burgess through a rear window thanks to that immovable back wall.

Nevertheless in spite of this bagful of technical problems, the Abbey achieved its world-wide fame; and this in a playhouse where it was advisable for all major exits to be made on stage right for the simple reason that on that side there was a wide and capacious scene dock, into which even a motor-bike could, if necessary, be ridden into the distance – (as occurs in George Shiels's *The New Gossoon*)[5] – while on stage left there was little room left for any sort of exit apart from a short flight of steps up to a tiny hall; the rest of this particular area was usually regarded as the sacrosanct property of Barney the prompter and U. Wright, the electrician, one of the most traditional members of the company who was usually asked to play small but important parts which required his constant appearance on the stage as well as his attention to the switchboard. (His 'U' actually represented 'Udolphus', his Christian name, although Yeats used to refer to him regularly as 'Uranus'.) It had also to be remembered when planning movements on the stage that, for some unknown reason, the arch of the proscenium had been planned (or left from other days) between eight or ten feet off-centre of the stalls, which left a considerable portion of the stage out of sight of customers seated at the left end of the front rows.

Apart from these problems there was, however, a pleasant sociable sort of life backstage, with friends of the players visiting the greenroom even during performances. This was a feature that was not usually frowned on by the authorities – as would certainly be the case today, as the stage was well within earshot – and the old troupers of the company were well able to keep a familiar play going with a few gag lines while some missing party dashed down a short flight of stairs muttering 'Excuse me. That was my cue'. More serious was the problem presented by an occasional visitor who, on entering by the doorway from the lane, would find himself unable to get to the greenroom without crossing the stage, and might indeed do so while the curtain was up. Even this intrusion has been known to be covered up by somebody speaking an additional line such as: 'Oh yes. That was the brother I mentioned. He's just coming back from Mass.' They were real pros – that small prewar company!

And let it be remembered that in spite of all these perils and handicaps, the management of this 'National Theatre Society', whose premises went up in smoke about twenty years ago,[6] survived at least three departures of most of its principal players to pastures elsewhere. It faced two riots and recognised two Nobel Prize-winning authors.[7] It also defeated two determined attempts at mob censorship, not to mention a third by the Lord Lieutenant. And all of this to the music of a very accomplished five-piece orchestra, intruding on the front row of the stalls, while delighting the public with everything from Bach to Antheil.[8]

One other feature does remain, however, apart from this courageous tradition – the familiar insignia that is to be seen on all its old programme covers and that still ornaments the notepaper and flyleafs of its more prosperous successors. There are some who insist that the picture is supposed to represent Maud Gonne – a lady who protested more often than she played: others insist that it is Kathleen Ni Houlihan. For years until recently, nobody has been able to say who designed it, and now I am afraid that it has slipped my memory again.[9] Anyhow, this figure is of a good-looking girl, stripped to the waist, and holding in one hand a somewhat out-of-date bow and arrow, while she fixes her black hair with the other. Meanwhile, she is either urging on or restraining an Irish wolf-hound from attacking the sunrise. Or maybe it is the sunset. A somewhat ambiguous picture that may be intended to influence the pit or reassure the stalls – whichever way you may interpret it.

Let us end by comparing this image with the escutcheon of the very competent offspring of the Abbey's Peacock[10] – the Dublin Gate Theatre[11] – a playhouse that used to be noted, amongst other things, for the length of its performances. This other design has been interpreted in the malicious way of our native city, as representing Micheál MacLiammóir, dressed as Harlequin and trying to prevent the curtains from closing in time for all of us to catch the last bus home.

NOTES

Denis Johnston (1901–84), playwright. He made an immediate reputation with the impressionistic *The Old Lady Says No* (1929). *The Moon in the Yellow River* (1931) confirmed his reputation. Johnston is one of the very first writers to do original scripts for television and radio. See Denis Ireland, 'A Journalist and Denis Johnston', *Irish Bookman*, 1 (Sept 1946) 13–23; Hilton Edwards, 'Denis Johnston', *Bell*, 13 (Oct 1946) 17–18; Micheál MacLiammóir, 'Yeats, Lady Gregory, Denis Johnston and Theatre Nights', *Bell*, 6 (Apr 1943) 33–42; 7 (Mar 1944) 487–95; Gene A. Barnett, *Denis Johnston* (New York: Twayne, 1978); Harold Ferrar, *Denis Johnston's Irish Theatre* (Dublin: Dolmen Press, 1973); Robert Hogan, 'The Adult Theatre of Denis Johnston', in *After the Irish Renaissance: A Critical History of the Irish Drama Since 'The Plough and the Stars'* (Minneapolis: University of Minnesota Press, 1967) pp. 133–46; and Joseph Ronsley (ed.), *Denis Johnston: A Retrospective* (Gerrards Cross: Colin Smythe, 1981).

1. *King Lear*, directed by Denis Johnston, was presented at the Abbey Theatre on 26 Nov 1928. This was the Abbey's first effort at Shakespeare. Cf. 'Some people said that Yeats invited me to direct *Lear* because he had refused to present *The Old Lady Says No!* But it wasn't for that reason at all. It was because the Abbey had never played Shakespeare and wanted a director who could approach the play from a new angle; at least that is what Yeats told me' (Denis Johnston quoted in *A Paler Shade of Green*, ed. Des Hickey and Gus Smith (London: Leslie Frewin, 1972), p. 63).

2. The new Abbey Theatre opened in 1966.

3. The Marlborough Street premises had formerly been a bank and then, temporarily, the City Morgue.

4. Johnston's great contemporary, Samuel Beckett, provides a gloss here. In his first novel, *Murphy* (1938), the hero asks that his 'body, mind and soul . . . be burnt and . . . brought to the Abbey Theatre, Lr Abbey Street, Dublin, and without pause into what the great and good Lord Chesterfield calls the necessary house, where their happiest hours have been spent, on the right as one goes down into the pit, and I desire that the chain be there pulled upon them, if possible during the performance of a piece, the whole to be executed without ceremony or show of grief' (London: Picador, 1980, p. 151).

5. *The New Gossoon* was first staged at the Abbey Theatre on 19 Apr 1930.

6. On 18 July 1951.

7. W. B. Yeats won the Nobel Prize for Literature in 1923; and Bernard Shaw, in 1926.

8. George Antheil (1900–59), American composer, who shocked audiences of the 1920s with his use of jazz rhythms and mechanical devices in symphonic music. He did the music for Yeats' *Fighting the Waves* at the Abbey, 13 Aug 1929, the revision of *The Only Jealousy of Emer*.

9. It was designed by Elinor Monsell, whose work Yeats saw at a Dublin exhibition and found her treatment of epic themes so much in keeping with his ideas that he commissed her to make a device for the theatre. The resulting woodcut, showing Queen Maeve hunting – the Abbey Theatre's 'wolfhound' device – has been used by the theatre ever since. The following note, probably by Yeats, appeared in *The Abbey Theatre, Dublin: Programme for the British Association Visit, September 1908*:

It is the work of an Irish artist, Miss Monsell, now Mrs Darwin, and represents Queen Maeve, the heroic queen of ancient Irish legend. The dog is the Irish wolf-hound, and it is not known, whether it was with intention or not, that Miss Monsell put into the background the raying sun, which is one of the symbols of Ireland.

See Liam Miller, *The Noble Drama of W. B. Yeats* (Dublin: Dolmen Press, 1977) p. 112.

10. The Peacock Theatre opened on 13 Nov 1927 as the experimental annexe to the Abbey Theatre. See C. P. C[urran], 'The Peacock Spreads His Tail', *Irish Statesman* (Dublin), 19 Nov 1927, pp. 255–6.

11. The Dublin Gate Theatre was founded in 1928 by Hilton Edwards and Micheál MacLiammóir. Its first home was the Peacock Theatre.

The Abbey Theatre*

LORD DUNSANY

There are in Dublin three theatre companies; which, in order of their seniority, are the Abbey Theatre, the Gate Theatre and the Longford Players. In a way the Gate Theatre might be called the child of the Abbey Theatre, and the Longford Players the child of the Gate; but the metaphor is a bad one, and one would better convey the relation between them by saying that the Longford Players were a heresy broken off from the Gate, as the Gate was heretical to the Abbey. The Abbey, which is about as old as the century, derived its sustenance from the munificence of the late Miss Horniman. Others helped, but no one should speak of the Abbey without remembering her name, and without it there would have been no Abbey to speak of. Miss Horniman must have been not merely generous, but she must have seen with considerable insight the possibility of a new kind of drama arising far from cities, or at any rate free of the influence of cities, which was at that time gripping the drama very tightly. Supporting her vision materially, she endowed the Abbey, and that vision became a reality. So much for the Abbey Theatre's material side; but the theatre had not been going long, when there came to it an inspiration that gives it a place above the Gate Theatre or the Longford Players: this inspiration was Synge. His material was the talk of the Irish peasasntry, and one does not have to examine his plays very closely to find three prominent ingredients; poetry, humour, rather grim, and satire. The first two of these are so inherent in the diction of the Irish people that one cannot at once distinguish between raw material and workmanship, as sometimes in jewellery the curve of a large pearl will be used untouched, by a jeweller, for the shape of a figure of which it forms a part. As for the satire, when first a Dublin audience saw Synge's *The Playboy of the Western World*, instead of regarding satire as one of the spices in a work of art, they concentrated their attention on it and booed the play. It was rather as though you offered a plate of roast beef, with all necessary vegetables and condiments, to someone not quite familiar with them, and as though he started his meal on the mustard, and were sick. But in course of time Irish audiences got over the bitter taste, and came to enjoy the play. This play was followed [sic] by *Riders to the Sea*, *The Shadow of the Glen*,[1] and

---

* Extracted from *My Ireland* (London: Jarrolds, 1937) pp. 259–63. Editor's title.

others; and, when we lost Synge in 1908,[2] he had left dramatic work that blew fresh on the theatre, as though someone in a scene in a drawing-room comedy had opened the window to air blowing fresh over cornfields. This breeze affected to some extent the whole contemporary theatre, and, for the Abbey Theatre, remained an inspiration; but too soon the inspiration wore a groove, and the grim mood of Synge turned towards sordidness, when his pen was in other hands; and many subsequent plays were written, not only for the Abbey, with Synge's material but without his inspiration. This was forced on my attention some ten years after Synge's death, when I saw a play in a theatre in Londonderry and was introduced afterwards to the manager; and, being more critical than tactful, said something about the play being 'Synge and water'. To which the manager answered: 'Who is Synge?'

And talking of Northern Ireland, I believe that Kipling was Irish on his mother's[3] side; and only a few days ago I happened to be reading one of his poems called 'The Gift of the Sea'. When telling of the power of Synge to those who did not know him I used nearly always to quote the great ending to his *Riders to the Sea*, when the woman whose last son is drowned, triumphantly says that the sea can do no more harm to her now. And what should I see, when I read Kipling's poem the other day, but this, the second verse:

But the mother laughed at all.
'I have lost my man in the sea
And the child is dead. Be still', she said,
'what more can ye do to me?'

The very idea that makes the apex of Synge's play. This poem was written before 1896. I do not wish to belittle Synge because a single gem in his jewellery was cut by another man. But I think Kipling should have the credit of that particular gem.[4]

Although many subsequent writers have worked the same mine as Synge, which is, as I have said, the natural talk of the Irish peasant, I think that Synge threw up most ore in each spadeful. And this is the reason that I have chosen him as representative of the Irish playwrights of this century. I used to think that Lady Gregory probably took notes of amusing things that were actually said by Irish people; and her plays had to me the appearance of containing large pieces of real conversation. But Synge seemed to me to be more in touch with their thought. If I am right in this, then their methods of workmanship would be exactly opposite: Lady Gregory would hear some witty remarks, and one would expect her to write a play to contain them; whereas Synge, inspired by some dramatic idea, would set out to make his play, using the talk of the people to do it, much as an architect would plan to build a house first, and would afterwards buy bricks for the building of it. The Abbey Theatre also turned out many fine actors and, if I choose one as representative of them, it will be Fred O'Donavan [sic],[5] partly because of his acting of a part more than twenty-six years ago which is very vivid in my memory yet. And Miss Sara Allgood and her sister, Miss Maire O'Neill, are two magnificent actresses.

NOTES

Lord Dunsany (1878–1957), fantasist, playwright and short story writer. His first play, *The Glittering Gate* (1909), was written in response to a request from W. B. Yeats for a production for the Abbey. However, the glorification of Ireland, one of the principal aims of the Irish Literary Revival, had no place in his canon. See Mark Amory, *A Biography of Lord Dunsany* (London: Collins, 1972); Edward Hale Bierstadt, *Dunsany the Dramatist* (Boston: Little, Brown, 1917); and Ernest A. Boyd, *Appreciations and Depreciations* (Dublin: Talbot Press, 1918).

1. *The Shadow of the Glen* was first produced in 1903; *Riders to the Sea* in 1904; and *The Playboy of the Western World* in 1907.

2. Synge died in 1909, not in 1908.

3. Alice Macdonald.

4. Synge's biographers point out that in a letter to Synge one of the Aran Islanders he befriended used just Maurya's sentiment, though not her exact words. See David H. Greene and Edward M. Stephens, *J. M. Synge 1871–1909* (New York: Collier, 1961) pp. 111–12.

5. For a note on Fred O'Donovan and his recollections see p. 101.

Thoughts on the Abbey Theatre*

SEAN O'FAOLAIN

A couple of years ago[1] when the Abbey was, patently, in bad straits (artistically and financially) the directors proposed a new policy, part of which was to produce, at intervals, European masterpieces. Against this my friend, Frank O'Connor,[2] and I wrote energetically in the press: we said that there was no real shortage of Irish plays, as had been argued by Yeats,[3] but merely a lack of enthusiasm on the part of the directors: and I

*Extracted from his Preface to *She Had to Do Something: A Comedy* (London: Jonathan Cape, 1938) pp. 17–19. Editor's title.

wrote an 'open letter' to Yeats begging for a return to that intimacy in the theatre which had been such a large part of the charm and appeal of the original Abbey – the Abbey of the days when, for example, the actors were encouraged to wear heavy countrymen's boots during the day so as to develop the typical countryman's walk, when we who looked at these plays as boys were excited beyond expression at finding common things presented to us with a fidelity and affection, that, translated into realism and lyricism, produced a drama then almost unique in Europe. I felt that even if there were no new plays by Irish dramatists intimate production of the old ones would show embryo dramatists what was expected of them by the traditions of the theatre. As it happened the Board of Directors was energised by new blood and it dropped the idea of continental plays and within the last three years a new Irish play has been produced, fairly regularly, each month. But of that old electrifying blend of realism and lyricism, which I call 'intimacy', there has been small sign. Actually I can only remember two or three plays that got it, and the best of these was not an Irish play; that was Obey's *Noah*.[4] It came across the footlights in all its freshness in Teresa Deevy's *Katie Roche*,[5] and in the little one-acter by Frank O'Connor and Hugh Hunt, *In the Train*.[6] There was a snatch of it in the two curates of Paul Vincent Carroll's *Shadow and Substance*[7] – the rest of which play is theme and nothing but theme: and there were chunks of it in *A Passing Day* [*sic*],[8] the best play to date of George Shiels. Whenever he gets half a chance that talented actor Cyril Cusack, one of the most promising of the younger men, puts it, out of his own genius, into parts that without him barely smell of it. For the rest the whole point of the argument – as far as I was concerned, a wholly literary argument – against producing continental plays has been vulgarised into the notion that Irish plays are better than continental plays just because they are Irish. The Abbey has now fallen to the depths of producing plays in Gaelic, in spite of the fact that not one solitary play in Gaelic exists, i.e. a play worth calling a play, and that among Irish writers there are only two who know enough Gaelic to write in it, Frank O'Connor and myself, neither of us dramatists by nature or training.[9] There, again, is the influence of the audience, at any rate of the public, the old tyrannical conspiracy of the multitude against the artist.

I still do not believe Yeats was right to propose that continental plays be produced *because* there is a lack of plays by Irish authors. That is not an artist's reason for doing anything. Experiment has proved that the plays are there: which merely means that a little excitement and enthusiasm and controversy will always provoke people into writing who might otherwise be overcome by the general inertia. I believe that further experiment would prove that really good plays are there: which merely means that a high ambition, greater enthusiasm and a controversy kept on the artist's plane (not the plane of the political-minded, fat-headed nationalist) would provoke people to write up to the highest standards set them. At present the highest standard set to Irish dramatists is summed up in what has become a backstage cant in the Abbey – 'P.Q.' – short for Peasant Quality. Actors are chosen for P.Q. Plays are approved if they seem to have P.Q. And, what is the result? The audiences are injected with the virus of P.Q. and we are back to the old vomit of the Abbey – the ineffable 'peasant play'.

NOTES

Sean O'Faolain (1900–), short story writer and man of letters. His play, *She Had to Do Something*, was performed at the Abbey Theatre in 1937. See O'Faolain's autobiographical memoir, *Vive Moi!* (Boston, Mass.: Little, Brown, 1964); Paul Doyle, *Sean O'Faolain* (New York: Twayne, 1968); Maurice Harmon, *Sean O'Faolain: A Critical Introduction* (South Bend, Indiana: University of Notre Dame Press, 1966); Maurice Harmon (ed.), *Irish University Review*, 6 (Spring 1976), Sean O'Faolain Special Issue; and Donat O'Donnell [Conor Cruise O'Brien], *Maria Cross* (Oxford: Oxford University Press, 1952).

    1. 1936.

    2. For a note on Frank O'Connor and his recollections see p. 150.

    3. 'We have got to make a fresh start', Yeats announced in an interview published in the *Daily Express* on 31 Dec 1934. In the forefront of the Abbey Theatre's critics were Sean O'Faolain and Frank O'Connor, two of Ireland's most promising young writers at the time. They maintained that there was no 'slackening of activity amongst Irish dramatists', but that dramatists were discouraged from writing for the Abbey by the discourteous treatment they received. At the same time they, and others, strongly deplored Yeats' announcement that 'from now on the theatre's policy would be orientated to include regular productions of contemporary continental plays'.

    4. *Noah*, by André Obey, was presented at the Abbey Theatre on 11 Nov 1935.

    5. *Katie Roche* was performed at the Abbey Theatre on 16 Mar 1936.

    6. *In the Train* was produced at the Abbey Theatre on 31 May 1937.

    7. *Shadow and Substance* opened at the Abbey Theatre on 25 Jan 1937.

    8. *The Passing Day* had its première at the Abbey Theatre on 13 Apr 1936.

    9. Although both Sean O'Faolain and Frank O'Connor wrote plays, they are primarily considered among the most accomplished short story writers of this century.

Myself and the Abbey Theatre*

FRANK O'CONNOR

When I first knew the Abbey Theatre it was already drifting rapidly to the devil. After the Civil War there was a complete change of mood throughout the country, which gave rise to a realistic movement of which O'Casey and O'Flaherty[1] were the leaders. Synge was dead, Lady Gregory was dead, and there was no one connected with the theatre who understood what the realistic movement implied or how it could be directed. Yeats was completely at sea.

For a short time the theatre was able to keep O'Casey, but after him for years it was kept going by a handful of noisy farces. The old cry (again being raised) was up: there were no new plays. Even when the old plays were produced, as they occasionally were, it was usually impossible to see them for the acting.

It was not only that the Connemara [sic][2] girls in *The Playboy of the Western World* had permanent waves. It was that, for lack of careful production, the actors had gone to seed and shot up to several times their natural height, while those of them with real theatrical technique were able to dominate any scene whatever they played in. Under those circumstances real theatre was impossible.

Yeats, impressed by the unanimity of public protests and alarmed by the successes of Edwards and MacLiammóir, the rival company,[3] brought some new members, including Higgins[4] and Ernest Blythe,[5] on to the Board of Directors, and they decided to compete with Edwards and MacLiammóir in the production of foreign plays. The reason for Mr Blythe's appointment was that, as ex-Minister for Finance, he might be supposed to know how to save the theatre from bankruptcy, a familiar delusion of artists.

Hugh Hunt[6] had been brought over from England to produce these plays and Tanya Moisiewitch to design the scenery. Obey's *Noah* had been produced, a pietistic Spanish play about St Ignatius was in production, while *Coriolanus* and *Dr Faustus* were queueing up. By this

---

*Condensed from *Leinster, Munster and Connaught* (London: Robert Hale, n.d.) pp. 34–43. Editor's title.

time the theatre was in debt to the tune of £2500, and the bank had threatened to close it down.

It was at this time that I joined the Board, and the first task I set myself was to get rid of the crazy scheme for competing with Edwards and MacLiammóir. I have no interest in what I call museum theatre – Shakespeare, Ibsen, Chekhov, plays about periods remote in time or places remote in space – and I hold that if Shakespeare's company had a museum repertory to fall back upon instead of having to produce a new play every month, William Shakespeare would never have been heard of.

My second reason was that the Abbey Theatre is still the only possible market for Irish plays. Working at full speed, it can rarely produce more than ten plays a year, which is as though all the Irish writers were to be confined to one publisher capable of producing only ten books a year. If you cut that ten to five, as the Abbey Board proposed to do, and allowed for the inevitable plays of certain established writers, it was obvious that there would be nowhere for a young Irish writer of talent to begin.

The arrangement by which Hunt only produced foreign plays also ceased, because he was appointed manager and producer for the following two years.

For the first time in years the theatre began to be well and economically run. Within a year the debt to the bank was paid off and we were able to buy adjacent property with an eye on extension. And, in spite of the wails, there never was a time when we had not as many reasonably good plays as we could produce. For the whole year up to December, when Hunt got under way, the theatre had produced two new one-act plays. In 1936 it produced nine full-length plays; in 1937 ten, with three new one-acters.

This, again, was largely due to Hunt, who, eager for work, read every possible play, circulated it expeditiously and got snap decisions. But what was of more importance from my point of view was that, with the increase in the number of new plays, a new style of acting was developing which was the theatrical equivalent of the sort of short stories that Liam O'Flaherty was writing – delicate, precise and poetic in its own realistic way. Cyril Cusack[7] was the most remarkable of the new players.

It is clear to me now that where we really failed was in the lack of an administrator. Lady Gregory was that. When I was appointed managing director in an honorary capacity I asked Yeats how I should behave. 'I asked Lady Gregory exactly the same question when I was managing director,' he replied, 'and she said: "Give very few orders and see that they are obeyed."' Admirable advice! Admirable old lady, knowing perfectly that her poet would never discover that she was merely quoting Sancho Panza![8] Most of the Board were amiable but useless. Higgins was probably the ablest man on it, but he was a poet and excitable and truculent.

What sunk me was the damn classical repertory. I took advantage of my position as director, and Higgins and I both had a heavenly time reviving the plays we admired most – *The Shadowy Waters*, Lady Gregory's *Dervorgila*, Colum's *Thomas Muskerry* – while, with lamentable results, I tried to get *The Player Queen* produced again.[9] But they would not come right, not in Hunt's precise, delicate, naturalistic convention. They needed that stiff, rather declamatory technique of the heroic, romantic play.

Poor Yeats had every reason for alarm at what we were doing to his beautiful repertory. I wanted to see *The Player Queen*, his best play, on the stage, and suggested Jean Forbes-Robertson for the title part. Yeats, bound by a promise to some obscure English actress, would not let her have it. Instead, he offered us *Deirdre*,[10] a bad play and entirely unsuited to Miss Forbes-Robertson's coloratura style. He was first out of the theatre that night, bellowing with fury.

As potential heir to grandfather's musical box, Higgins was equally concerned with the traditions of the theatre. Hunt, brilliant with modern realistic plays and with an uncanny knack of squeezing poetry out of them, was lost when it came to what Higgins called 'porthery'. The production which roused Higgins's indignation was one of *The Playboy of the Western World*. Within the realistic frame of reference I thought it lovely. Anne Clery as Pegeen Mike was exquisite, and Cusack as the Playboy was superb, but hopelessly miscast.

Hunt being away, Higgins burst into Cusack's dressing-room and created a scene. Hunt, on his return, protested. I thought Higgins' criticism well founded, but his way of expressing it deplorable. Since then I have always had a sneaking respect for Rosencratz and Guildenstern, who had the misfortune to get mixed up in Hamlet's tortuous affairs.

Yeats returned to Ireland and took up the cudgels for his widow-presumptive. Instead of arguing it out over a cup of tea, he decided to descend like Zeus in wrath on an unsuspecting Board meeting. My recollection is that, as he usually did when he was looking for a fight, he moved me to the chair – it was the best way of preventing my flinging it at him.

Primed by Higgins, he made the bad mistake of beginning with a list of offences supposed to have been committed by directors during his absence. I took my chance and told him that he could have my resignation, but that I was not prepared to reply to greenroom gossip. (That really hurt him badly, because he was a most loyal colleague and had merely been caught on the wrong foot; over a year after he grumbled at me: 'I know you think I go round collecting greenroom gossip.')

Then he gave us a sales talk on the traditions of the theatre and how it differed from the naturalistic English theatre, all of which I could have repeated in my sleep. I replied that he might remember the tradition, but that nobody else did. I knew I was not being fair, because I had already given Hunt exactly the same sales talk in private; but I felt that, if Yeats insisted on establishing a party with Higgins against Hunt, I must back up my man.

It ended in a compromise, Hunt being debarred from future productions of the classics, while as an act of atonement to Synge's memory, *The Playboy* was to be produced again under Higgins's supervision.

I shall never forget that production. After 'porthery' what Higgins liked best was what he called 'Peasant Quality', which the players renamed P.Q. To me it seemed as great a confusion of literary planes as Hunt's naturalistic productions of poetic plays. He carefully trained the players to turn every 'st' into 'sht', so that 'Castlebar' became 'Cashtelbar'. I left after the first act, but Yeats thought it a splendid production, and, Synge's shade appeased, Mount Jerome had a quiet night.

That finished Hunt if only he had known it. It also finished me. Yeats, knowing he had only a short time to live[11] and wishing to provide for the two things nearest his heart, made Higgins director of his publishing business and managing director of the theatre.

To quiet me, who knew there was no work in the theatre for a salaried managing director, the appointment was made only for six months, but I knew that every Irishman approaches a job with an eye to the marriage service – 'till death us do part' – and a job is always self-perpetuating, never lacks an heir and, like other families of dubious origin, rapidly acquires respectability. Having no work to do, Higgins diverted himself by doing Hunt's.

Within a few weeks of his death, I realised that the Board was determined on forcing my resignation. Yeats was wrong about his own guile, but he understood me very well. Higgins, of course, retained his appointment until his death, and after his death Blythe became managing director.

The temporary appointment intended to bridge the gap between the departure of Hunt and the appointment of his successor has now lasted eight years. The home of comedy had ended its career in high comedy, with the family retainer inheriting the ancestral home, where his priceless collection of postage stamps is nightly on view.

But anyone who calls to ask me to join the Board of another theatre will be shot at sight.

NOTES

Frank O'Connor [Michael O'Donovan] (1903–66), short story writer and man of letters. From 1935 to 1939 he was director of the Abbey Theatre and worked in close contact with W. B. Yeats. Two plays by him were produced at the Abbey, *In the Train* (1937) and *Moses' Rock* (1938). His tumultuous tenure on the Board of Directors of the Abbey is sketched in his autobiography, *My Father's Son* (London: Macmillan, 1968). See also Roger McHugh, 'Frank O'Connor and the Irish Theatre', *Eire–Ireland*, 4 (Summer 1969) 52–63; Maurice Sheehy (ed.), *Michael/ Frank: Studies on Frank O'Connor* (Dublin: Gill & Macmillan, 1969); James H. Matthews, *Frank O'Connor* (Lewisburg, Pennsylvania: Bucknell University Press, 1976); Maurice Wohlegelernter, *Frank O'Connor: An Introduction* (New York: Columbia University Press, 1977); and James H. Matthews, *Voices: A Life of Frank O'Connor* (Dublin: Gill & Macmillan, 1983).

1. Liam O'Flaherty (1896–1984), novelist and short story writer.

2. They were Mayo girls. Connemara is in county Galway.

3. Hilton Edwards and Micheál MacLiammóir founded the Dublin Gate Theatre in 1928.

4. F. R. Higgins (1896–1941), poet.

5. Ernest Blythe (1889–1975), politician and theatre manager. See his recollections, p. 161.

6. Hugh Hunt was first invited by W. B. Yeats to become director of plays in 1935. He had a most distinguished career internationally as artistic director of the Old Vic in London. He left the Abbey in Oct 1938, to return years later (in 1970) as artistic director of the new Abbey and its official historian.

7. For a note on Cyril Cusack and his recollections, see p. 205.

8. Lady Gregory wrote a play called *Sancho's Master*, based on Cervantes's *Don Quixote*.

9. *The Shadowy Waters*, by W. B. Yeats, was first produced on 14 Jan 1904; *Dervorgilla*, by Lady Gregory, on 31 Oct 1907; *Thomas Muskerry*, by Padraic Colum, on 5 May 1910; and *The Player Queen*, by W. B. Yeats, on 9 Dec 1919.

10. *Deirdre*, by W. B. Yeats, had opened at the Abbey Theatre on 24 Nov 1906.

11. Yeats died on 28 Jan 1939.

Behind the Abbey Scenes*

ANN TREANOR

'For all the world like a carpenter's shop without the shavings!' was my first impression when I ducked my head and raised my foot and caught the hem of my dress in the heel of my shoe getting through the small door in the big gate of the scene-dock of the Abbey Theatre; and there I was 'behind the scenes' and with only the flimsiest excuse for being there!

Safely and unchallenged down the five or six steps, I stood for a moment to take my bearings, and when the floor *did not* open and swallow me I squared my shoulders, lifted my chin, and advanced on my tour of inspection.

** *Irish Press* (Dublin), 22 Mar 1938, p. 8.

Fifteen feet or so towards the stage the place widens to the right, and the carpenter's shop atmosphere gives way to that of a well-kept auction room, dusty enough and untidy enough to sustain the illusion. It only wanted a man with a bell to complete the impression, but although there was probably every other type of musical and 'effects' instrument, there was no large bell with a wooden handle!

The china dogs, bottles of 'whiskey', buckets, sofas, chairs, gramophones and general conglomeration of neatly stacked props raised a host of memories, not merely at the Abbey, but of innumerable experiences of country life in all parts of Eire.

I affectionatey regarded the dresser from the Playboy's kitchen, the Gossoon's motor-bike, the Invincibles' bar-counter, Maxine's camp-beds, and Kevney's blotting-paper (remember that business with the pens?). Hung on the walls were the scrolls, banners, pikes, hurling sticks, shovels, guns, 'holy' pictures, various anonymous objects, and a large crucifix, all used in the Abbey since the Abbey began.

A rosary hung from a rusty nail, and I thrilled a little to think how many stage mothers' sufferings it had made bearable through O'Casey's tragedies. The big bronze gong which crashes through your polite critique during the interval rises, impressive with the dignity of age and respectability, from the midst of a clutter of old pens, rolled photographs, labels, nails, property coins, a powder puff, a mirror off a motor car, a pair of bedroom slippers, and quite a decent Tyrolean hat.

Out from beside a radiator a gas stove jutts incongruously. One of its rings flared, for no apparent reason, and my tongue in my cheek said, 'Tut! tut! What waste!'

It is a very casual and friendly place – nothing fussy nor surprising about it, but just the sort of place in which you would expect the Abbey people to work. It could not be different and you would not want it to be.

Up those stairs was the famous greenroom, and on up to the right were the wardrobe and dressing-rooms, I guessed, wishing I had time to explore a little further; but I would have needed permission for that, and as people started to drift in – for a rehearsal, I supposed – I did not want to be a nuisance. Nobody bothered to inquire my business, so I did not have to use my excuse after all.[1]

NOTE

1. Cf. Ann Treanor, '"The Twisting of the Rope"', *Irish Press* (Dublin), 4 May 1938, p. 10 (on the rehearsal of a revival of Douglas Hyde's play at the Abbey); and Ann Treanor, 'Settings by Miss Moseiwitch' [*sic*], *Irish Press* (Dublin), 28 July 1938, p. 8. Both these later articles contain more specific details about matters behind the Abbey scenes, as if Ann Treanor had been invited back after the publication of her first piece.

Arthur Shields Remembers the Abbey with Pride*

MARION FITZGERALD

This past summer, Arthur Shields came back[1] to spend a holiday in Ireland. It was his third and longest visit since he left in 1939, and he spent it in County Wicklow, in a long, low house on the banks of the Avonmore.

I met him with his wife Laurie, his daughter Christine, a nephew and niece, a nephew-in-law, two grandnieces, a grandnephew, and an amiable boxer dog. It was a warm family group of which Arthur Shields was clearly the centre. It is not for nothing that he is known as 'Boss'.

Shields was born in North Great George's Street, one of a family of eight. His mother was German, his father Irish and a socialist. Until Arthur and his brother, 'Barry Fitzgerald', took to the stage, there had not been any professional acting in the Shields family.

'We moved house rather a lot, about twelve times in all. We were always having to move because nothing could be paid. There never was enough money in those days, and the family was big. Do you know, I can remember my father going on only one week's vacation?'

He left school at the age of fourteen, and did odd jobs in the *Evening Telegraph* office for a while, 'so that when I read *Ulysses* I could see all the different places. Then I went to work in Maunsel's, the book publishers. While I was there I also attended evening classes at the Abbey.'

Shields left Maunsel's when he got a contract with the Abbey in 1915.[2] His contract was for £1 a week, 'or £2 10 shillings[3] a week if we were travelling. When we travelled we stayed in theatrical digs, places like Mrs Yilke's, in Liverpool. All that street, Westland Row, used to be theatrical digs when I was young.'

Mr Shields' parents were delighted with his success on the stage. 'My father even went so far as to pay for my classes. Maureen Delany got her contract the same day I got mine. I was nineteen. Who was in the company then? Oh, Arthur Sinclair, Fred O'Donovan, J. M. Kerrigan, Ulick Wright, Harry Hutchinson.'

Before he joined the regular company he had played occasional parts

---

Irish Times (Dublin), 28 Sept 1964, p. 8.

at 5 shillings a night. In 1914, he played the part of Major Butterfield in *The Lord Mayor*, by Edward McNulty.

During his career at the Abbey, which lasted from 1915 until 1939, Arthur Shields reckons he played in some 134 plays, and in well over 200 parts because from one production to another they changed parts. 'In Yeats' *The Countess Cathleen* I played all the different men's parts at one time or another. You know, the Abbey at that time was a playwright's theatre, not an actor's or a producer's theatre.'

Mr Shields feels he was very lucky to have worked in the Abbey, 'firstly because I learned so much of value there, and also because I met some extraordinarily wonderful people there: Yeats, Lady Gregory, Lennox Robinson, many of the playwrights. Quite a number of distinguished people came to the greenroom of the Abbey, and even if some of the meetings were brief, they were wonderful – people like Shaw, Chesterton, James Stephens.

'In the Abbey in those early days we learned as we went along. In those years of the First World War we made our own scenery, we looked after our own constumes.' ('Yes', said his wife. 'He can iron most beautifully.') 'We painted our own scenery. We did bits of carpentry. Everybody pitched in. I did maybe a little more because I was made stage manager.

'The Big Strike of 1913 had just taken place; I can remember standing in Beresford Place listening to James Larkin speaking. He was a most dynamic speaker. My father was friendly with James Connolly. Dublin then was exciting, as far the labour movement was concerned, as far as the national movement was concerned, as far as the literary movement was concerned.'

He arrived back from an Abbey tour just in time to take part in the Easter Rising. He fought in the GPO,[4] and subsequently served time in Frongoch.[5] He was eventually released by an examining officer who had seen him in the Abbey and who told him to go home, stick to the theatre and forget about 'all this revolutionary nonsense'.

He went to the United States in 1939 because he was asked to play in a picture *Drums Along the Mohawk*. This was not by any means his first appearance in films. In fact, as far back as 1912 or 1913 he had appeared in a film about the life of St Patrick, in which he played the saint from the age of fourteen to twenty-one.

'When I went to America that time I had a return ticket to Dublin. But on my way home I went to New York and was asked to play in *Kindred* by Paul Vincent Carroll. I got injured in that play, and I went into hospital. I had broken ribs. While I was there they found I had TB, and told me to go to California or into a nursing home. I went out to California, with the help of John Ford, who gave me a couple of parts in some of his pictures.[6] He was very good to me.' But he has never become an American citizen.

As well as working in films, he has also appeared in a couple of plays in the United States, and he has directed one play, the first production by the New York Theatre Guild of Eugene O'Neill's *A Moon for the Misbegotten*.

'I met and had quite a lot to do with Eugene O'Neill. I had a great regard for him. He was very ill when I met him. He would have made a great priest. He had a way of looking at you that went right down deep and knew if you were telling the truth.'

At present he lives in Santa Barbara, California.

'We moved there from Los Angeles', his wife said, 'to get him away from the stupid rush of terrible television shows.'

'Santa Barbara is 100 miles away from Los Angeles,' said Mr Shields, 'so it's much easier to say no. What do I do?' He smiled blandly. 'I don't do anything – except collect stamps. I'm an ardent philatelist. I have quite a nice collection of Irish stamps.'

NOTES

Arthur Shields (1896–1970), actor who began to act at the Abbey Theatre as a young man. Influenced by the nationalist spirit of the literary revival, he joined the Irish Volunteers, and took part in the Easter Rising of 1916. See his earlier recollections, p. 133, and Quidnunc, 'An Irishman's Diary', *Irish Times* (Dublin), 3 July 1964, p. 7.

1. From California, where he had been living.
2. He had already appeared in Sheridan's *The Critic*, staged 26 Dec 1914, playing the Constable. His brother William (Barry Fitzgerald) also had a small part in the production, playing the Second Sentinel.
3. Two pounds and ten shillings. A shilling was equal to five (new) pence.
4. General Post Office.
5. Shields was interned at Frongoch in Wales, but was released after a short time and resumed his acting at the Abbey.
6. Including the film version of *The Plough and the Stars*.

Great Lady of the Irish Theatre*

SHELAH RICHARDS

Who, asked Yeats at the Arts Club in the 1920s, is the girl with a head like a lion? It was Shelah Richards' first meeting with the poet, and he

RTE Guide (Dublin), 19 Aug 1966, p. 15.

came to regard her so highly that he cast her as his Player Queen. She seems always to have had that knack of drawing the attention of the distinguished. Were this all, she might have been a hostess, a patron. But she was, and is still, a distinguished actress, so considerable that her name immediately comes to mind whenever great ladies of the Irish theatre are mentioned.

In recent years she has been a producer with Telefís Éireann,[1] whose soaring mast she can see from the windows of her dreaming pink house across the road. A gentle and airy place, full of books and prints, drawings and paintings – ancestors and fellow-actors, contemporary pieces and things a long time made. And, of course, Shelah Richards herself – casual in jeans, creosoting a garden table, remembering and half-acting all her years in the theatre.

There was nothing in her immediate family to suggest the stage as a career. They were bridge-playing, golfing people, her father a lawyer, her grandfather a law baron. But further back there were wilder growths. Malachi Who Wore the Collar of Gold is mentioned, and so, too, is St Brigid of Kildare. Her Roper cousins go back to Margaret, daughter of St Thomas More. And there are Wild Geese named MacMahon, gaily-uniformed young men smiling from faded portraits. And the Sheares brothers. And painter Nathaniel Hone.

But none of them actors. Nothing to suggest to lawyer Richards in Fitzwilliam Street that his daughter Shelah slipped through the study window every night. He had sent her to Alexandra College and a convent in Paris. Why should she want to be an actress, and slip through the study window, down to the Abbey Theatre? So her father never knew, not until his cronies at the club complimented him on how his daughter was doing on stage.

Lady Beatrice Glenavy and Lennox Robinson had much to do with her early career. And M. J. Dolan of the Abbey encouraged her when he heard that the Royal Academy of Dramatic Art had rejected her: 'There must be something in you to be turned down by that lot.'

There was. In no time at all she played Mary Boyle in *Juno*. And O'Casey cast her, against opposition, as Nora Clitheroe in the *Plough*. She remembers it all half-jokingly, all those halcyon Abbey days. 'And I think O'Casey fell a little in love with me. Maybe I shouldn't say that, because to date it does not seem to have been mentioned in any of the memorabilia. He was a marvellous person. During the *Plough* riots I was seen home every night by the police. . . . And then, well, I played about every juvenile there was.'

In Yeats' *The Player Queen* she followed Maire (Molly) O'Neill, who had played it ten years before. He had not allowed any actress to play the part in the meanwhile. 'Everybody said how glorious Maire O'Neill had been, and that intimidated me a bit. I was very young.' She talks on, sitting on a yellow couch, grey-haired, a practical romantic.

For many years she played leads in all the new plays at the Abbey. Playwrights wrote for her, audiences loved her. Eventually she went to New York with the Irish Players – 'and that was some advenutre' – with Sinclair, Allgood, O'Neill, each of them demanding separate rehearsals with their young colleague.

She left the Irish Players in Chicago. Back with the Abbey, she married Denis Johnston, whose play *The Old Lady Says No* was soon to be produced. It was not until 1938 or so that Shelah finally left the Abbey to go to New York with Gladys Cooper and A. E. Mathews in M. J. Farrell's *Spring Meeting*. It was around Munich time and she was advised to stay in America; but she elected to come home – she had two small children in Dublin.

During the war years in Dublin she ran her own company in the Olympia in partnership with Michael Walsh (Nigel Heseltine). Paul Vincent Carroll's *The Strings Are False* was a tremendous success. Dublin was avid for contact with the war situation and Carroll's play, which had been neatly edged under the nose of the German Embassy, was just what they wanted. Her company at the Olympia prospered, and among its first productions was O'Casey's *Red Roses For Me*[2] – one of Shelah's most satisfying memories.

Eventually she found the strain of being business manager, producer, director (and sometimes actor) far too nerve-racking. But memories are made of such challenges. She played St Joan, was asked by Yeats to take over the Abbey School of Acting, recommended Hugh Hunt to the directorate, employed such designers as Louis Le Brocquy, brought the mime Marcel Marceau to Dublin, produced an acclaimed *The Playboy* at Edinburgh with Siobhán McKenna, was magnificent in Congreve's *The Way Of The World*, produced Synge in Salzburg.

And since television came, she has been with it. Plays, serials, feature programmes. Wherever the theatre action has been in Ireland, Shelah seems to have been there. Already, she is proud of having a small family dynasty in theatre and television. Her son Mícheál, her daughter Jennifer.[3] her niece, the film star Geraldine Fitzgerald, 'and a raft of other nieces and nephews in the business.'

NOTES

Shelah Richards (1903–85) joined the Abbey Company in 1924. See the notice which appeared to mark her eightieth birthday, when a presentation was made to her at the Abbey Theatre: 'It Was Exciting', interview with Fintan O'Toole, *Sunday Tribune* (Dublin), 22 May 1983, p. 17.

1. The Irish Television.
2. *Red Roses For Me* had its première at the Olympia Theatre, Dublin, on 15 Mar 1943.
3. Jennifer Johnston (1930–   ) is a novelist.

Meet Mr Blythe*

Mr Ernest Blythe looks well against the black-and-old-gold of the Abbey's interior decoration. He sort of belongs. I could not tell why at first. Then it dawned on me. For black-and-old-gold are the predominant colours in Chinese lacquer-work, and if anyone in Dublin has the air of an ivory Buddha it is Mr Blythe. His glinting eyes, behind his large round spectacles, his chrysoprase smile, the shining baldness, the gleaming teeth, the hands folded in repose across the stomach – all these are the carven Buddha's.

There is a friendly and glossy benignity about Mr Blythe, a sort of Nonconformist heartiness. One shudders to think just how many times he has been apostrophised as: 'Hail to thee, Blythe spirit!' There is a clinical air about him, too, that reminded me once or twice of a Christian Scientist (*all* Christian Scientists are successful businessmen) and once or twice of an expensive West End dentist. Even his prim Southdown accent (how different from Mr St John Ervine's synthetic ruggedness!) has all the overtones of Nonconformity about it. You expect him at any minute to rise from his chair and ask an imaginary congregation to join in Praise.

Well, that is Mr Blythe on the surface – the impression the casual visitor who had not quite caught his name might carry away. And then one remembers Mr Blythe's remarkable career as a politician, as a fighter for Irish freedom, a man of fierce courage and terrific sticking power, and (occasionally) ruthlessness. One remembers how as a young man from the North he once took a winter's job as a labourer on a farm in the Gaedhaeltacht for a few shillings a week – to learn Irish. And one begins to wonder where the mask ends and the man begins.

Mr Blythe has a despairing way of conducting conversation at arm's-length. He has an equally despairing way of answering an awkward question with: 'Well, I wouldn't like to say.' But his smile never dims, and the inflection of his voice remains on the same level

* *Bell* (Dublin), 3 (Oct 1941) 49–56. Presumably by Sean O'Faolain, who founded the *Bell* in 1940 and was its editor from 1940 to 1946.

somewhere up among the leger lines. Everything is for the best in the best of all possible worlds. Remembering the building's original function, one is tempted to assume that the motto he has adopted for the Abbey is: *De mortuary nil nisi bonum.*[1]

'What', I asked Mr Blythe, 'would you do about the theatre in Ireland, if, say, you were Minister of Fine Arts and had oodles of money?'

'Well, I'd build an opera-house and form a national opera and ballet-company and . . .'

'But, I mean, what would you do about the Abbey?'

Mr Blythe ravelled his brow and then, as quickly, unravelled it.

'All the Abbey needs, to my mind,' he said, 'is a larger stage and a larger auditorium. It could do with better equipment in the way of scenery and lighting. But that's really about all.'

'I seem to have read somewhere', I said, 'that Mr Yeats' policy originally was to keep on giving the audiences the best plays till they liked them. Would that be part of your policy – if you had unlimited money? Is it, in fact, the Abbey policy to-day?'

Mr Blythe looked at me earnestly – perhaps he was not sure what I meant by 'the best plays'.

'It all depends whether the best plays, as you call them, played to decent audiences. As far as I'm concerned, a play's a failure if it doesn't ultimately draw an audience. It's a miserable failure, in fact. I don't think anything's so discouraging for either the actors or the playgoers as a house that's more than three-quarters empty. It doesn't do anybody any good – not even the author.'

'But, supposing you were convinced of a play's outstanding merit, and you'd money to do so, wouldn't you think it worth while to keep it going till it did catch on? Barry Jackson, I remember, used to do that frequently. And one of his early "flops", *The Farmer's Wife*, after it had got into its stride, ran in London for four years.'

'We should certainly give such a play every chance to catch on', said Mr Blythe reflectively, 'But we shouldn't keep it running indefinitely with microscopic audiences.'

'Microscopic audiences.' I had a brief vision of Mr Blythe on all fours somewhere in the stalls, glass in hand.

'There's been a lot of talk', I went on, 'about the new policy of long runs at the Abbey – *The Rugged Path, Strange Guest, Trial at Green Street Courthouse, The Money Doesn't Matter,*[2] and so on. Would it be fair to describe it as a new policy? Or just an accident?'

'It's certainly not a new *policy*. We've never had plays before – at least in my time – which it was possible to run for more than a few weeks. Only two of the plays you mention had long runs.'[3]

'What, frankly, do you feel about these long runs and the audiences they attract?'

Mr Blythe gave a polite little Nonconformist gurgle and peeped at me over his spectacles.

'We've no pledge against making a little money if it comes our way – if that's what you mean.'

'So it's not a case of *The Money Doesn't Matter*, after all.'

A frown – and at once I realised the importance of being earnest.

'Of course, only a very small proportion of the audiences who helped to make the long runs will become regular patrons of the theatre', Mr Blythe went on. 'Most of them are not regular playgoers and came only because they heard their friends talking about these particular plays. However we have evidence that some of them will come again. It's very useful to widen the circle.'

The circle? I had a brief vision of masonic signs – of circles, of compasses and squares.

'You do, of course, realise the perils of a long run', I went on. 'I mean in a small city like Dublin? It can't be particularly good for your actors – whether they're in the show or out of it?'

Mr Blythe looked at me hard – as if I had spoken lightly of the GAA.[4]

'I haven't heard any complaints from the actors who were in the plays', said Mr Blythe. 'Of course, it's hard on the actors who are out for several weeks. A policy of long runs would make it impossible for us to produce as many new plays as we wish to, because it would of course end our policy of frequent revivals. If a popular play is given only a short run it makes it easy a little later on to stage a play that is likely to run only, say, a week, because there is always something ready to follow the piece which is not commercially successful. On the other hand, if all our popular plays were run for as long as there was support for them, a play which failed would either have to be followed by another new play which might not have been sufficiently rehearsed or be continued for a fortnight or three weeks to empty houses.'

'What efforts does the Abbey make to encourage new writers?' I asked. 'How do you discover them? Or do you just wait for them to queue up?'

'I'm afraid there's not much queuing-up these days', said Mr Blythe. 'All we can do – normally – is to wait for the plays to be sent in to us. We have had a number of competitions for new plays in the past and will hold another after a suitable interval. There's no use trying a competition every year as it only results in plays which had been rejected in previous competitions being sent in again. It usually takes an interval of about two or three years for new writers and new plays to come forward.'

'Is there any truth in the extraordinary stories I've heard of plays sent in to the Abbey being kept unacknowledged for years – until the moss grew on them?'

'It's certainly not true today. Is it, Mr Gorman?'[5] and he turned over his shoulder to a little whitehaired man in the corner, tapping vigorously at a typewriter.

'Certainly not', echoed Mr Gorman.

'At one time we tried to have every play read by the directors,' continued Mr Blythe. 'That, of course, meant delays.'

'And nowadays?'

'Nowadays, new plays are first sent to our play-readers. The job of weeding-out is consequently much easier.'

'Do you reject many plays?'

From the promptness of his answer, it was obvious that Mr Blythe had not been Minister for Finance for nothing.

'Up to three hundred a year', said Mr Blythe. 'But since the war, it's become smaller.'

'On what grounds do you usually reject plays?' I asked.

A long draw at an imaginary pipe, and Mr Blythe was off into the dialectic of drama.

'One thing I'd like to say – we've never rejected a play because we didn't think it would pay. The fact that we can't use the commerical argument has made the Theatre many enemies. If we were a commercial theatre we could say to an author that though we thought his play good we didn't think the public would appreciate it. As it is, we can only say that a play doesn't merit production – which is the sort of criticism which most authors resent. Whenever we reject a play by someone of prominence, we say: "There goes another enemy for the Abbey." As you must know yourself, Dublin is full of people who seem to be agreed that masterpieces are being rejected every month and that anything successful is bound to be bad.'

Perhaps I did. It did not seem to make much difference to Mr Blythe whether I did or not.

'In what direction does your own – and that of the other directors – lie? Is it for comedy or tragedy?'

'The directors', said Mr Blythe emphatically, 'have no preference. They are keenly on the lookout for good plays of any sort. Audiences, of course, prefer comedy.'

Mr Blythe, I gathered somehow, did not care for audiences.

'Hasn't Sean O'Casey done something to educate audiences to appreciate tragedy?'

'I'm afraid not. In his plays the tragedy is interlarded with comedy and he may have done something to make sections of the audience impatient of tragedies not so interlarded.'

'Supposing I were to send you a comedy, would it have a better chance of acceptance?'

'No.' Mr Blythe was again emphatic. 'A good tragedy stands the same chance of acceptance as a good comedy – but it does not stand the same chance of repeated revival.'

'Why not?'

'We can't put on a play again and again unless there's a certain public demand for it.'

'I seem to remember', I said, 'that while the Abbey produced what I think is the best play of the last thirty years – I mean *The Moon in the Yellow River*[6] – they rejected *The Old Lady Says No*. Why was that? Were they afraid of faction-fights among the audience or what?'

'It might interest you to know', said Mr Blythe, 'that, though the Board of that day felt *The Old Lady* wasn't quite up their street, as you might say, they actually subsidised its production – in a small way, of course – at the Gate. The reason they didn't do it was simply that the Abbey producer[7] at the time thought that it needed a different technique from his.'

'So that plays submitted to the Abbey have also to conform to the Abbey producer's technique?'

'Hardly. I think *The Old Lady* stands alone.'

'Which brings me to the point', I said, 'of the Abbey producer. I'm not, of course, speaking in terms of personalities.'

'Heaven forbid!' said Mr Blythe gaily.

'But has it ever occurred to you – with all due respect to the work of Mr Dermody[8] and Mr Hugh Hunt before him – that it's a bad and tiresome business for your actors to have the same producer year in and year out? Why not do what the Church does – hold a Mission once in a while, and have a change-round of preacher? Invite guest-producers – people like Denis Johnston, Stanley Ilsley,[9] Louis d'Alton, Liam Redmond. There are heaps of them. Give poor Mr Dermody a rest now and again and time to think up new ideas and go scouting round the countryside for new talent.'

'It's certainly an idea', said Mr Blythe, though a trifle doubtfully.

'And some day, don't forget, some one'll be sending you in a play with instead of a list of characters, "Seumas O'Heffernan", "Brigid, his wife", "Sorcha, their daughter", and so forth, just the names: "F. J. McCormick", "Maureen Delany", "Eileen Crowe", "M. J. Dolan", and the rest.'

But Mr Blythe was obviously thinking of something else. He gave me no answer.

'Most people who've never had a play produced at the Abbey, I imagine, would like to know just how much they'd get for it', I said after a respectful interval. 'How, for instance, it would compare with the money they'd get for a first novel.'

Mr Blythe rubbed his hands – gesture of men in the money.

'Well, in the first place, no matter who the author is, he gets £15 down.

That's to say, it works out at £5 an act for a three-act play. He gets that on acceptance of the MS. After that, of course, everything depends on the takings at the box-office. If a play is successful the author may make as much as £20 or £25 a week, though £25's the limit. Which, I think, compares pretty favourably with what the ordinary writer would get for a first novel which might take him a twelve-month to write.'

'Getting back to my original hypothesis', I said. 'Supposing you were Minister of Fine Arts, what would you do about entertainment in general in Ireland?'

Somehow I felt as if I had struck a gong – a great bronze gong. I was on the right track at last.

'If times were normal', answered Mr Blythe, rising suddenly to enthusiasm, 'I'd establish an Irish *film* industry. I think it's absurd for us to spend the sums we do spend on the Diplomatic Service and on the army and the air force and to have the country flooded with foreign films and produce none of our own. I believe that for £200,000 we could establish an Irish film industry, which would prevent the national individuality of the country being destroyed. If there were no other way of getting the money I should scrap the Diplomatic Service and reduce the army.'

'There's just one other question I'd like to ask, Mr Blythe', I said, taking a deep breath. 'It's about. . .'

'Is it about *The Money Doesn't Matter?*' cut in Mr Blythe.

'It is, as a matter of fact.'

Mr Blythe suddenly discarded a full fifty per cent of his benignity.

It was Mr Gorman who saved the situation.

'You're wanted on the telephone, Mr Blythe', he said, and proceeded to show me out.

NOTES

Ernest Blythe (1889–1975), politician and theatre manager. As Minister for Finance he gave the first direct grant to the Abbey Theatre. He was managing director of the Abbey from 1941 to 1967, retiring at seventy-seven. His policies drew sustained criticism. It was said that he engaged players for their knowledge of Irish rather than for their acting ability, that he rejected good plays and put on bad ones, and that he favoured kitchen comedies to swell box-office receipts. In 1957 he published *Trasna na Boinne* (Dublin: Sóirséal and Dill, 1957), an account of his life until 1913. His writings include *The Abbey Theatre* (Dublin: The National Theatre, [1965]) and 'Gaelic Drama' in *The Irish Theatre: Lectures Delivered During the Abbey Theatre Festival held in Dublin in August 1938*, ed. Lennox Robinson (London: Macmillan, 1939).

1. A pun on the tag *'Die mortuis nil sisi bonum'*, one must speak nothing but good

of the dead, the joke being that the Abbey was (partly) built upon an old mortuary or morgue.

2. *The Rugged Path*, by George Shiels, was first produced at the Abbey Theatre on 5 Aug 1940; *Strange Guest*, by Francis Stuart, on 9 Dec 1940; *Trial at Green Street Courthouse*, by Roger McHugh, on 6 Jan 1941; *The Money Doesn't Matter*, by Louis D'Alton, on 10 Mar 1941.

3. *The Rugged Path* and *The Money Doesn't Matter*.

4. Gaelic Athletic Association.

5. Eric Gorman, who for many years played small parts at the Abbey. He was the original Uncle Pether in *The Plough and the Stars*. See recollections of him by Seamus Kelly, p. 192.

6. *The Moon in the Yellow River*, by Denis Johnston, was first presented at the Abbey Theatre on 27 Apr 1931. The play has frequently been revived since, most recently in Aug 1983.

7. Lennox Robinson.

8. Frank Dermody.

9. Ilsley was part of a famous duo, Ilsley and McCabe(Leo) who managed the Olympia Theatre with the slogan 'World Theatre on Your Doorstep' in the 1940s and the 1950s.

Ernest Blythe and the Abbey*

TOMÁS MACANNA

I first met Ernest Blythe when, a few days after I arrived in Dublin to join the Customs and Excise some time in the late October of 1944, I presented myself at the Abbey Theatre, armed with a sprawling letter from Lennox Robinson, three words to the page, to say that he had seen my work at the Dundalk Little Theatre and thought that I was quite good as a scenic designer. I had no appointment, but found myself courteously received in a tiny paper-stuffed office above the foyer and proceeded to offer my services not alone as a scenic artist, but as a playwright, play director, actor and general theatrical messiah, all in my best Christian Brothers' Gaelic.

He pointed out to me, reasonly enough, that he could hardly sack the resident designer, Alicia Sweetman, or anybody else for that matter, to accommodate my youthful ambitions, but if I wished to come in from time to time to help paint the scenery he would have no objection but not to expect to be paid for it. So next day, in between an early morning and

Threshold (Belfast), no. 26 (Autumn 1975) 100–5.

late night shift of duty I presented myself at the stage door, was conducted across the stage where Joseph Tomelty's *The End House*[1] was in rehearsal, and up to the paint frame where a small creased man informed me that Miss Sweetman had departed that very morning apparently after a heated argument about the artistic merits of a backcloth for *John Bull's Other Island*, and that he, Seaghan Barlow, was now in charge, and needed no assistance whatsoever.

Almost immediately at the whim of the Revenue Commissioners, I found myself on the way to Ballyshannon and my next contact with Blythe was an invitation to contribute to the Christmas Gaelic Pantomime which I accepted with enthusiasm, informing him that if he was stuck, I would be happy to direct it and design it as well. He wrote back to say that this would not be necessary as he had Carl Bonn and Frank Dermody; but when next I was in Dublin, perhaps I would call to see him.

So once more I found myself in the same tiny office, this time with a Donegal blas on my Irish, to be told in his own dry, very precise, blasless idiom that there would be a vacancy very soon in the theatre and if I was willing to learn and not regard myself as a sort of Gaelic-speaking Orson Welles, sent by Yeats or Gregory or the rest of them, from Dundalk (via Ballyshannon) to save the Abbey from its long-expected demise, he was willing to give me a job. His well-known dedication to the Irish language[2] and the influence this was having on Abbey policy[3] had meant the creation of a new position in the theatre, that of Gaelic producer, and this was the position he offered me. That was in June 1947. On and off, I have been with the Abbey Theatre since, and for twenty years of my time there, the presence of Ernest Blythe, his personality and policies, dominated my artistic life.

Yeats had invited Blythe to join the Abbey Board of directors in 1935, possibly influenced by the fact that the theatre's survival had been assured by the annual subsidy, the first in an English-speaking country, granted by Blythe twelve years before when he was Minister of Finance in the Cosgrave government. It was however by the unanimous request of his fellow directors that he became managing director in 1941, a position he retained until his retirement in 1967, a span of twenty-six years, almost one-third of the theatre's existence. No other manager, not even Yeats, held such a dominant position, and certainly not for as long a continuing period. Even before I joined the Abbey I had been told so many things about him – that he was utterly ruthless, a fanatic for the Irish language, with little or no artistic judgment, and certainly the decisive influence that had brought the once-famous theatre to its ever-present lamentable state. I was hardly a few weeks in the theatre, when, during an indifferent production of *The Plough and the Stars*, Valentin Iremonger and Roger McHugh rose during the interval and denounced the management, before walking out in what seemed an ineffectual protest,[4] but rapidly became a newspaper controversy with everybody throwing in his piece, including Bernard Shaw and Paul Vincent Carroll who demanded the managing directors' resignation by return post.

Blythe ignored the storm completely, refusing to comment himself, or allowing anyone else to comment. He later told me that he had not read one single word of the controversy, so that, when the whole affair had ended, he could meet with and speak to even the most vicious of the participants – some of them playwrights of note – completely without prejudice, although he did have the last word in a way when he had both Iremonger and McHugh turned away from the box-office some time afterwards. When Ria Mooney replaced Michael J. Dolan as senior producer in the next year it was claimed that the critical tirade had had some effect, but the truth of the matter was that Blythe himself, as severe a critic of his own theatre's standards as the most vehement outsider, was well aware for the need for change. Some years later the BBC played a mean trick on him when, in the one-sided programme one invariably expects on the Abbey Theatre, he was made seemingly to dismiss all comment and criticism by saying 'I don't give a damn!' a phrase deliberately selected from a much longer context to accentuate what was assumed to be the definitive trail of his very northern personality. But my experience of him was that he did very much 'give a damn' provided that it was so to speak his own particular damn.

Yeats ruled the Abbey by a sort of aloof awareness: an unlikely admixture of the mystical and the practical. Blythe ruled by force of character at once down-to-earth and commonsensical. With the exception of Lennox Robinson who seemed to be always hovering in odd corners of the theatre, we never saw the other directors. By tram or bus, and later by an aged Ford Eight, Blythe arrived sometimes before noon, hat on the back of his head and more often than not his raincoat slung over his shoulder. Rehearsals started at eleven o'clock, mornings only, and before ending at one the stalls door would open and the familiar bespectacled figure would slide into a right-hand seat, to watch for a few moments. If the rehearsal was of a play in Irish, there might be a few comments, mostly to correct pronunciation. At dress rehearsals there would certainly be comments, very much to the point, and in my own experience both helpful and devastating. He had a horror for pretention and a good eye for practical details, especially in a realistic production. Anything overdone or too theatrical he would spot at once; his attitude was that our work must reflect life as it was; our stage had to reflect its natural image and never exaggerate it; indeed it was preferable to diminish it. Here he was overmuch influenced by tradition, so much so that he was always wary of any new approaches to our many revivals.

I produced all the plays in Irish, mostly one-acts presented after, not before, the main attraction; and of course the Christmas pantomimes, eighteen in all between the Abbey and the Queen's. My work was completely in contrast to that of Ria Mooney:[5] where she found herself producing play after play in the same naturalistic style, I was romping through Ghéon, Jalabert, Benevente, Molière and Chekhov in styles ranging all the way from late Guthrie to music-hall. Here, surprisingly, I found great encouragement from Blythe. So long as I made sure that the Irish spoken by the actors was correct, I could do as I wished. I found however, that he regarded all this theatrical exuberance as being much easier to produce than the strictly naturalistic play: I carried out his main policy of making Irish entertaining and colourful to our audiences, while enjoying myself hugely in the process, even if fretting somewhat at not being given the odd English production. But he sternly kept me to my task and it was only in later years that I realised how wise he had been in so limiting me at the time. He was allowing me to develop my own style in a way unique for the staid and tradition-bound Abbey, so that when Brecht and Lorca came into our repertory in the later days at the Queen's, he simply handed me the scripts and gave me my head, without interference.

Of course there were differences, mostly at pantomime time. Every Christmas presentation had to be built up from scratch, a mad rush of ideas and improvisations, part music-hall and part Aldwych farce, put together in a frenzy of anarchical fervour that left us all in a sort of technicoloured haze over Christmas. Blythe insisted on supervising the script as it came together in bits and pieces, especially the songs which were translated from current popular hits. He was most insistent that the Irish should be grammatical and that not one single word of English appeared in the show, even by way of explanation. This led to many clashes and as far as I remember, I resigned at least twice. On the second occasion I sent him up a hasty note telling him that all was over between us, and was improvising a dramatic farewell to the bewildered cast on the stage when suddenly the iron door to the foyer banged open and there he was, a formidable and angry figure standing towards me, my note in his hand. The cast which had been expressing life-and-death support for me a moment before, melted mysteriously away, leaving me face to face with what looked like a doomsday situation. He handed me my note and for once spoke in English. 'Never resign' he said, 'Too many people want you to and then abandon you. Besides, if you want to change this theatre, you can only do it from the inside.'

I found myself with my note in my hand, and there he was walking away from me back up to his little office, humming a tune, a sure sign that he had got something off his mind.

The least that can be said of Ernest Blythe and the Abbey is that, in good times and bad, he kept it going; no mean feat as I can assert from my own experience. But over and above that he kept the theatre true to iself, not at all interested in striving to maintain an international image but, one feels, certainly aware that to achieve such an image a theatre must be, paradoxically enough, first and foremost national. Under him many new playwrights saw their plays produced; he was willing always to give the benefit of the doubt to new work, even though it took the best efforts of both players and producers sometimes to keep the curtain up and hold an audience to the end. He made the Abbey company fully professional, gradually getting rid of the amateurs and the semi-professionals. He did not, contrary to general belief, limit entry to the company to Gaelic speakers only: what he did do was to bring the Gaelic theatre home to its proper place in the Abbey, and merely asked of the young talent that he engaged, that it have sufficient knowledge of the language to make the Gaelic productions fully as professional as the English productions. In this he succeeded.

He kept the company together after the disaster of the fire in 1951 and managed to maintain it at the Queen's with a ludicrously inadequate subsidy over fifteen years. And finally he coaxed a brand-new theatre from a reluctant, if sympathetic government: two theatres[6] in fact, standing on the site of the old Abbey, no insignificant monument to what was in fact a lifelong dedication to the arts.

Behind the blunt northern manner there was a man of great understanding and humanity. His office door was open to all, staff and players alike. The disappointed and the untalented vilified him, and indeed the press critics, knowing full well that he would never reply to them, threw whatever ethics they should have held to the winds whenever they wrote about him. It was significant that when he died[7] most of the commentaries on his life dealt with his political career and little, if anything, was heard about his Abbey Theatre years. Perhaps it was too early, perhaps the venom would still have been in evidence; it was, after all, much easier to write about the political past, things over and done with, than to venture about the more recent artistic years of his life. Whatever the reason, the later life of Ernest Blythe as director of the Abbey has never been properly and fairly assessed. In time it will be, by enthusiastic American academics if by nobody else, and it may well be that the verdict will surprise everybody, though hardly Ernest himself, were he alive to read it and did not dump it into the wastepaper basket as he ususally did.

NOTES

Tomás MacAnna (1926–) has been with the Abbey Theatre since 1947 when he joined the company as director of plays in Irish. Later, he was appointed stage designer. In 1972, he was appointed to the Abbey's Board of directors, and from 1966 to 1968 and 1973 to 1978, he was the theatre's artistic director. His writings include 'Nationalism from the Abbey Stage', in *Theatre and Nationalism in Twentieth-Century Ireland*, ed. Robert O'Driscoll (Toronto: University of Toronto Press, 1971) pp. 89–101.

1. *The End House* was produced at the Abbey Theatre for the first time on 28 Aug 1944.

2. Blythe's devotion to the Irish language revival never faltered. He encouraged Micheál MacLiammóir and Hilton Edwards to found a Gaelic theatre – the Taibhdhearc – in Galway, and founded An Gúm to publish books in Irish for the government.

3. On the Abbey Theatre's policy of producing plays in Irish see Earnan de Blaghd (Ernest Blythe), 'The Abbey Theatre and the Irish Language', *Threshold* (Belfast), 2 (Summer 1958) 26–33.

4. On Saturday 7 Nov 1947, Valentin Iremonger rose in the stalls just before the curtain went up on the last act of the revival of *The Plough and the Stars*.

Ladies and gentlemen, just before the show proceeds, I would like to say a few words. When the poet Yeats died, he left behind him to the Irish nation as a legacy his beloved Abbey Theatre, then the first theatre in the world in acting, in production and in the poetic impulse of its tradition. Today, eight years after, under utter incompetence of the present directorate's artistic policy, there's nothing left of that fine glory. Having seen what they did to O'Casey's masterpiece tonight, in acting and production, I, for one, am leaving this theatre as a gesture of protest against the management's policy.

Quoted by Donal Dorcey in *The Story of the Abbey Theatre*, ed. Sean McCann (London: New English Library, 1967) p. 156. The *Irish Times* endorsed the protest. See also Quidnunc, 'An Irishman's Diary', *Irish Times*, 10 Nov 1947, p. 5.

5. Ria Mooney (1904–73), actress and producer. In 1924 she joined the Abbey Theatre company by invitation, after giving a striking performance at the Dublin Arts Club in Chekhov's *Proposal*. She was the personal choice of Sean O'Casey for the part of Rosie Redmond in the first production of *The Plough and the Stars* in 1926. In 1944, she became director of the Gaiety Theatre School of Acting, but she later returned to the Abbey Theatre as the first woman producer there, a post she held for fifteen years. See Micheál MacLiammóir, 'Some Talented Women', *Bell* (Dublin), 8 (May 1944) 117–27.

6. The Abbey Theatre and the experimental Peacock Theatre.

7. Blythe died on 23 Feb 1975.

The Abbey Theatre*

P. S. O'HEGARTY

The Abbey is degenerate! Its best actors have left it! The remainder are thinking of leaving it! The directors are incompetent! They do not know a good play when they are offered it!

So! Now, where and when have I heard that before? I heard it first in 1903, when Dudley Digges, Maire Quinn and P. J. Kelly left for America, and scarcely had the echoes of it died away when it was heard again, in 1908, when Willie and Frank Fay left, and again when the sisters Allgood left, and again when Arthur Sinclair and Fred O'Donovan left, and again and again as J. M. Kerrigan and others, down to the Shields brothers, left. In the history of the Irish National Theatre, this particular Jeremiad is like a recurring decimal. In 1913, for instance, an article appeared in the Dublin *Saturday Herald* of 19 July entitled 'The Decadence of the Abbey', in the course of which the writer said:

> General dissatisfaction prevails throughout the city at the protracted absence of the Abbey Company. This year, so far, there have been only two performances of the No. 1 Company, and these at high prices for the benefit of the Art Gallery. It is further stated that the Irish Players are again going to America next January for a six weeks' season in the Fine Arts Theatre, Chicago. What has been the result of all this touring and exploiting of the Abbey Company abroad? A marked deterioration in the acting.
>
> It was felt in Dublin, and has been the subject of sorrowful comment among playgoers. During the Court Theatre season there has been much outspoken criticism. Friendly critics have sounded a note of warning, and they have not hesitated to point to the American tour and the music-hall engagements as the cause of the decadence. The situation is grave, indeed, to all interested in the movement.

and he goes on to quote, with approval, unfavourable references to the acting and the performances generally by F. A. Baryhan and John Palmer – the two stodgiest of the then dramatic critics of England. The

*Irish Times (Dublin) 6 Sept 1944, p. 3.

article is not signed, but it was written by W. A. Henderson. As Lemmy Conlin would say, does time stand still or does it?

The truth is that the Abbey Theatre is not degenerate. The best acting in Dublin (and to hell with Mr Richard Watts,[1] metaphorically speaking) is still to be found there, and the best actor is Mr McCormick, without detracting in any way from Mr MacLiammóir, who is the most brilliant in parts that interest him. If, from time to time, some of its best actors have left it, and if some of the present lot are thinking of leaving it, well, they will simply leave room for other talent. Consider all those who have left the Abbey, from Dudley Digges, in 1903, to Arthur Shields recently. What happened to them? Their places here were filled adequately, with two exceptions, and with one exception, they have not reappeared anywhere in the acting firmament. Dudley Digges alone came to anything. The remainder, who might have become forest trees at home, became simply leaves in a forest. They were too Irish to get into the framework of the slick cosmopolitan acting of England and America. In the case of two of them, William and Frank Fay, the theatre suffered an irreparable loss, a loss which is still felt and will continue to be felt to the end of its career. Nobody that ever surveys the history of the Abbey but will regret the irreparable loss to it of these two men of genius dissimilar, but each essential to the proper development of the theatre, and, alas! lost to it.

What masterpieces has the theatre rejected? Or even very good plays? I can only remember three – Shaw's *John Bull's Other Island*, David Sears' *Juggernaut*[2] and Denis Johnston's *The Old Lady Says No*. Of these, Shaw's play is not a masterpiece. (Shaw's masterpieces are *Man and Superman* and *Saint Joan*.) But it is a good play, and should have been played. *Juggernaut* is not exactly a very good play, but it has something; it gets down, better than anything else that I am acquainted with in prose, the spirit of temper of the Irish Volunteers at the best period of the Black-and-Tan fight. Mr Johnston's play is an authentic undeniable masterpiece, and I shall never understand why the Abbey did not play it. In the case of it, and of the Shaw play, they explained it by alleging difficulties of casting; but, while we accept that, we do not believe it. (Mr Yeats [was] alleged to have said of Mr Johnston's play 'He is attempting to write plays with a cinema technique.') But what other really good plays has the Abbey rejected? *The Silver Tassie? The White Steed? The Pipe in the Fields?*[3] None of these are good plays and to hell with New York, metaphorically speaking, and they were rightfully rejected. Where, oh where, are these acknowledged masterpieces? There are none. Some years ago the directors asked me to read the plays sent for a couple of competitions. The first competition produced Mr Carroll's *Things that Are Caesar's*,[4] and the second produced Miss Connor's *Mount Prospect*.[5] Outside these two, in the couple of hundred others, there were not half-a-dozen which could be regarded as capable of being moulded into even tolerable plays. To write a play it is not enough to buy pen, ink and paper, or to borrow a typewriter. Nor, to act, is it enough to go upon a stage and 'saw the air'. Both arts have to be studied, and they must be studied with patience and humility. Many an indignant performer is receiving X pounds per week who is really worth only half that, if anything at all; and many an indignant playwright has had his play put on because there was nothing else available at the moment, or because it had a good first act, or simply to encourage him. The present directors of the theatre are Lennox Robinson, Ernest Blythe, Dick Hayes and Roilbeárd Ó Faracháin. Can it be said, with even a pinpoints justification, that they know nothing about the theatre? Mr Robinson[6] is our most experienced playwright and a master of stagecraft and production. He has a first-class dramatic intelligence. Mr Blythe[7] and Mr Hayes have learned about plays where most people do – by years and years of attendance at theatres, by reading and discussion. Mr Ó Faracháin is one of the younger men, a poet and a writer of distinct imagination and power. What the directors are entitled to, from critics generally, is a little humility.

But the *Irish Times* called in the heavyweights – Shaw, O'Casey and Carroll. Mr Shaw is, of course, a privileged person. He may say what he chooses. Dramatic art owes him too much, and Ireland is too largely indebted to him, for anybody to cavil at anything he may say. But he is a very careful person – unlike Messrs O'Casey[8] and Carroll.[9] He never guesses. If he does not know the answer he lies low, like Brer Fox. And, in answer to your query, he appears to have said nothing in several words. He does not appear to have agreed that there was a decline in the Abbey, and he characterised one of your questions as thoughtless. But the other two jumped in with characteristic thoughtless foolhardiness. Mr O'Casey gave you an intemperate opinion on the disadvantages of Irish and the advantages of 'socialism of the USSR brand', which he is apparently unaware is not socialism at all; and Mr Carroll breaks in with a solemn and pompous attack on 'Dublin's censorious, provincial and pietistic attitude'. It has been well said 'What do they know of Ireland who only England know', and Messrs O'Casey and Carroll, who live in England and Scotland, respectively, know nothing about Ireland, and less about the Abbey. I gather that they both desired to say that the Abbey has declined, but they are in no position to know, and they have given no reasons for this belief, save Mr Carroll's crack about Dublin's censorious, pietistic and puritanical atmosphere. It is easily seen he has not been an attendant at the Dublin theatres of the past five years or so. His statement is, plainly, not true. The matter with both of them is a very large swelled head, entirely without justification, and the cure is a little humility. Mr O'Casey has not written a good play since *Juno*, and he will not write one until he again tries to portray men and women, and recognises that he is neither a prophet nor a philosopher, but just a Dublin chiseller. Mr Carroll has not written a good play since *Shadow and Substance*. That is what is eating them.

Now, what about this Gaelic? The prime sin of the present directors is, apparently, that they are 'breaking the tradition' of the theatre by playing plays in 'Gaelic'. I have observed that the people who do not like the Irish language always refer to it as 'Gaelic', doubtless, so as to put it on a level with Esperanto. But its proper designation in English is Irish. Chambers's dictionary defines Gaelic as 'the Scottish Highland dialect'. It defines Irish as 'language of the Irish, a form of Celtic'. The Irish language is the national language of Ireland, and is one of our two official languages. Now, cast your eye on any Abbey programme – it will be seen that the plays are presented by 'The National Theatre Society, Ltd.' Chambers defines national as 'pertaining to a nation; public; general; attached to one's own country'. By what process of reasoning can it be held to be inappropriate for the National Theatre Society to produce plays in the national language? There is no other country in the world in which such a suggestion would be seriously made. Not alone is the production of plays in Irish not a breach of the tradition of the theatre, but it is a part of its tradition; for at the third performance of the Irish Literary Theatre, of which the Abbey is a continuation, the plays performed were *Diarmuid and Grania*, by George Moore and W. B. Yeats, and *Casadh an tSugáin*, by Douglas Hyde, performed in Irish, and on 15 January 1912, the Abbey produced another play in Irish, *An Tincéar Agus an Tsídheóg*, again by Dr Hyde. It is the critics, not the directors, who are ignorant of the theatre's tradition. Nor is there any truth in the suggestion that a knowledge of Irish is likely to unfit anybody for acting, or for distinction in any art. Mr MacLiammóir is a fluent speaker and writer of Irish, as well as English, and it has not prevented him from being not alone a brilliant actor, but the most many-sided talented person in Dublin, and Messrs O'Flaherty, O'Faolain, O'Connor and Corkery do not write any less well in English because they are all fluent speakers and writers of Irish, three of the four not being native speakers of Irish.

As this question of Irish has been raised at all let me carry it a little farther. The opposition to the Irish language is an opposition to the very idea of an Irish nation. It is a hankering back to the idea of British domination, a hope for the re-establishment of Humpty Dumpty. But not all the king's horses nor all the king's men can put Humpty Dumpty together again! The community for which the *Irish Times* speaks, or for which it is presumed to speak, has learned nothing in twenty-two years of Irish freedom. It hopes that a government will some day arise here which will recede from the principle that the Irish language should be taught to all Irish children. It is a vain hope. The quarrels amongst us as to how far teaching through the medium of Irish should be carried, and the occasional irritated letters to the papers about Irish, and Ernest Blythe's unjust and untrue notes about Michael Tierney,[10] and other similar things, are only quarrels about details, not about the principle. Despite all the growling and rumbling, the policy about Irish which has been followed since 1922 would be upheld on a plebiscite by an overwhelming majority. And no other policy is even remotely likely. What happened in 1922? I remember, I was sitting one evening in 1924 at a dinner in the Town Hall at Stockholm, mosaic and all, as one of the Irish delegates to the Universal Postal Union Conference of that year.[11] The buzz of conversation was powerful, and you had almost to shout to your next-door neighbour. Suddenly, there came a complete silence, one of those queer, accidental silences that occur sometimes at these gatherings for a few seconds. And then it was broken by a single voice saying 'You know, what really happened in Ireland was the resurrection of the Gael.' It was the voice of one of my fellow delegates, P. J. Keawell, who had been one of those who founded the Gaelic League with John MacNeil, and who was explaining what had happened to one Wang, delegate from China. Swift and Molyneux and Lucas, Tone and Davis and Mitchel, Parnell and Griffith – that was what they led to, and there was nothing else they could have led to. The 'Anglo-Irish' rejected them, but the Gael accepted them. It was the resurrection of the Gael that made possible the things that these great Irishmen, from Molyneux down, hoped for. But you people have not yet discovered that. You go on making us blush for your intelligence with puerile arguments against Irish. For instance, the suggestion that teaching Irish is hindering education. The argument goes like this: the English language, good! English and French, or German, or Spanish, or Italian, better! English and Latin, excellent! English and Greek, superb intellectual training! But, English and Irish – no damn good! Shaw makes his Swiss take pride in his three native languages. Well, we have two. Your Englishman has only one. Go to!

It is true that the Abbey today is not as good as it was fifteen years ago. But neither is the Gate nor its offshoots; nor Jimmy O'Dea, nor his offshoots. There are many reasons which might be suggested. The growth of the cinema which, itself not an art at all, has yet debased dramatic art and debased public taste. The growth of a materialistic outlook upon everything, especially in this country. The growth of small repertory companies, which dissipate both the available acting talent and the available public. The domination of the human mind by science, which takes richness and imagination out of thought and language. The growth of luxury and ease, the annihilation of time and distance. In short, modern progress, which is turning mankind into ants and destroying character. There are others. But at any rate the reasons are general, and not particular to the directors of the Abbey. Nor is the decline peculiar to drama. Poetry and prose are equally affected.[12]

NOTES

Patrick Sarsfield O'Hegarty (1879–1955), public servant and writer. He was a regular contributor to the *Irish Book Lover* and *Irish Freedom*, which he edited between 1911 and 1914. His books include *John Mitchel: An Appreciation* (1917), *The Indestructible Nation* (1918), *A Short Memoir of Terence MacSwiney* (1922), *A History of Ireland Under the Union* (1922) and *The Victory of Sinn Féin* (1924). See P. S. O'Hegarty, 'Bibliographical Notes: The Abbey Theatre (Wolfhound) Series of Plays', *Dublin Magazine*, 22 (Apr–June 1947) 41–2. 'The P. S. O'Hegarty Collection' is in the University of Kansas Library; see survey of this Collection in Frank C. Nelick, 'Yeats, Bullen, and the Irish Drama', *Modern Drama*, 1 (Dec 1958) 196–202. The following article is in the form of a 'Letter to the Editor' in reply to a number of letters on the condition of the Abbey Theatre which started in the 28 July 1944 issue of the *Irish Times*.

1. Richard Watts Jr, American drama critic.

2. *Juggernaut* won the drama prize at the Tailteann Games in 1928, and was staged at the Gate Theatre in 1929 after rejection by the Abbey. It was published by the *Midland Tribune* (Birr) in 1952, with a foreword by Maurice Walsh.

3. *The Silver Tassie*, by Sean O'Casey; *The White Steed*, by Paul Vincent Carroll; and *The Pipe in the Fields*, by T. C. Murray, respectively. However, *The Silver Tassie* was later produced at the Abbey Theatre on 12 Aug 1935 and *The Pipe in the Fields* on 3 Oct 1927.

4. *Things That Are Caesar's*, by Paul Vincent Carroll, was first presented at the Abbey Theatre on 15 Aug 1932.

5. *Mount Prospect*, by Elizabeth Connor, had its première at the Abbey Theatre on 22 Apr 1940.

6. See Lennox Robinson's recollections, p. 123.

7. See Ernest Blythe's recollections, p. 161.

8. See Sean O'Casey's recollections, p. 197.

9. See Paul Vincent Carroll's recollections, p. 188.

10. Michael Tierney (1894–1975), President of University College, Dublin.

11. From 1922 to 1944, O'Hegarty served as Secretary of the Department of Posts and Telegraphs.

12. O'Hegarty also defended the Abbey Theatre in 'Art and the Nation', *Irish Freedom* (Dublin), no. 16 (Feb 1912) 8; no. 17 (Mar 1912) 2; no. 18 (Apr 1912) 7; and no. 19 (May 1912) 2. However, in 'About Drama', *Inis Fáil* (London), no. 46 (Aug 1908) 5–6, he had expressed the view that the Irish dramatic movement was not progressing.

F. J. McCormick*

EILEEN CROWE

In 1931 a man named Otto Kahn advanced £1000 towards an Abbey tour of America. On the first tour we did *John Ferguson* and *The Whiteheaded Boy*. Peter [F. J. McCormick] loved it. He was interested in everything, and America was something in those days. New York was a wonderful city, but most of us felt that if we were going to live in America it would be in San Francisco. When we returned in 1936 to make the film of *The Plough and the Stars* in Hollywood, Dudley Digges, who had already settled there and was very kind to us, said: 'Listen, don't stay in Hollywood when you finish the picture. Go home. They want you there. But if you want to come back later, then come back.' Of course, when we arrived home Peter and I did not want to go back. Both of us were always home birds.

I had joined the Abbey School of Acting in October 1921. During the time of the curfew the company was away touring. The Abbey had fallen on bad days and the theatre was closed. Michael Dolan was head of the School of Acting at the time. I think I had 30 shillings a week; the highest salary was £4 a week – a ridiculously small salary to pay players. But there was no money. Seaghan Barlow, the stage carpenter, did wonderful work in making sets out of next to nothing, and he kept the theatre going, really. I was only six weeks in the School of Acting when I was given the lead in the revival of *The Revolutionist* by Terence MacSwiney. Sean O'Casey's first play, *The Shadow of a Gunman*, was produced in 1923 just after the players – Arthur Shields, Maureen Delany, Gertie Murphy (who married John McCormick's brother) and others – came back from their tour of America and Australia. I heard them talk about the strange man who went to rehearsals, and after the dress rehearsal went around and shook the hand of each of the players, thanking them for appearing in his little play.

I went to the first night of *The Shadow of a Gunman*. At the end of the first act I remember my hands were tingling because I had clapped so much, as had everyone in the audience. I went to the greenroom after the performance and found O'Casey sitting in a corner by himself, looking very frightened. I said to him: 'Are you the author of this play?' He said:

---

*Des Hickey and Gus Smith, *A Paler Shade of Green* (London: Leslie Frewin, 1972) pp. 37–42.

'Yes.' And I said: 'Heavens!' I just could not say enough enthusiastic things about it. The next day I had a very lovely letter[1] from him saying that he had not realised when he talked to me the night before that he was talking to the Countess Cathleen and Nora Helmer.[2] We became great friends afterwards, until the break-up.[3] And then a lot of people were not friends any more.

Like all the other players, Peter had to go away to make a living when the Abbey closed.[4] He joined a touring company with *Paddy, The Next Best Thing*,[5] and toured England as well as Belfast and Cork. As soon as the tour finished he came back to the Abbey. I remember seeing him in a play shortly after he returned. Several of us in the School of Acting regarded him as a matinee idol. We were not friends at all in the beginning. I was playing the young girl entering the convent in *The Kingdom of God*[6] by Martinez. In the second act she becomes a nun looking after a home for old men, and in the last act she is in charge of an orphanage. In this last act one of the former pupils of the orphanage, a matador, comes to present her with a bull's ear. Peter was stage manager, because in those days you could be playing big parts, as he and Arthur Shields were, and stage managing at the same time. He was so thorough in everything he did that he went out and bought a real bull's ear for this scene. Nobody knew of this until I opened the handkerchief which the matador gave me and saw the ear. Fortunately, it was the dress rehearsal. When we came off Arthur Shields attacked Peter for being so inconsiderate. But, of course, he was only trying to have everything exactly right. The two of them nearly had a fight, which was very unusual for actors in those days. I remember saying that day to someone: 'If Peter Judge was the last man in the world I wouldn't marry him.'

It was not very long afterwards that we became more than friends. We were married in December 1925. Nobody had known of our plans. We told the others in the company only the night before we were married and asked them to come to the wedding. When I went to Lennox Robinson, he said: 'I was wondering when Peter was going to make an honest woman of you.' We were playing in *Grasshopper*[7] that evening, a play translated by Padraic Colum from the German of Count Keyserling, and it was an embarrassing, but very lovely experience. The evening papers had got hold of the news, and I am sure the audience applauded us for a full seven minutes.

I played Mary Boyle in the first performance of *Juno and the Paycock* in 1924. Peter played Joxer Daly. It was his great part. When Sydney Morgan played Joxer in London afterwards, he said: 'I can only copy McCormick.' But he liked *The Shadow of a Gunman* best; that was his favourite. After the first night of *Gunman*, Sean O'Casey said to him: 'That wasn't my character.[8] But don't change him. He's much better than the character I wrote.' He and O'Casey were firm friends. O'Casey was quite different from any author the players had met. Peter was the one who befriended him and took him out to meals, partly because he was sorry for him, partly because he liked him and partly because he wanted to talk about the characters in the plays. He considered O'Casey a great playwright, but I remember someone in the Abbey saying to us: 'O'Casey is not a playwright. He's a reporter, and his plays will be forgotten in ten years.'

O'Casey wrote the part of The Covey in *The Plough and the Stars* for Peter, but he was cast as Jack Clitheroe. Peter had been very good to O'Casey in the early days, before he was recognised publicly. But on the fourth night of *The Plough* when the audience were in uproar and Peter, who was one of the cast, was trying to keep them quiet, he said: 'Don't blame the actors. We didn't write this play'. I think O'Casey never forgave him for that.

O'Casey had been a very happy man, but he became very bitter after the Abbey refused *The Silver Tassie*. Of course they should have put it on. After all, O'Casey had achieved great things for the Abbey with his first three plays. But his break with realism in the second act may have frightened them off. But we played it afterwards.[9]

Peter was born in Skerries, where his father was the manager of a brewery. He went to the convent school and had a happy boyhood. He became a boy clerk in the Post Office in London and fed himself on rice which did terrible things to his digestion. His name was Peter Judge, but when he was moved to the Civil Service in Dublin he did not want them to know he was acting, because they would not approve of it, so he decided to take another name. I think F. J. McCormick was a name he saw on a poster. He was in the Abbey company before I joined them. When I came to the Abbey School of Acting he was away touring. Frank Fay had left many years before, but he was living in Dublin and they had engaged him to teach in the School of Acting. He selected me immediately and told me he would make my voice the talk of the world within six months. He had been touring England in Shakespeare and told me I must drop my 'h's. We were rehearsing *The Shadowy Waters* and when I spoke the line: 'Why is the moon so pale?' Lennox Robinson asked me: 'What has the letter "h" done to you?'

'Mr Fay told me to drop my "h"'s', I answered. The next day Yeats sent for me, and said: 'My compliments to Mr Fay, but would you please put back the "h".'

I remember the morning Arthur Griffith was buried. We had been rehearsing, and Lennox said to Michael Dolan and myself: 'We'll go down to Beresford Place to watch the funeral.' We went down, and at the head of the cortège was Michael Collins,[10] a magnificent figure in his uniform. Lennox said: 'Oh, Michael, please give us a wedding for a change. We have had too many funerals.' A week later Michael Collins was dead.

I earned more money than Peter when I joined the company, because Lennox Robinson thought that I was the most wonderful thing that had ever happened. He gave me a rise, which I did not appreciate at the time, and which was unfair. I had £10 and Peter had five, which was ridiculous. Peter was interested in everything. He had a great interest in photography. He felt that every time a play was staged it would be sensible to take a photograph of the set to show the positioning of the furniture and props, so that there would be no dispute afterwards. He was asked by the management to take the photographs, and for taking them he got 10 shillings a week. Actors would be asked to play big parts and stage manage at the same time. Peter was stage manager when he was playing Jack Tanner in *Man and Superman*, one of the longest parts in any play. How could they have asked him to do that? But they did. It was inhuman to expect actors to do that sort of thing, but they could not afford to pay a stage manager at the time.

Despite the small salaries the Abbey was a happy place in those days, and I do not think any actor wanted to go anywhere else. Peter was happy in his work, and we had a marvellous variety of parts. In later years we were cut down to kitchen comedies and kitchen tragedies, but in the early days we played practically all of Shaw and Ibsen. The players were extraordinary content, much more so than people are now with larger salaries. I loved playing with Peter. There was no feeling of acting a part. He was the character he was playing and you were the character you were playing. When he played a big part my own part suffered very often because I would become so nervous and worried about him that I would almost forget what I was doing. As soon as he got news of a part, he studied all he could about it. He had a wonderful sense of humour and he was kind. On one occasion an actor was cast as Captain Boyle, who was a fine actor indeed, but completely unsuited to the part. On the first night Peter went down to the Abbey and played his own part with his back to the audience to help the actor, and when he was off stage he stood behind the window prompting him.

Peter liked to play classical parts, but costume plays were not always popular in the Abbey. He was magnificent in Shaw. He played Oedipus and Lear. One Sunday night we put on *Oedipus* for a charity audience in New York with just a curtain at the back of the stage. During an exit, Peter stepped off the stage into space, because it was so dark. But despite his fall he came on again and finished the play. He received all sorts of offers at a time when we could have used the money, but he never wanted to leave the Abbey. When he finally appeared in the film *Odd Man Out* it made him an international name. They were making *Odd Man Out* and *Hungry Hill* at the same time, and he moved from one set to another. It was too much. Immediately afterwards they asked him to play in another film. I was so upset at the time that I do not remember the name of the film or the Irish location at which they were filming on the east coast. They were working nights and Peter had a gruelling time. He had to give it up.

Two Cities offered him a £2000 yearly retainer and he was offered a five-year contract by Hollywood. He enjoyed making films, but the only thing that tempted him was an invitation from Olivier to play the First Gravedigger in *Hamlet*. He was very ill at the time, and Olivier offered to finish the film without Peter's scenes, and wait for him. Stanley Holloway played the part afterwards, and said he could not hope to be as good as F.J. On the day Peter died, the surgeon said to me: 'Which one of us wouldn't wish to go at the height of one's fame?'[11]

When you consider the international exchange of actors today, perhaps Peter's full potential was never realised. But he was happy. He was happy playing all those wonderful parts. What upsets me is that his greatness is only for those who saw him and remember him. Nowadays, when so much great acting is preserved on film for posterity, all that remains of Peter's work is *The Plough and the Stars*, *Hungry Hill* and *Odd Man Out*. I do not remember him talking about the parts he would like to have played. Each part as he played it was his life for the time being.

NOTES

'F.J. McCormick', stage name of Peter Judge (1889–1947). After a brief career in the Civil Service in Dublin and London, during which he acted in amateur dramatic societies, he became a member of the Abbey Theatre Company in 1918. He acted in over 500 plays at the Abbey, and was particularly noted for his performances in plays by Sean O'Casey. He toured America five times, and played three major film roles. In the new Abbey Theatre there hangs a composite portrait of him entitled *The Empty Throne*. (Cecil Salkeld's picture emphasises McCormick's versatility.) When leading members of the Abbey Company – including Arthur Shields, Barry Fitzgerald and Sara Allgood – left Ireland for America, McCormick stayed on, and his widow, Eileen Crowe, continued as a member of the Company. She died in 1978. For more on McCormick see Gabriel Fallon, 'F. J. McCormick: An Appreciation', *Studies* (Dublin), 36 (June 1947) 180–6; Gabriel Fallon, *The Abbey and the Actor* (Dublin: The National Theatre Society, 1969) pp. 53–7; and 'F. J. McCormick: A Symposium of Tributes', *Capuchin Annual* (Dublin), 1948, pp. 149–225. See also Eileen Crowe's own recollections, p. 130.

1. This letter is not included in *The Letters of Sean O'Casey*.
2. Nora is the heroine of Ibsen's *A Doll's House*.
3. The Abbey Theatre turned down O'Casey's *The Silver Tassie* in 1928.
4. Cf. 'There was a dreadful day in the spring of 1921 when the Company had

to be dismissed by me. . . . One actor, F. J. McCormick, sold all his books to keep himself alive' (Lennox Robinson, *Ireland's Abbey Theatre: A History 1899–1951* (London: Sidgwick & Jackson, 1951) p. 120).

5. By Mackay and Ord.

6. A translation of *The Kingdom of God*, by Gregorio Martínez Sierra (1881–1947), was presented at the Abbey Theatre on 3 Nov 1924.

7. *Grasshopper*, a play in four acts by Padraic Colum and E. Washburn Freud, founded on a play by Keyserling, was first performed by the Abbey Theatre on 24 Oct 1922.

8. McCormick played the part of Seumas Shields in the first production of *The Shadow of a Gunman* on 12 Apr 1923.

9. *The Silver Tassie* was produced at the Abbey Theatre for the first time on 12 Aug 1935. It had opened at the Apollo Theatre, London, on 11 Oct 1929.

10. Michael Collins (1890–1922), revolutionary leader.

11. Cf. 'McCormick's untimely death in April 1947 was a shattering blow to our Theatre' (Robinson, *Ireland's Abbey Theatre*, p. 156).

The Death-watch Beetle*

DONAGH MACDONAGH

Visitors to Dublin, particularly those who are connected with the theatre, generally make a pious pilgrimage to the Abbey Theatre, and then sometimes wonder why.

The building itself has changed little since the Yeats fire burned behind those walls; the facade has been modified by the addition of a modern chromium canopy and the lobby is bright-walled and brightly lighted, which was dim and oak-lined in the old days. Over the box-office, which has a slot into which the 'House Full' notice neatly slips, is a portrait of the founder, an urbane work by Sean O'Sullivan,[1] which shows the Old Man in a rich, poetic garment, gazing with interest towards the money-changing below. Round the walls are other portraits, the best of them by the poet's father, John Butler Yeats, which mirror the faces of those who made the Abbey great – Augusta Gregory, Miss Horniman, Frank Fay, Lennox Robinson. In the summer months visitors peer respectfully at these, and their progression from picture to picture is described by the Abbey staff as 'doing the Stations of the Cross'.

An electric bell rings and the enquiring stranger follows the crowd down a few steps into the auditorium – should he be late he will find the door closed in his face, since the Abbey has in recent years imposed the

Drama (London), no. 12 (Feb 1949) 4–7.

excellent rule that the doors close at the rise of the curtain. Inside he will find as curious an architectural eccentricity as any in the history of the theatre, but so many famous voices have echoed from these walls that the oddity of design merely adds to the interest of the place.

The orchestra is playing the overture to *Oberon*, the curtain, a worn black with vertical gold strips and two obvious if symmetrical patches, is obscured by a safety curtain which slowly descends and rises to reassure the nervous. The house is full, the bewildered stranger is examining his programme, which bears on its face a huntress, and an elkhound from the William Morris kennel. He finds that he is now in *Amharclann na Mainistreach*, 'The Theatre of the Monastery', where people with Gaelic names, printed in Roman type, are playing the parts of characters with readily understandable English names. This curious linguistic ambivalence is symptomatic of the Abbey today.

The last patron slips down the steps, a head is withdrawn from a door beside the stage, a gong sounds, another, the house lights dim and go out; a third gong and the dusty curtain rises on a cottage interior. But no famous Abbey actor takes the stage – they are all dead or in Hollywood or Elstree.[2]

Ah, it is a poor thing when a great institution comes to the end of its days, and when those who saw it in its might mourn its decay and popularity. The Abbey in the days of its greatness was empty of the populace, but now, in its old age, 'with flattering tongue it speeds the parting guest'.[3]

In the early days Yeats was sometimes furious if some meretricious quality in a play secured it a fleeting popularity, and the indiscriminate laughter of those whom he considered the mob would send him raging from the theatre. Today those who mocked and rioted at *The Playboy of the Western World* and *The Plough and the Stars* pack the theatre of his dream.

It was the theatre of Yeats. The plays, with the exception of those of Synge and O'Casey, were seldom great; the sets were never extraordinary, the lighting consisted of an unchanging amber, but the acting and the cold high integrity of the poet made for greatness. The Abbey was Yeats. While he lived it lived too, and when he died it died with him.

He had made it out of nothing, in a dead time in a moribund country, when English touring companies came to Dublin as one more step on their provincial Calvary, when the English domination of Ireland seemed complete. But in those frozen years at the end of the nineteenth century a new national movement was formed which was to sweep the English from the country, a new theatrical movement which was to make the name of Ireland famous in the intellectual world, and a language movement which in the end would help to destroy the Abbey from within – the resurgent Irish Republican Brotherhood, the Abbey Theatre and the Gaelic League, a strange and portentous triple birth.

The Abbey was founded principally for the production of Yeats' verse plays, those static masterpieces which require a small drawing-room full of friends, rather than a large theatre, for their appreciation, but it was not until Synge came back from Paris to transfer the colours of the western world to his palette that the Abbey came alive, with riots and enthusiasm and John Butler Yeats.

> upon the Abbey stage, before him a raging crowd,
> 'This land of Saints', and then as the applause died out,
> 'Of plaster Saints', his beautiful mischievous head thrown back.[4]

The Abbey from its inception to the death of Yeats was a theatre, with all that that means and implies. Its directors, its producers, technicians, actors were men of the theatre who thought and lived in terms of the theatre; and week after week, to empty houses, they produced plays which, successful or unsuccessful, were produced because they had or promised theatrical qualities, not because they seemed likely to fill the theatre and run for months. It was unusual for any play to be retained for more than a week, and the 'House Full' notice provided a loom for spiders. Occasional American tours produced enough funds to keep the doors open, and in later years a government grant paid some of the outgoings.

With the death of Yeats came popular success. An adaptation of a Toller play, *Blind Man's Buff*,[5] by Denis Johnston, had once run for a few astonishing weeks, but the first record-breaker was a tendentious work entitled *The Rugged Path*,[6] by George Shiels. This glorified duty to the state, and civic conscience, ran for many weeks and started the directors on the primrose path of compromise. 'Let us', they said, 'produce a number of such popular works, and, with the money thus questionably earned, put before the public works of art which will educate them, improve their taste in plays, and persuade them to give the superior works of the theatre that enthusiasm which they now reserve for the inferior.' The result was of course inevitable. The directors are still searching for popular successes, but their good intentions have long since been used for paving-stones.

About 1942 the Abbey directors took over another theatre, the Comhar Dramíochta, or Drama League, a 'little theatre' for the production of plays in Irish, and with the Comhar came its government grant.[7] The intention was that the Abbey would run a bilingual company which would be able to leap without pause from one language to another, and the members of which would be equally brilliant actors in either language. The result of this manoeuvre was also inevitable; the present Abbey company is in the main bilingual, but the Holy Ghost has been remiss in imparting the gift of acting with that of tongues.[8]

As I write a typical neo-Abbey success is packing the theatre nightly. It is entitled *The King of Friday's Men*,[9] and concerns a landlord with a weakness for exercising the *jus primae noctis*,[10] a shillelagh-fighter who rescues the maiden from his horrid designs, an old lady who smokes a pipe, a girl who has submitted to the *droit de seigneur*,[11] and who is now dressed like the doxy she is and various other characters from the old melodrama stage. As few of the modern playgoers have ever seen any of the older plays which so pleased the audiences at the Queen's Theatre when Yeats was endeavouring to combat that form of entertainment, they mistake the situation for one of originality, and are persuaded by the fine language in which the piece is written that they are witnessing a work of art. The play, I understand, is to take the London stage shortly, and it will be interesting to see how its qualities travel.

It does not seem likely that under its present Board of directors any renaissance may be expected at the Abbey in the near future. The Board has that nose, so envied by other commercial managements, which recognises a box-office success, but the 'fascination of what is difficult' they have never felt or have left long behind. Sometimes as the enthusiastic applause of the audience brings down the curtain on yet another success I imagine that I can hear a small and ominous sound somewhere in the fabric of the Abbey, the tick of the death-watch beetle, whose advent presages the fall of ancient structures.

NOTES

Donagh MacDonagh (1912–68), poet, playwright, lawyer, ballad writer, broadcaster and editor; son of Thomas MacDonagh, one of the executed leaders of the 1916 Easter Rising. He became a popular broadcaster on Radio Éireann, which provided him a platform for his lifelong interest in folk ballads. His own plays are either poetic dramas or ballad operas. His most successful play was the exuberant *Happy as Larry* (1946), which was successfully produced in London and New York, and which has been translated into a dozen European languages.

1. Sean O'Sullivan (1906–64), painter. He had a remarkable feeling for personality and executed many portraits of distinguished Irishmen, including Eamon de Valera, Douglas Hyde, James Joyce and Brendan Behan.

2. Elstree Studios (ABC film studios) between Watford and Barnet, Hertfordshire, England.

3. W. B. Yeats, 'Youth and Age', *Collected Poems*.

4. W. B. Yeats, 'Beautiful Lofty Things', *Last Poems (1936–9)*.

5. *Blind Man's Buff*, based on a play by the German dramatist Ernst Toller (1893–1939), was presented at the Abbey Theatre on 26 Dec 1936.

6. *The Rugged Path* opened at the Abbey Theatre on 5 Aug 1940. It ran for twelve weeks.

7. In Mar 1942, Ernest Blythe persuaded the Gaelic theatre organisation, An Comhar Dramaíochta, to sub-let its production of plays to the Abbey. Thus he

was able to lay hands on this organisation's annual grant which, at the time, amounted to £600.

8. The Abbey's Gaelic policy, however, based on what appeared to be linguistic rather than artistic grounds, seemed to some a betrayal, or at least a distortion, of the Abbey's primary purpose, and disruptive of its regular work. Joseph Holloway wrote in his diary for 30 May 1943: 'It is a pity to see the childish efforts of the Gaelic three directors of the Abbey to graft on the Gaelic Theatre to the far-famed Abbey, and to behave like children in interfering with the regular work of the theatre by encroaching on their rehearsals and interfering in many ways with the Abbey's players' progress' (*Joseph Holloway's Irish Theatre, 1926–1944*, vol. 3, ed. Robert Hogan and Michael J. O'Neill (Dixon, California: Proscenium Press, 1970) p. 89).

9. *The King of Friday's Men*, by M. J. Molloy, had its première at the Abbey Theatre on 18 Oct 1948.

10. The right of the first night; the reported claim of the feudal lord to the virginity of the bride of his vassal on the first night of her marriage.

11. *Jus primae noctis.*

Can the Abbey Theatre be Restored?*

PAUL VINCENT CARROLL

When W. B. Yeats was hurriedly summoned to the Abbey Theatre stage in 1924, during the deliberately conconcted hullabaloo against O'Casey's *The Plough and the Stars* [*sic*][1] he calmly adjusted his monocle and said to the hooligan demonstrators in the audience, 'You have disgraced yourselves – again!' His 'again' was a reference back to the much earlier riot during the staging of Synge's *The Playboy*.

This dramatic reproof by Yeats will be remembered in Irish social and dramatic history whenever organised bigotry and narrow nationalism combine to confine a passionate nation's art and drama within mere conventional limits. If its message and implications are allowed to die, then Ireland will dwindle inevitably into a smug peasant pocket republic, renowned for her drolleries instead of her art. Such must not be allowed to happen, for the Irish soul has made, and must continue to make, superb contributions to the beauty and aestheticism of this unbalanced world.

It has been artists of fearless courage such as Yeats and Lady Gregory who have blazed the Irish trail of dramatic achievement through the

* *Theatre Arts* (New York), 36 (Jan 1952) 18–19, 79.

jungles of misrepresentation, clerical opposition and press vilification, and placed Ireland proudly on the artistic map of the world. In the past, Ireland, through her artists, has placed at least five stage masterpieces (*Juno and the Paycock*, *The Plough and the Stars*, *The Playboy of the Western World*, *Riders to the Sea*, *The Whiteheaded Boy*) in the world gallery of dramatic art – an amazing achievement for so small and so sparsely populated an island. But it has ever been the gifted few, and not the loud-mouthed many, who have been responsible for this achievement, and on account of this, the artistic destiny of the race must at all costs remain in the hands of the minority of genius. But unfortunately, since the death of Yeats in 1939, and of his superb bodyguard of artists, the Abbey Theatre has been in retreat, and Ireland has at the moment no artist fearless enough to rally this broken and disrupted creative force.

Many unworthy factors have contributed to this deplorable retreat. First, the unofficial interference of the government in Abbey policy as the price of a rather stingy subsidy. Second, the very powerful unofficial clerical censorship, and the bullying tactics of certain lay bodies and organisations who throw the balls made by their clerical directors. Third, the deplorable policy of the Abbey directorate to submerge criminally the Anglo-Irish achievements on which the Abbey was built, and replace them by an insane policy of purely Gaelic culture, expressed through the medium of the native language, of which the majority of the Irish people know little and care less.

No one of course, let me hasten to add, could reasonably quarrel with an Irish government for opening a new theatre in Dublin, exclusively featuring native plays in the Gaelic language, such as we already have on a small scale in Galway.[2] But when it comes to disembowelling the famous Abbey tradition to satisfy the racial whims and tempers of a handful of doctrinaires, that is a different matter and once that commands the attention of that English-speaking world that has garlanded the Anglo-Irish genius with very coveted international laurels. And mark that when I use the term 'Anglo-Irish', I mean men who love the Irish nation passionately but who write superbly in a form of English that they have moulded to Irish requirements in beauty and art. Yeats and his splendid contemporaries such as AE [George Russell] and Lady Gregory all had an English strain in their blood, but if they had not been really *very great* men and women, they would have taken the *wrong* side in the Irish revolution. But did they? Did any single one of them? That is the question that the narrower type of nationalist in Ireland hates to answer, because the answer chokes him!

The difficulties I have quoted above are the difficulties that must be faced unflinchingly in the future Ireland, for since the death of Yeats, the Abbey had been going from bad to worse until finally it went up in smoke and ended fifty years of world fame in flaming tongues of fire.

As an art theatre, its policy has degenerated into a please-the-multitude cringing, its acting has become slovenly and impoverished – the death of F. J. McCormick struck the final blow – its new playwrights are hamstrung by unofficial censorships that intimidate them into the mediocre and the commonplace, and its audiences have degenerated into a guffawing mob of courting couples and soda-pop swillers. Veterans of its history such as Michael J. Dolan, its oldest living actor, and Ria Mooney, its present thwarted producer, could not without strong directorial support and good will stem the downward flop to mediocrity in all its branches.

There is no doubt whatever that a new Abbey will soon arise. But what sort of an Abbey will it be? Ireland without her Abbey is like Rome without St Peter's, or Paris without its Louvre. If the Irish government rebuilds the theatre, which I hope it will not, there is little hope that the Abbey will re-arise as the proud, independent theatre that it was. It will amost inevitably come under subtle government control and be subject to the numerous national taboos of the ignorant and the smug pietistic provincialists. If, on the other hand, the American people, who have always loved the Abbey because of its artistry and because it is the legitimate mother of countless small theatres scattered over the United States, decide with their usual generosity to rebuild it in a finer and architecturally more beautiful form, they should demand in return that it be handed over to the rightful artists of creative Ireland, and that no governing body in Ireland, either lay or clerical, shall have any control over it, offical or unofficial.

Unoffical Irish censorship in all its insidious forms has, since the Revolution in 1916, been the curse of Irish creative art. We, the playwrights, poets, writers and artists of the race, have been accused of all sorts of ridiculous crimes, including belittlement of the Irish people, misrepresentation, anti-clericalism, pro-Englishism and anti-nationalism.

To be sure, we are anti-clerical. Any intelligent Irishman is. But those of us who are Catholic are certainly not anti-Catholic, and those of us who are not Catholic are definitely not anti-Christian. And apart from the running-sore problem of Irish partition, we admire the English people for their wonderful literary heritage, just as we love the younger American people for their superb efforts to find a sanctuary for the immortal arts of a beleaguered and heartbroken Europe. The other charges are too contemptible to need refutation – we just love Ireland, the mystical, mysterious, unutterable Ireland that gives us our strength and artistic inspirations.

In reality, we, the accused, belong to *the rebel mind* of a passionate and age-old nation. That is the simple truth. It is the first and last duty of every creative writer in every country to swim against the current of popular opinion, provided always that he swim loyally within the Constitution that embodies the soul of the nation. This is the only spiritual means by which we can keep healthy conflict alive and preserve the nation from smugness, ennui and artistic and spiritual stagnation. We, therefore, make no apologies. The cry of 'Wolf! Wolf!' against a creative writer, who is loyal to his homeland, but blindingly aware of its deficiencies, is the very lowest and meanest weapon in the armoury of noddles, humbugs and doctrinaires.

When the new Abbey Theatre arises in Ireland, it will be a mere pretentious counterfeit institution unless it is ruled by artists of the mettle of Yeats, AE and Lady Gregory. It must allow its playwrights to dramatise the burning contemporary problems that are now politely but firmly taboo. It must be the death chamber of mere post-revolutionary pietism. It must thrash out on its boards, with high dramatic tension, such burning questions as the alleged strangling of the civil law by clerical law, or the drama of the recent extraordinary liaison between the richer members of the medical profession and certain dignitaries of the Irish hierarchy that brought about the disgrace of a brilliant Minister of State and the actual fall of the legitimate government.[3]

And when the new Abbey rises resolutely to its old fearless eminence, and the intimidating riots start again – for the riots are by no means over in uneasy, groping modern Ireland – there must be someone worthy of the Yeatsian tradition who will advance aristocratically to the footlights and thunder:

'You have disgraced yourselves – AGAIN!'

NOTES

Paul Vincent Carroll (1900–68), playwright. In 1921, disillusioned with Irish provincial life, he emigrated to Glasgow, where he taught in state schools. His first play, *The Watched Pot*, was produced at the experimental Peacock Theatre in 1930. *Things That Are Caesar's* (Abbey Theatre, 1932) launched him on his career as a playwright. After the success of *Shadow and Substance* (Abbey Theatre, 1937) he became a full-time dramatist. This play won the New York Drama Critics Circle Award for the best foreign play in 1938. *The White Steed*, first produced in New York, received the same award in 1939. Carroll's portraits of clergymen and clerical life in his best plays have not been surpassed on the Irish stage. See Paul Vincent Carroll, 'The Irish Theatre (Post War)', in *International Theatre*, ed. John Andrews and Ossia Trilling (London: Simpson Low, 1949) pp. 122–8; and Paul A. Boyle, *Paul Vincent Carroll* (Lewisburg, Pennsylvania: Bucknell University Press, 1971).

1. *The Plough and the Stars* was first produced in 1926, not in 1924.
2. *An Taibhdhearc*, founded in 1928 by Hilton Edwards and Micheál

MacLiammóir. After MacLiammóir, other managers were Frank Dermody and Walter Macken.

3. Dr Noel Browne, Minister of Health in the Coalition government of 1948–51, tried to introduce welfare legislation known as the 'Mother and Child Scheme', which was strongly opposed by the Catholic hierarchy. After vainly attempting to fight the clerical opposition and the passivity of his own party, Clann na Poblachta, Browne resigned on 11 Apr 1951, and shortly afterwards the government fell. See F. S. L. Lyons, *Ireland Since the Famine* (Fontana, 1973) pp. 560, 572–9.

An Irishman's Diary*

QUIDNUNC [SEAMUS KELLY]

Smooth Work

At midday yesterday the President of Ireland proved himself a good mason. At least I thought so until I mentioned it to another spectator at the laying of the foundation stone of the new Abbey, and was told: 'He's not so good – he should have left the mortar rougher.'

It was a rather disorganised occasion; sheep mixed with goats regardless, and the one man who started his theatrical career with the Fays, before the Abbey was founded, was buried in the background until Dr John Larchet discovered him for me. He is Seaghan Barlow, who met Willie Fay, then running his Comedy Combination company, at the back of Walker's shop in High Street, Dublin, in 1902, got roped in, and has been with the theatre ever since.

Came the Dawn

Other veterans present were: Dr Larchet himself and Eric Gorman, who was with his wife, Christine Hayden. They joined the old Abbey in November 1908 (the play then running was *When the Dawn Is Come*, by Thomas MacDonagh); Michael Cunniffe, the first native Irish speaker to join the Abbey; May Craig, and Felix Hughes, who joined as a boy in 1910 (his first part was in *The Shuiler's Child*). Eric Gorman is still the theatre's secretary,[1] though we are unlikely to see his incomparable Uncle Pether again – nor are we likely to see May Craig's equally memorable Jenny Gogan.[2]

Eileen Crowe was there, bringing back to the mind of everybody who

---

Irish Times (Dublin), 4 Sept 1963, p. 8.

loved the Abbey memories of F. J. McCormick, Michael Dolan and Maureen Delany. Siobhán McKenna was there, talking to Ria Mooney, but neither her husband, Denis O'Dea, nor his Abbey contemporary, Cyril Cusack, appeared. Fred Johnson, who worked with both the Abbey and Gate companies, arrived, and explained that it was by accident, not by invitation, as he chatted with John McCann[3] TD,[4] currently the Abbey's most successful playwright. Most of the present players turned up, and everybody was delighted to see that Harry Brogan,[5] like Seaghan Barlow, broke out from his sick-bed for the occasion.

Resting?

Apart from the President, the state was represented by the Taoiseach[6] and Mrs Lemass, and the Minister for External Affairs, Mr Frank Aiken, while Mr James Dillon and Mr Brendan Corish[7] showed the flag for the Opposition.

At the luncheon later, Mr de Valera[8] looked almost coy when it was disclosed that he had once been an actor, playing the part of a doctor. He was, it seems, described by the then critic of the *Irish Times* as 'a tall, dark cadaverous young man'. The Taoiseach, too, emerged as a one-time Thespian who had played the part of Sir Lucius O'Trigger in *The Rivals* (opposite one James O'Dea, if I am not mistaken). No curtain was lifted on Mr Dillon's dramatic past, but he made one of the cracks of the day when he said, 'A politician without enemies is a cipher; a theatre without critics is a nullity.'

Abbey Aristos

From the founding families, I saw Mrs W. B. Yeats, her son Michael and her daughter Anne, whose latest one-woman show opened in the Dawson Gallery yesterday afternoon. Frank Fay's son, Gerard, now London editor of the *Guardian*, was there with his wife, and presumably his memories of the days when he was a boy actor in Dublin.

Before the stone was laid I had a look at the inscription. It reads: 'Ar 3 Meán Fomhair 1963 do leag An t-Uachtarian, Eamon de Valera, cloch-bhoinn seo Amharclainn Nua na Mainistreach . . . le omos do[9] William Butler Yeats, Augusta Lady Gregory, John Millington Synge, Frank J. Fay, William G. Fay.'

A whisper from some prompt corner or other tells me that the initial intention had been to include only the names of Yeats and Lady Gregory on the stone, and from another prompt corner I am urged to ask about omissions. In common gratitude one might have expected to see the name of Miss Annie Horniman, who after all put up the money before there was an Irish state to subsidise an Irish national theatre. And where was the name of Douglas Hyde, An Craoíbhin Aoibhinn,[10] first President of Ireland, first playwright in the Irish language, and one of the Vice-Presidents of the original Irish National Theatre Society when it was founded in 1903?[11]

NOTES

On 3 Sept 1963, the foundation stone of the new Abbey Theatre was laid. 'Quidnunc' was Seamus Kelly (1912–79), who was also the *Irish Times* drama critic.

1. In 1966, Eric Gorman, after thirty-two years as Secretary of the Irish National Theatre Society, retired and his place was taken by John Slemon, a young and energetic accountant.

2. Both parts are in *The Plough and the Stars*, by Sean O'Casey. Gorman and May Craig appeared in the RTE television production of the play in 1966, directed by Lelia Doolan. Gorman played his original part, May Craig the Woman from Rathmines.

3. John McCann (1905–80), playwright and politician. In 1954, he lost his seat in the Dáil, but by then his plays were being produced by the Abbey Theatre. Such pieces as *Twenty Years A-Wooing* (1954), *Blood is Thicker Than Water* (1955), *Early and Often* (1956) and *Give Me a Bed of Roses* (1957) probably became the Abbey's biggest box-office draws during its long exile in the Queen's Theatre.

4. Teachta Dála (Member of Dáil Éireann, the Irish Parliament).

5. Harry Brogan (1905–77) was born in Holywood, County Down, and came to Dublin as an infant. In 1926 he got his first walk-on part at the Abbey in *Androcles and the Lion*. In 1936 he became a permanent member of the Company and one of the most popular comedians.

6. Prime Minister. Sean Lemass (1899–1971) became Taoiseach in June 1959.

7. Brendan Corish (1918–   ) became leader of the Labour Party in 1963.

8. Eamon de Valera (1881–1975), President of Ireland. He was elected President in June 1959; and was re-elected in 1966, when he was eighty-three.

9. On 3 Sept, 1963, the President, Eamon de Valera, laid this foundation stone of the New Abbey Theatre . . . to honour. . . .

10. The Sweet Little Branch (pen name of Douglas Hyde).

11. At the meeting of the Irish National Theatre Society on 9 Aug 1902, Douglas Hyde was elected Vice-President; the other two Vice-Presidents being AE [George Russell] and Maud Gonne. W. B. Yeats was elected President.

The Abbey Theatre in London*

PETER DAUBENY

I had wanted to present a season of his [O'Casey's] work in London, and was already in touch with the playwright at his house in Torquay, when plans for the first World Theatre Season began to take shape. I decided to bring to my first World Theatre Season the Abbey Theatre playing O'Casey, and for this purpose I determined to repair the breach between Ireland's national theatre and one of its finest playwrights.

I was delighted and honoured to receive a letter from O'Casey's wife Eileen, in which she said:

I am thrilled that you have chosen to bring Sean's two plays, *Juno and the Paycock* and *The Plough and the Stars*, over from the Abbey Theatre to be presented at the Aldwych in the World Theatre Season this year. Sean, I know, is also happy that his plays are to be presented in London. I know he has written to you.

I am doubly pleased because, after the Bishop [*sic*] of Dublin had banned *The Drums of Father Ned* – which was written for the Tostal – Sean banned the performances of all his plays in Dublin. Joyce and Beckett were to have been performed, as you know, that year, but they withdrew their plays in protest.[1]

Sean took a while to decide to lift the ban. I know it was his great respect and admiration for the work you have done in the theatre, and the fact *you* have chosen his plays to come to the Aldwych, that made him decide to do this. Having decided, he could hardly let down the Abbey players by not allowing them to perform and rehearse the plays in Dublin before coming to London.

Although I have always felt that Sean should do exactly as he wanted about his own work, I am delighted he has written to Ernest Blythe, saying he will lift the ban temporarily. I am most pleased that the younger generation in Ireland can now see his plays. There is no doubt that this gesture of his is entirely due to you.

In the months preceding their visit, O'Casey became my one great telephone friend. We never met, but we rang each other almost daily,

* *My World of Theatre* (London: Jonathan Cape, 1971) pp. 286–8. Editor's title.

and seemed to talk for hours. He was very happy that two of his plays should be chosen that year to honour Shakespeare.

'The best way to honour him, of course,' he wrote to me, 'is to know and love him; but it is good and proper to honour him in a tribute from one who loves true men and true poets. You have done richly in assembling this tribute in London. I am grateful to you for thinking of a place for Ireland and for me among those who come bearing the gold, frankincense and myrrh of Drama as an offering to the Poet!'

But when I actually went with John Francis Lane to see the plays in Dublin I experienced a degree of dismay. The Abbey Theatre Company were performing at the old melodrama theatre, the Queen's, while they awaited completion of their new building, which was to open in July 1966. After the old Abbey had been burnt down in 1951, the company, crossing the Liffey to the Queen's, had suffered a deterioration of spirit. It was hardly surprising. The place was like a drill-hall and, however full it might be, always felt empty. The productions seemed crammed with faults: some poor acting and very poor sets. The actors always looked cold.

I argued bitterly with the Abbey directors, insisting that changes must be made before the productions came to London. When I described my problems to O'Casey he wrote of one of the directors, 'He is a mass of obstinacy, so full of his own importance that he will listen to no one; insensitive, too, utterly impervious to anything said to him. He hasn't the faintest idea of what is Drama, and less about the art of actor; he has become a human limpet fastened to the Abbey Theatre.'

The plays, nevertheless, arrived, despite a strike threat by the Abbey Players themselves, and were received by a muted press. They were, however, enormously successful. We had full houses every night and long queues for return tickets.

'I accept the praise in your letter with humility,' O'Casey wrote to me, 'for, looking back at the plays and all else, like Gogol, I find little to brag about, but remain dissatisfied that all could not have been better shaped and the plays given a fairer habitation on the stage.'

NOTES

Peter Daubeny, CBE (1921–   ), English actor and producer. In 1964, he became Artistic Director of the World Theatre Season; and, in 1966, a Consultant Director of the Royal Shakespeare Company. Volume I of his autobiography, *Stage by Stage* (London: Jonathan Cape) appeared in 1952.

1. In 1958, John Charles McQuaid, the Archbishop of Dublin, refused to say an inaugural Mass for the Dublin Theatre Festival which was scheduled to contain works by O'Casey, Joyce and Beckett. The Festival director hastily

cancelled the production of *Bloomsday*, an adaptation of Joyce's *Ulysses*. O'Casey and Beckett then withdrew their plays, and the Festival for that year was abandoned. See Robert Hogan, 'O'Casey and the Archbishop', *New Republic*, 138 (19 May 1958) 29–30; and Sean O'Casey, 'Abbey Can't Have My Plays', *Sunday Press* (Dublin), 27 July 1958, p.1 (interview).

Abbey Has Been Deteriorating for Years*

SEAN O'CASEY

Sean O'Casey had not read the statement from the Abbey Theatre directors when I spoke to him, and he was not interested in it. 'There's no need to read it to me', he said. 'I can guess what they said. They probably said: "How could O'Casey know anything about it?"'

He said that he did not need to see the Abbey production at the Aldwych Theatre[1] to give an opinion about it. 'I judge from the world around me. I can see things and understand things and give opinions about things without seeing them. It is a well-known fact for years now that the Abbey has deteriorated. Who is going to say it has not? It has been going on for years.

'Years ago[2] a public protest was made from the audience against the quality of the production and acting in *The Plough and the Stars*. About a week before the Abbey Company went to London a serious article appeared in the monthly magazine, *Focus*,[3] and the writer actually suggested that they should be prevented from going because of the inferior quality of the production. Why didn't the Abbey directors exclaim against this article?'

Mr O'Casey went on to say that many visitors to Ireland dropped in to see him when they came to Britain and they all said that the Abbey was a sorry spectacle.[4]

'What the hell does Blythe know about the drama, anyway?', O'Casey asked. 'He knows nothing about acting or drama. He may be a good manager in a financial sense but he doesn't understand the drama. I have a letter from him in which he condemns himself. He says they weed

* John Howard, '"Abbey Has Been Deteriorating for Years", Says Sean O'Casey', *Irish Times* (Dublin), 4 July 1964, pp. 1, 11.

out a number of plays that have been submitted until they have about ten
left. Then they read these again and select two or three which they
consider to be the best and they finally select the one they think will fit
the house. That is no way for a national theatre to select a play. They
neglect what they think would be a better play if they think it would not
make money.

'It doesn't matter if I was at the Aldwych or not. They had to get three
of the old troupers – Eileen Crowe, May Craig and Eric Gorman – to
play three very important parts. Why had they to do that if the quality of
the acting in the present company is so fine as Mr Blythe and the other
directors make out? If they are producing such fine actors why had they
to get a man of over eighty and a woman of seventy to take over these
parts? Will the directors answer that?'

O'Casey seemed in great form as we spoke and before finishing he said
he would like to tell people to go to the Abbey and judge for themselves.

'One last thing . . . it has not been pleasasnt to have to say these things
about the Abbey. I would love to see the Abbey the finest company in the
world. That is my feeling.'

Mr Blythe, when asked about O'Casey's charge that in a letter to the
playwright he had said that they eventually chose a play that they
thought would fill the house, and therefore chose plays for their money
potential, commented:

'That is entirely wrong. We never reject a play on the basis that it may
not make money, when we find that it is a good play. If we think that a
play is good we give it a chance whether we feel it would fill the house or
not. But we *do* recall plays that have filled the house and we do *not* recall
plays that have not. That is a different thing. It would be senseless to
recall a play that has proved it will not make money and that the public
have rejected. I may add that if there is a good play that we think will not
fill the house at its first presentation, we may not put it on immediately,
but eventually we *will* put it on.'

A statement issued by the directors of the Abbey Theatre indicated that
'The directors of the Abbey Theatre have read with great interest Mr
Sean O'Casey's announcement that they have been dead for years. They
would like to assure Mr O'Casey that, as in the case of Mark Twain, the
rumour is greatly exaggerated. Dead men tell no tales, not even that of
Juno or *Plough* or *Gunman*.

'Mr O'Casey's statement that the directors know nothing about
acting or the Drama is patently absurd. The longstanding involvement
of each of them in various aspects of the work of the theatre is common
knowledge.

'As to Mr O'Casey's reference to the managing director, the point is
that his relationship with the Board is precisely that of the managing

director of any ordinary business establishment, except that the directors of the Abbey Theatre have always taken a bigger share of control of its work than is customary in a commercial concern. In particular, they have always retained control of the two most important functions in the theatre, the acceptance and selection of plays, and the assessment of the producer's casting proposals.

'In spite of differences of opinion with Mr O'Casey, the directors share his enthusiasm for the idea of making the Abbey Theatre the best in the world, and all their efforts are directed towards the end.'[5]

NOTES

Sean O'Casey (1880–1964), playwright. His early realistic plays (1923–6) portrayed life in the Dublin slums. His next play, *The Silver Tassie* (1928), was rejected by the Abbey Theatre. This was a bitter blow to O'Casey and estranged him from the directors. He wrote seven further full-length plays, but none of them had either the success or the critical acclaim of his first three. His six autobiographical volumes [reprt in 2 vols: *Autobiographies* (London: Macmillan, 1963)] throw a great deal of light on his relationship with the Abbey.

1. The Abbey Theatre presented *Juno and the Paycock* at the Aldwych Theatre, London, on 20 Apr 1964, during the World Theatre Season. See Peter Daubeny's recollections of this production, p. 195.

2. In 1947, when the Abbey Theatre revived *The Plough and the Stars*.

3. John Gossen, 'Fit for a Festival?', *Focus* (Dublin), 7 (Apr 1964) 78. In this article Gossen said, 'The current production – judged professionally – is lamentable.'

4. Similar views were expressed by the actor and director, Jack MacGowran, *The Times* (London), 18 Mar 1967, p. 7 (interview).

5. See also Ronald Ayling, 'Sean O'Casey and the Abbey Theatre Company', *Irish University Review*, 3 (Spring 1973) 5–16.

The Abbey Theatre*

GERARD FAY

To write about the Abbey Theatre is, for me, almost an act of autobiography. My father, Frank Fay, was one of the founders, with his brother Willie, and the other Willy (Yeats) and Lady G. From the strictest historical point of view I suppose that neither Yeats nor Lady Gregory was a 'founder'. They came in, as did Miss Horniman, after the

* *Ireland of the Welcomes* (Dublin), 15 (July–Aug 1966), 28–32.

amateur group started by the Fay brothers had been going quite a while and had taken over from the Irish Literary Theatre with such important plays as AE [George Russell]'s *Deirdre*, Yeats' *Kathleen Ni Houlihan* and a whole series of plays including one in Irish at the Camden Street Theatre which had been adapted from some sort of warehouse. When the company and its theatre were thoroughly well established (at the Abbey, with Miss Horniman's money) Frank and his brother Willie Fay left in 1908 after a stupid quarrel contrived by lesser persons who thought the Fays were getting too big for their boots.[1]

Willie Fay never returned to Dublin, except once in the 1920s to be interviewed for the job of first director of Radio Éireann, which was then known as 2 RN. Frank settled again in Dublin after wandering all over England in minor touring companies and made a living as a teacher and producer with occasional leading parts at the Abbey. I went to all his performances and played in several of them, under Lennox Robinson as director. I have been going to the Abbey ever since, so I might say that my connection with it and sometimes my despair about it cover forty-five years.

It is possible, without being fanciful, to trace a direct line of descent from Dublin's early Abbey – the theatre of which I have direct personal knowledge – to London's national theatre, of which I also have quite a bit of knowledge since I have been writing about it steadily since 1936. Miss Annie Horniman, whose family were of the big tea company, paid for the building of the original Abbey, out of the profits of some shares she had in the Hudson's Bay Company. When she left after a long drawn out struggle against Yeats, Lady Gregory, Synge and the Fays she went to Manchester and started a repertory theatre called the Gaiety. Lilian Baylis[2] in London used the Gaiety as her model for the Old Vic. Here is a curious parallel – the first performance of the company which became the Irish National Theatre Society was in the Coffee Palace, Townsend Street, Dublin, which was part of the temperance movement of those days, still running on the inspiration left behind by Father Mathew. The Old Vic was originally called the Royal Victoria Coffee Music Hall, and was part of an exactly similar English temperance movement. What the world theatre owes to tea and coffee!

The Old Vic, originally devoted entirely to Shakespeare, spread out as a general repertory theatre, spawned an opera company and a ballet (now one of the greatest dance companies in the world).[3] And the Old Vic was the main foundation on which the national theatre is to be built. When London gets its £10 million theatre on the South Bank, it will be possible to follow the line over from the Liffey-side to Thames-side.[4]

The Abbey's influence ranges much more widely. One of its early historians, Fr Dawson Byrne in *The Story of Ireland's National Theatre: The Abbey Theatre, Dublin* (Talbot Press, Dublin, 1929) attributes the start of the 'little theatre' movement in the United States to the inspiration of the Abbey and gives a list several hundred long of 'little theatres' which, he said, 'have sprung from the Abbey' – among the most famous the Washington Square Players which became the American Theatre Guild and the Provincetown Players which first unleashed the power of Eugene O'Neill on the world theatre. It is certain that Abbey influence, sometimes directly applied by the Fay brothers, was strong in the British repertory theatres such as Birmingham, Liverpool, Leeds, Oxford, Cambridge and Glasgow. I have heard it said that Edward Stirling's English Theatre in Paris was modelled in part on the Abbey and I knew of a plan for the Fays to go and play there, but it fell through, and my first visit to France had to be made in less artistic circumstances. It is also certain on the other side of the picture that the French theatre was a strong influence on the Abbey, for much of the style of acting and production was based on Frank Fay's enthusiasm for Antoine's Théâtre Libre which in its origins and methods had many resemblances to the early Abbey.

Three cities, London, New York and Hollywood, have drawn heavily on the Abbey for acting talent, sometimes by drawing away with tempting salaries the best actors and actresses, sometimes through young, partly trained players who lean heavily for reputation on a brief stay at the Abbey and a thin plating of its technique.

NOTES

Gerard Fay is a journalist and drama critic, and the author of *The Abbey Theatre, Cradle of Genius* (Dublin: Clonmore & Reynolds, 1958).

On 18 July 1966, the fifteenth anniversary of the burning of the Abbey Theatre, the new Abbey opened its doors. Designed by the Irish architect Michael Scott, it occupies the site of its predecessor in Lower Abbey Street. The first production was a gala presentation of the Abbey's history down to the burning, dealing with the plays, playwrights, actors and actresses who made the theatre famous.

1. Cf. 'It was a clash of personalities. Yeats immensely admired his work as a comedian, and his brother's as a beautiful speaker of verse, and the comedian brother had contributed so much to Lady Gregory's comedies. But neither she nor Yeats were disposed to let the reins slip from their hands. It is difficult, thirty and more years after, to judge who was most in the right; doubtless there were wrongs on both sides' (Lennox Robinson, *Ireland's Abbey Theatre: A History 1899–1951* (London: Sidgwick & Jackson, 1951) p. 56). William G. Fay and Frank Fay resigned from the Abbey Theatre on 13 Feb 1908.

2. Lilian Baylis (1874–1937), English theatre manager.

3. Sadler's Wells.

4. An issue and a dream since the time of David Garrick (1717–79), a British

national theatre finally came to realisation only in 1963, when the Old Vic formally ceased to exist, and in its place a new National Theatre Company moved into its premises in the Waterloo Road, pending the building of a special theatre designed for it on a new site on the South Bank. The new National Theatre opened on 4 Oct 1976.

The New Abbey Theatre*

WALTER MACKEN

How do you feel about your new appointment, Mr Macken?

My feelings about this appointment are mixed. As a writer who has lived for fifteen years in the West[1] it is quite a wrench to go and live again in a city. On the other hand, anyone who has ever worked for the Abbey will tell you of the sort of disease it engenders, a sort of love–hate relationship.

It has an attraction for people who have ever worked there, which cannot be put into words. A good number of the company are my friends; we know one another well, and I'm looking forward to working with them again.

What exactly are your functions?

Only time will tell. Everyone will have to become involved in the new theatre, you who ask the questions, and your readers, with the directors, the shareholders, the company, the technical staff, the office staff; in fact everybody in the country who has the interest of the theatre at heart.

After all, the new Abbey will belong to the people, since in a way it was their money that made it possible. It will be up to us, inside, to aim at high standards of production, acting and presentation, and the people outside to support and criticise.

So as I see it, one of my main functions will be to have everybody in Ireland talking, eating, writing, dreaming Abbey Theatre.

Do you consider the new post as an indication of a change in policy or just as an extension to it?

You must realise that the Abbey Theatre as such has been away from home and wandering in lodgings for a long time, fourteen years.

---

*Interview by Colm Cronin; condensed from *The Irish Press* (Dublin), 27 Jan 1966, p. 7.

Conditions were not easy. The Queen's Theatre was a difficult one to function in successfully for many reasons.

Going into a new theatre will mean part of the battle won already. The basic policy of the Abbey will not change. It was created to provide a place where Irish drama could be encouraged and performed. This will remain its primary policy.

Accepting that you will be greatly responsible for the selection of new plays, do you, as an Abbey playwright, think that you know the type of play that the Abbey needs?

Who knows what 'type' of play any theatre needs? The age of O'Casey, Synge, Yeats, was a different time. You had all the drama of poverty, insurrection, patriotism, Irish mythology. These are different times. They will provide different themes, which our playwrights will have to search out for themselves.

They will have to look around at this odd, modern Ireland and see the drama in it. It's there, somewhere, but it needs their inspiration to find it. While man lives he is dramatic. It is just that playwrights have to look at the change in his environment.

What do you really think of the present state of Irish playwriting, and is it all that bad?

As long as young men are writing plays, I don't care what kind of plays they are writing. All plays cannot be works of genius. Most theatres in the world have to get by on good plays, competently written, until the outstanding playwright comes along.

No person can become a really good playwright overnight. It takes time. But there must be somewhere that he can see his plays performed, so that he can learn from them to do better.

Would the presentation of contemporary European plays help the lethargic condition prevalent in our theatre today?

I think a national theatre should display to its own people the arts and cultures of other nations. Contemporary drama is an expression, as seen through the eyes of the artiste, of the lives and loves and hatreds and moods of his own people.

You could get a deeper insight into the people of Finland, Russia, Scandinavia, Italy, Spain, France, etc., by seeing them through the eyes of their playwrights, than you would be travelling ignorantly.

Is enough being done to encourage new writers?

I don't think enough is being done to encourage new writers. Having once been a new writer myself, I can sense what should be done in the way of encouragement, and will try and do it.[2]

Have you any opinions on the frequency of revivals at the Abbey, and how do you feel about the staging of the theatre's classics?

In any repertory theatre, revivals are at times necessary, depending on the success of new plays, or their abrupt failure, you must always have plays to fall back on. The more prosperous the state of Irish playwriting becomes, the less need there will be to fall back on revivals.

When you ask about the theatre's classics, you are talking about the theatre's traditions. They are part of the foundations and they must be displayed at the ripe times. You build on tradition, learn from it, but you must not become obsessed by it.

What do you think of state-subsidisation of the theatre?

At the present day, there are very few countries which do not provide some form of subsidisation for their theatres. The idea of the state subsidising art used to be the bogey of our generation, but in practice it has worked fairly well in other countries. The ideal subsidisation is the support of the people.

NOTES

Walter Macken (1915–67), playwright, novelist and actor. When he was seventeen he joined the Taibhdhearc na Gaillimhe, the Irish language theatre in Galway. In the 1940s and 1950s, he was a prominent Abbey actor. He also played leading roles in the film versions of his own *Home Is the Hero* and of Brendan Behan's *The Quare Fellow*. Early in 1966, he became artistic adviser to the Abbey Theatre, but he gave up the job after a few months to devote full time to writing.

1. Walter Macken was born and died in Galway.

2. Cf. 'There is nothing in Ireland to encourage anybody to write a play, except his own dedication' (Wesley Burrowes, 'Writers Are Not Encouraged', *Irish Times* (Dublin), 18 Mar 1968, p. 10).

Cyril Cusack Talks*

FERGUS LINEHAN

Cyril Cusack is small and neat and, in conversation, shows the same apparent abstraction, punctuated with sudden twinkles, which marks his style as an actor.

Acting is, of course, what he has spent the greater part of his life doing, both his mother, who is still alive, and his stepfather having been in the profession. He began as a small boy playing in a silent film based on Kickham's[1] *Knocknagow* and shot, unusually for the period, on location at Mullinahone in 1916 or 1917.

'I like to think', he says, 'that right from the beginning I was a pro. I was a plump little boy, but I was playing the part of a lad who has been evicted with his family and was starving. I was meant to sit with my father in the film on the side of the road and the lady of the Big House gives us soda bread and buttermilk, which I was to wolf down. I was wearing corduroy breeches with holes in the back and I sat on a clump of nettles. But I sat my ground until the scene was shot. Similarly, I was touring in Oxford recently with the British National Theatre in *Spring Awakening* and the hotel went on fire. The only think I reached for was the waistcoat I wore in my entrance in the play.'

Acting may have been in the blood – there is an ancestral connection with the famous music-hall comedian Dan Leno, too – but it was not the only thing he ever wanted to be. Journalism beckoned at one stage, and the Indian Civil Service ('whatever that was. My mother thought it would be good'). Then there was a period as a student at UCD,[2] where he was a contemporary of President Ó Dalaigh,[3] and an ambition to be a barrister ('another form of acting, I suppose'). But the money was not forthcoming and a long and distinguished career in the theatre and films got under way.

It is a career which has taken him all over the world and made him probably the best-known Irish actor abroad, but he still regards Ireland as his home. 'I get an enormous welcome in odd areas when I come back', he says. 'People stopping me in the street and that. Mind you I get it in cockney-land, too. There they say: "Haven't seen you on the telly lately." Here it's more likely to be: "Jaysus, you must be makin' a packet!"'

Irish Times (Dublin), 3 Jan 1975, p. 10.

Despite his ancestry and the fact that he is the father of two actress daughters,[4] he says that the stage is not a profession which he would advise people to follow. 'It's true', he admits, 'that, as Father Ronald Knox said, it's the most brotherly and sisterly profession in the world, but the actor has a constant problem of personal identity – I mean the actor who's an artist, not a handyman. If you asked me for my New Year resolution, it would be to find out who I am.'

He speaks with affection of the days of the theatrical touring companies and regrets that they have largely passed. 'A touring company was really a communications centre. I remember how when we'd be going down from the station the people in small country towns would wave to us from across half doors. A training? If it was, it was because one found one's audience and had a relationship with it. Nowadays acting has been demoted by the cult of the director, which has infiltrated the theatre, possibly because of the influence of the cinema. The academic influence hasn't been a good one either.

'When people asked me whether I preferred the theatre or films, I used to say that all the media were the same to me. Now the relationship with a live audience seems to me to count for more. The celluloid effect tends to be a superficial one. They say six million people see you when you act in a film, it may only be 600 in a play. But the effect on the 600 may be truer and more lasting. The stage can be spiritual as well as physical. Nowadays the physical aspect – in the line of sex anyway – has overstepped the line of true communication'.

He speaks too of the sense of tradition that exists among actors, an invisible thing that passes down so that they feel in communion with the Garricks, the Keans and the Irvings. ('Do you know I was in Bristol recently and the great-grandmother of the landlady I was staying with had given a bouquet to Mrs Siddons?')

To the suggestion that this tradition is in danger here, he says: 'Yes, it just seems to hang on by a thread. It's asked, where are the actors of my age? Actors leave this country not for mercenary or career reasons, as is sometimes suggested, but to find artistic fulfillment. In the Abbey there was always a clash between the literary mind and the actors. Yeats wanted a literary theatre, but of course this wasn't and isn't possible. The actors left and made the name of the Abbey famous all over the world. I've worked with or met every member of that early company and I'm convinced that the true founders of the Abbey were the Fay brothers. Nowadays the clash seems to have developed into something worse, though. It seems now to be on a mercenary level'.

None the less he has no desire himself to get involved again at either the administrative or the directorial level. In his time he has written two plays,[5] had his own company – the first Irish one to play in Paris – and published a volume of poetry,[6] an art which he still practises. 'I try to arrange my thoughts poetically between the times allowed by this ridiculous (twinkle) profession'.

In the end, though, he remains the complete actor, stressing again his belief that the function of the director has been overstressed in the modern theatre and that the actor must re-assert his lost independence, 'not in vanity, or for mere effect or innovation, but in self-assessment'.

Reminiscences are many – *Odd Man Out*, 'a bad book made into a very good film. I nearly fell into a wind machine and was killed while it was being made'. A play about Roger Casement by Roger McHugh, which packed the Theatre Royal in Waterford for a week and then came to Dublin where 'nobody but Mr and Mrs de Valera came for three weeks!'[7]

'An actor only finds ecstatic self-fulfilment about three times in life, though', he says. 'The first time it happened to me was when I was young and playing in Eugene O'Neill's *Ah, Wilderness!* here and in London. George Bernard Shaw came to see it – I remember seeing his silver beard in the audience. He said afterwards that he never went to sleep once. A second time was much more recently, the production of Chekhov's *The Cherry Orchard* at the Abbey in 1968. Madame Knebel, who came from the Moscow Arts to direct it, knew the Chekhov family. The first time we met her she said through the interpreter – she only spoke Russian – "you are the born Gayev". It was one of those miracles, Chekhov, you know, recognised the creativity of the actor. After the first production of *The Cherry Orchard* he said to Stanislavsky,[8] who had played Gayev, that it was not as he had conceived the part, but better.

'The third time I had this feeling was in between the others, and oddly enough it was on celluloid. It was as the Whiskey Priest in the film of Graham Greene's *The Power and the Glory*. An extract from it was shown here recently in a television programme about Greene. I met three priests in the Shelbourne[9] here and one of them said to me that it was the best retreat he's ever had.'

NOTES

Cyril Cusack (1910–   ), actor, poet and playwright. He acted at the Abbey Theatre from 1932 until 1945, when he formed his own company, Cyril Cusack Productions, with which he worked both in Ireland and internationally until 1961. He later returned to the Abbey as a shareholder at the invitation of the Minister for Finance. In 1968 he revived Boucicault at the Abbey and then took the production to the World Theatre Season at the Aldwych Theatre, London. When he gave this interview, he was appearing in *The Vicar of Wakefield* at the Abbey. For more on Cusack see 'Every Week a Different School', in Des Hickey and Gus Smith, *A Paler Shade of Green* (London: Leslie Frewin, 1972) pp. 23–35.

1. Charles J. Kickham (1828–82), novelist and Fenian. Today he is remembered mainly for his long novel *Knocknagow; or, The Homes of Tipperary* (1879), which has gone through many editions and is still in print.

2. University College, Dublin.

3. Cearbhall Ó Dalaigh (1911–78), fifth President of Ireland (in succession to Erskine Childers) from 1974 until his resignation in 1976.

4. Cusack's eldest daughter Sinéad, who began her career at the Abbey Theatre, appeared with her father in the films *David Copperfield* and *Toys*, and opposite Peter Sellers in *Hoffman*. She is now a member of the Royal Shakespeare Company. His second daughter Sorcha won good notices for her performance in Harold Pinter's *The Homecoming* at Trinity College, Dublin. She was later a member of the Abbey company, appearing as Nora Clitheroe to her father's Fluther Good in the 1976 Jubilee production of *The Plough and the Stars*. His third daughter Niamh was given a tiny part in the film *I Was Happy Here*.

5. *Tareis an Aifreann* (Dublin Gate Theatre, 1942) and *Mr O* (Dublin Theatre Festival, 1961).

6. *Timepieces* (Dublin: Poetry Ireland, 1970).

7. Cyril Cusack Productions presented *Roger Casement*, by Roger McHugh and Alfred Noyes, at the Gaiety Theatre, Dublin, on 10 Mar 1958.

8. Konstantin Stanislavsky (1863–1938), who produced and staged Chekhov's plays at the Moscow Art Theatre.

9. Shelbourne Hotel, Dublin.

I Modelled Joan on My Mother*

SIOBHÁN McKENNA

I came to the Abbey Theatre from Galway in 1944. The first English play in which Denis[1] and I appeared together was *The End House* by Joseph Tomelty. Two years later we were married and we began making films. While Denis was in *Hungry Hill*, I was in *Odd Man Out*. When I arrived at the Abbey Theatre Barry Fitzgerald, Sara Allgood and others of that period had gone and, unfortunately, Yeats and Lady Gregory had gone. But I feel that the actors who were there when I arrived were far greater because they were now professionals and had the best of both worlds. I am not denying talents such as Barry Fitzgerald's, but I had never seen him on the stage and could not imagine him being anything like F. J. McCormick. McCormick was the greatest actor I have ever clapped eyes on. And when I saw May Craig in *The Words on the Window Pane* by Yeats,

*Extracted from Des Hickey and Gus Smith, *A Paler Shade of Green* (London: Leslie Frewin, 1972) pp. 49–51.

who had directed her in the play originally,[2] she was overwhelming. And there were other extraordinary people like Cyril Cusack, Brid Ni Loinsigh, Liam Redmond, Harry Brogan, Fred Johnson, Denis and Mick Dolan, who in his own way was as perfect as McCormick. There were so many talented people that I could never understand how I managed to get my nose in edgeways.

When I first went to the Abbey it was not in my nature to call anybody 'Mister' or 'Missus' or 'Miss' because it was the Galway tradition always to call people by their first names to show that one loved them. My father was always called Eoin. But I respected the Abbey Players and if I went up to the greenroom and a senior player, as they were termed, was there I would think twice before I went in. They called me 'Miss McKenna', which I found very strange and foreign, and then I remember Mick Dolan suddenly calling me 'Siobhán'. You had to earn your place.

During my first year at the Abbey I was asked to star in a film, *I See A Dark Stranger*, which Deborah Kerr later did. I went to McCormick and he advised me: 'Please stay for at least three years. You could become an overnight star, but I also think you could become a real actress.' I turned the part down, although it was a leading part, and my first screen appearance was to be a tiny one in *Hungry Hill*. I was able to do it during the Abbey holidays when Denis did *Odd Man Out*. We had arranged to get married in Galway at this time and when they wanted to build up my part in *Hungry Hill*, I made the excuse that I wanted to go to Paris with my father because he had not had a holiday for a long time.

In those days I used to read the notices. If I got a good notice I would be up the stairs to Ernest Blythe's office. I used to get 5 shilling rises and within the space of two years I was on top salary. When I was earning £2 5 shillings a week my flat was costing me 15 shillings and that was simply because my landlady in Northbrook Road liked me.

She gave me a marvellous room with wood panelling and a big fire. I never told my father and mother what I was earning. I had come up to Dublin to study for my MA and had drifted into the Abbey. My mother used to send me farm eggs because they were fresh; she never realised she was sending me my food. I would live on bread and butter and egg and tea and on payday treat myself to a bun in the Country Shop in Stephen's Green. When I became ill my cousin came to see me. I had been in bed for three days and when she opened the cupboard it was bare.

You had to supply your own clothes at the Abbey for modern plays. Eithne Dunne, who used to play sophisticated parts, had left when I arrived and they probably thought: 'Well, here's a girl who could dress herself.' May Craig was generous to me and I shall not forget her kindness. She would give me her pearls, and when I played the Woman from Rathmines in *The Plough and the Stars* she gave me a long fur coat and made me a hat with a feather in it. McCormick and Cusack and Denis were in that production.[3] When I played a very sophisticated part I wore my little black dress and May, who had been sent a present of a hat by friends in New York, said: 'I have the perfect thing for you, Siobhán.' It was a toque of little flowers in pink, mauve and blue which she set on one side of my head. I remember it so well. But I told her: 'But you can't give me this. You haven't worn it yet. People will say "Look at May Craig in the hat Siobhán was wearing in that play!"' So she went out and bought pieces of tulle and a kind of crown and turned it into a new hat for me.

I think actors should go abroad for experience. In those days once you left the Abbey you did not come back, and that was much too harsh. Yet when Denis and I got married and went away to make films they were very amicable. We never left the Abbey officially. We were never rebels. We have both gone back to play there. When we were offered contracts in Hollywood, Denis thought it might be pleasant for a while, especially to have one's own swimming-pool and all that. But I would not consider it. I had heard the stories about Sara Allgood and Barry Fitzgerald, of how they had gone out for one picture and found the life so comfortable that they had not come back. Apart from Barry Fitzgerald, the great ones settled down to playing little parts. Years later I went to Hollywood to make a television film. It was neither city nor country and the smog was terrible. I thought: 'My God, where did I get my wisdom?'

NOTES

Siobhán McKenna became one of the postwar Abbey actresses to achieve recognition outside Ireland. The world saw Siobhán McKenna's Joan of Arc and Pegeen Mike. She made an occasional return to the Abbey Theatre in the late 1960s – as the Countess in *The Cherry Orchard* and as Cass in Brian Friel's *The Loves of Cass McGuire*. In 1970, she achieved an especial ambition to present her favourite Irish writers to audiences outside Ireland when her one-woman show, *Here Are Ladies*, was staged at the Criterion Theatre, London. It was after the run of this show that she gave this interview.

1. Denis O'Dea (1903–78), her husband. Like Eileen Crowe and F. J. McCormick, Siobhán McKenna and Denis O'Dea had married during their time in the Abbey Theatre.

2. At the Abbey Theatre on 17 Nov 1930. May Craig played Mrs Henderson, coached by Yeats himself. See Liam Miller, *The Noble Drama of W. B. Yeats* (Dublin: Dolmen Press, 1977) p. 288.

3. In Sept 1945. F. J. McCormick played Fluther Good, Cyril Cusack played the Young Covey and Denis O'Dea played Jack Clitheroe. It was directed by Frank Dermody.

The Abbey and the Future*

FERGUS LINEHAN. Well, we'll start with you, Tomás MacAnna, as a present member of the Abbey company. What effect you hope the new theatre will have on you, your work and the work of the Abbey in general?

THOMÁS MacANNA. Well, first we start with the big advantage of moving into a new theatre, designed specially for plays, a building without any of the handicaps which one associates with the theatre in the olden times. Of course, the Queen's was a variety theatre, which was meant to be only a temporary abode, an abode which lasted for years. In the new theatre the actual operating costs will be cut and, of course, the new facilities are going to make it easier for us to devise new and exciting productions.

LINEHAN. Are you satisfied with the theatre from a technical point of view, from what you've seen of it?

MacANNA. From a technical point of view, I'm going to talk now as one who hasn't worked in the theatre as such, just gone along and seen it. I think it's going to be very satisfactory. There is the novelty of a new theatre, new paint, new walls. A theatre where the dust isn't accumulating on your script when you leave it down for two minutes. I feel the main thing about moving into a new theatre is this: that you have an opportunity of breaking with a certain tradition of writing. You must remember to a certain extent, we have the players (there's never been a shortage of good players in Dublin), set designers, technicians and so on. The question is have we got the dramatists who are content to devote more time and not give us once more a re-hash of themes and characters which we see over and over again?

LINEHAN: Could I ask you, Seamus, do you think this is what we're going to get from the new Abbey, something new, in fact?

SEAMUS KELLY. Tomás MacAnna spoke about need for new dramatists and the adequacy of current actors. I didn't hear him say anything about need for new managements, need for a new directorial slant. In my quite honest opinion, until there is a complete overthrow of the people in power at the Abbey at the moment, and there's no point in putting a tooth in this, the new Abbey will offer us nothing better than the old Abbey outside the mechanics it has.

Irish Times (Dublin), 18 July 1966, p. 8; 19 July 1966, p. 8; and 20 July 1966, p. 10.

LINEHAN. Hilton, what do you think about this question of management – do you think it's essential?

HILTON EDWARDS. I would say it's not only a change of policy. I'm very impressed by what Mr MacAnna said about the promise of new techniques and so on. As I see it at the moment, not knowing the new theatre, I have to bear in mind that the theatre is only an instrument. Now I would say that the first experience of this instrument would be a rather awkward one – there would be a period of trying to get used to it. Against this, there is the great novelty of an audience coming into a new building, and I think that the first six months will be a sort of research as far as the audience is concerned by which time the company should have got used to the new instrument. On the other hand, I don't think any theatre, or any theatre movement, is dependent on an instrument, any more than the public is really dependent on it. I'll put it another way. I understand that very, very fine photographs can be taken with a very, very primitive camera, and I'd like it better to see a very fine photographer moving a very primitive camera, than a less skilled photographer getting tied up with the more complicated machine. Therefore I'm still concerned with the company, the two Ps, the policy and the personality, more than I am impressed necessarily with a theatre.

JIM FITZGERALD. One thing I'd like to say. What astonishes me about the architecture is that it seats 600 plus people; this to me expresses an immense pessimism about the theatre, that a national theatre in a country whose theatrical traditions are enormous should be built in such a manner that large space is given to the stage and the auditorium is cut down to such a size. Is it actually possible that a management of a national theatre should build what amounts to only 250 seats more than the Gate, which was built out of nothing?

MacANNA. I myself would be quite happy to have an auditorium of 1000, 1200. But I think this was discussed pretty thoroughly and I would agree with an audience of approximately 700. What we are concerned with particularly is the intimacy of the play in this auditorium and we feel that the whole point of the old Abbey – one of its advantages was that it was a most intimate theatre to play in.

FITZGERALD. But architecturally nowadays, this problem has been solved.

BARRY CASSIN. Chichester, Nottingham, I think.

MacANNA. Quite possibly so, but nevertheless I do think that a 700 maximum auditorium is to my mind good for Dublin.

KELLY. I don't think the physical dimensions of a theatre matter all that much. Let's get back to policy. I think the Abbey, certainly the new national theatre, should have a basic repertory of, for want of a better term, Irish classics, and play them like the Comédie Française.

MacANNA. That's what we intend to do.

KELLY. Well, no one's said that.

MacANNA. We're back to the subject of the Queen's. The overheads were absolutely enormous, the overheads in regard to hiring lighting, staff and so on. The fact of the matter is, Seamus, that if a play went in the Queen's, you ran it for as long as it possibly could take. We had runs in the Queen's of astronomical length. We had *This Other Eden*, I think it went for something like thirty-two weeks, we had *Home is the Hero*. This was necessary – it was not policy of the Abbey, it was policy of the Abbey in the Queen's. It was survival. The result was that a play which took in money was allowed to take in as much as it could possibly at the box office, so that we could pay the rent, the overheads, the overdraft.

KELLY. Well then, why were so many plays admitted that weren't worth a damn moneywise?

MacANNA. Well there, you're asking me a question which I cannot answer. I have no way of knowing when I read a script, when I work in a play, when I'm at the dress rehearsal of the play, and I'm sure that every producer present will agree with me, that that play isn't going to fall flat on its face in one night, or pick up and go. We don't know.

KELLY. We are outnumbered by four directors. Would you people agree that the new national theatre, in putting on O'Casey's, and putting on Synge's and putting on Yeats' and putting on, if they do, Gregory's or even T. C. Murray's, should try very hard to mount and play them as they were mounted and played in the classical Abbey?

MacANNA. No. Under no circumstances.

KELLY. That's what I meant by the Comédie Française.

MacANNA. Imitations can kill a theatre stone dead, imitation of your own past. The hand of the past has reached out many times. I'm not worried about the Comédie Française, I'm worried about the Abbey.

EDWARDS. Forgive me, even the Comédie Française, quite some time ago, had to make a break from their very early tradition. I think taking the best in one's tradition . . . and retaining it, is a very, very important thing. I think that if one just remains in tradition one becomes a museum and nothing else. What interests me is this: I feel the need in this city, of course, of the Abbey with its here-again traditional policy. But the very fact that I started my own policy some thirty-five years ago makes me feel the need in this city for something more than just gazing perpetually at what I might disrespectfully call the national navel.

T. P. McKENNA. I haven't said anything so far, I think we'd better get down to basic facts, and I'm going to set down a few. It should be possible to discuss the Abbey, to be inside the Abbey, the ex-Abbey, and to discuss it on altruistic motives, and that is from the point of view of the past and the future, without regard to personality or politics. I'm going to propose two things: one is that the Abbey has lost the confidence of Irish writers: secondly, that it has lost a following or audience. Now these are two inescapable facts, and from these must come two conclusions. In moving to a new building we could discuss at length the merits of the building – but the building is now a fact, and it is a bit late for that – but taking the building for what it's worth, once you move into it, as Hilton says, a building itself does not necessarily mean it's going to be a stimulation, and that it's going to change everything else. The two problems which face the Abbey are to regain the confidence of Irish writers and to regain a following or an audience. Now I think this is the big question that should be discussed here – how can this best be done – because I think nobody can deny that this is not true.

FITZGERALD. A Board of directors is the only answer, it's hatefully obvious that it's an old man's theatre.

KELLY. You wouldn't suggest that the theatre regain the confidence of Irish actors as well?

McKENNA. Well, that as well, but I think that is, to a lesser extent, important.

FITZGERALD. It seems to me, it should be clear to almost everyone in this room that you can't any longer, in a population of our size, enclose into a hot house a national theatre. It must be possible for Barry Cassin or Jim Fitzgerald or Tyrone Guthrie or Hugh Hunt, who was there earlier, or for new young directors to work there. It must be possible for actors of world fame whom the Abbey claims. It should be possible for a younger Board, or a more intelligent Board, or even an older Board who are actually theatrically minded rather than business-minded, it should be possible for them to invite all the available talent, even the rather suspicious –

MacANNA. I'll say something to Jim Fitzgerald here and now. It will be possible. You may think I'm talking through my hat but I know, I can't explain how I know this thing. I know that the new generation there and people who are moving in there will make this possible.

CASSIN. Surely Tom MacAnna's own position here must be the clearest on this. Recently you did *Yerma* and you did the Brecht, which from the traditional Abbey line is quite a break.

EDWARDS. The new policy will not include the strict inclusion of only Irish plays? I think this may be necessary to get an audience back, but one thing I'd like to suggest. I think that what is lacking at the present moment is that we are still remaining in what I would call the early theatre. Now when I first came here, there was a young nation, a young theatre, a child-like theatre, now I think it's sort of at the teenage stage, in which it's a little adolescent and a little wilful, but I think that very, very soon we've got to look forward to it becoming adult, and I think to become adult, to put ourselves on a par with the rest of the theatres of the world. We've got to attract our audiences. And this doesn't only mean in the material we choose, but in the manner we choose.

McKENNA. This is to be the national theatre. Whether it's to be on the old principle of the National Theatre Society, which was a private company, or a national theatre, properly subsidised with a Board of directors, and an artistic director and all that goes with it. I think, trying to be constructive, that we must take a look at the other national theatres, and the nearest and the newest one is probably the national theatre which was set up in England, which is accepted now as being a success; it is running to ninety-eight per cent houses and it has a policy. Now to my mind, the new Abbey Theatre must have an articulated policy. They must declare what their intentions are: it mustn't be something vague: 'We hope to do this or that' – it must be, here and now, a completely articulate policy which might suggest containing the best of the past with a new vista for the future.

What happened with the national theatre in England was that they appointed as artistic director an accomplished experienced man of the theatre and he was complemented by a literary director so that, side by side, you had a man who had in one sense the confidence of the writers, and on the other side the confidence of theatrical people. Now, this has been conspicuously absent in twenty-five, thirty five years of the Abbey.

EDWARDS. This must be done by people. May I suggest that the building won't do this; the only thing that can do this is people. As I said, policy and personality. Now one's got to find the kind of people who will dedicate themselves to this, who are capable of teaching, of leading, of creating style and selection. Now, I am certain they are in the country. Can they be made to be incorporated in the Abbey? Can they be made to work in a team together? Who's going to do this? The only way you can really do this is by two things: (a) dedication, or (b) cash. Now, dedication lasts for a certain number of years as I happen to know, and then, rather like cash, one becomes bankrupt of it. I'm inclined to become a bit bankrupt of dedication.

McKENNA. But surely, the virtue of a national theatre must be, as you say, dedication and cash, and that's where subsidy is absolutely essential.

KELLY. As a non-cash-paying customer of all your theatres, could I ask you, particularly the four directors who are present to give me six ideas for plays for your new national theatre?

FITZGERALD. I'll give you an indication of what might be done, without limiting myself to six plays. Point one, there should be an area of contact involving the universities, and going backwards from them to the schools. A second thing a national theatre should do is to keep abreast of developments, especially in a small country where experimentation is limited to some degree by finance. It should keep abreast by doing European plays which we haven't seen – Dürrenmatt, Frisch and so on. We have not seen the *Marat/Sade*. It's our business, if we have a national theatre, to show these (and most of the time failing) to do, but he taught European theatre how to handle a total theatre. I would also like to see a theatre which is alive – if it has no plays, we'll do poetry readings; if it has no poetry, we'll borrow. It's got a duty to keep its playwrights – our small company of playwrights – aware of European and world developments in theatre. It has not done this so far. It should declare its policy to do that now, or begin to do it. It must encourage Irish playwrights, and the way you encourage them is to show them techniques which our country is too small and too poor to develop ourselves.

McKENNA. I think that Fitz is absolutely on the ball. I think that this is a very articulate and useful statement. This is what I meant earlier, by that word 'education'. Only a theatre subsidised in its own house and being able to afford to do it can bring European theatre to the doorstep here and allow the Irish writers to get into the mainstream of European writing.

EDWARDS. I can no more than Fitz (who has frankly not attempted to do so, without notice), name half-a-dozen plays at this moment, and even if I could, I should hesitate to do so because it should look as if I'm laying down unasked advice to an Abbey Board that isn't present. This may be a heresey from your point of view, but I have always been more concerned in the manner than the subject-matter. I would point out that you can go and see a performance of *Macbeth*, and say, 'Oh, God, this is superb this is wonderful.' Six months later you can go and see another performance of *Macbeth* and think it is dire and ghastly, and not one word of the script has been altered. Now it is quite obvious that the right play and a good play is the *sine qua non*.[1] But I don't think people realise quite as much that the accent to get an audience in, is not only upon the play, the literary theatre, but on the treatment, the personalities playing it, how the play is handled. I remember, not mentioning names again, that the Gate Theatre had been let some time ago, and six plays had been put on there by independent producers (not our management) many many years ago, and these plays all failed. I went to see these plays and I was convinced at the end that none of them had been presented to the public. The words were spoken from the stage, but because of the way they were presented, none of them were fairly represented to the public. It was this that taught me that more than half the battle is *how* a thing is presented, and this I think, brings us back to the fact that while I cannot mention the type of play, I entirely agree with Fitz, that what is wanted is more extended knowledge and a greater variety of approach.

MacANNA. You've asked me for six plays. I'll tell you what we intend to do. We have this opening History of the Abbey – we'll not talk about that at the moment, let it speak for itself. Then we have a new production of *The Plough and the Stars*; then we have a new play by Louis MacNeice which is based on the story of Everyman. It is a modern Everyman which takes place in a television studio. Following on that we have a new play by Michael Judge, who has written a play about the 1916 celebrations.

EDWARDS. I thought 1916 had been mentioned in the Abbey before?

MacANNA. Not 1916, the 1916 Celebrations. It's a new play by Michael Judge who has gained some reputation as a television writer. Following on that we have a new play by the young fellow McKenna, who wrote *The Scatterin'*. This play is about Bantry Bay and the landing of the French, and it combines music, ballet. It is the total theatre that Jim Fitz was talking about a while ago. I also intended to produce *Arturo Ui* by Bertold Brecht, which I was asked to do some time ago.

EDWARDS. If what Mr MacAnna says is correct – I've no reason to believe that he's not absolutely clear and sane – we've very little to worry about, except the fact that I do think in general in the theatre, we are still being very, very shoddy. This may be a lack of money, but I think it is a very, very important thing, because you see, with the films and the television I think the public are becoming alive to the discrepancy between that and our very, very shoddy theatres.

CASSIN. It's more than money – it's lack of ideas.

EDWARDS. But also it's lack of carpentry, lack of painting, it's lack –

KELLY. Hilton, I seem to be doing nothing but stopping you all night, but I would like, before we leave the main line, to ask Barry for his ideas for a new national theatre.

CASSIN. Six plays? I would like to see one of the Greek plays, tragedy or comedy; I would like to see *Marat/Sade* – somebody mentioned that one as being one of the plays of the new wave: and I would like to see a Brecht. Don't ask me to mention names, other than that I'd like to see plays representative of something of the past, and of the movement, or movements that are going on at present. This is the great thing that we lack here from an audience point of view. I think that part of the duty of a national theatre is that it must look further than within its own walls. I'm not naming myself, one way or the other, let's leave me out of this but I think the national theatre should embrace everyone working within the theatre within the nation, it needs them. There should also be the opportunity of, call it a scholarship, call it whatever the hell you like, to send somebody abroad where they'll learn something, then bring them back and get the work out of them by all means.

KELLY. I haven't been deliberately ill-mannered in confining the question to you four fellows. Now I'd like an actor's view. [To T. P. McKenna]: What would you pick?

McKENNA. Well, I don't know why you keep insisting on the six plays, but if I were to choose six I'd choose, first of all, *The Playboy of the Western World*.

KELLY. Thanks be to God somebody's picked an old Abbey play.

McKENNA. I would suggest that for the Abbey, you would have to balance the progressive writing of today with the masterpieces which we've had. I think, there is a danger here that we might get carried away so that people will say: 'Ah, now they want to change the Abbey and all the traditions of our theatre.'

FITZGERALD. Traditions, me . . .! there are no traditions.

McKENNA. There *are* traditions.

FITZGERALD. No, there are *not* traditions for young players.

McKENNA. I'm not talking about traditions of style, or anything so generic as that, but I don't think it's fair to say there aren't any traditions in the Abbey, there is a tradition –

EDWARDS. Of style, too.

McKENNA. Yes, but I think that thing has become fuzzied and lost definition. I mean it's impossible to define what that style was. I've never been able to find out what it was. It seems to have got lost somewhere along the way. You can't get a definition of acting style from reading a book. You might from a film, but I would suggest, with all respect, even acting styles keep changing anyway, even within a company. I'm told the Moscow Arts Company are not quite the same as they were.

EDWARDS. If you're putting the mirror up to nature with national idiosyncrasies, one thing hasn't changed – I've experienced this quite lately. I've had lots of American actors in the last few weeks who were offering themselves for Irish parts and I made what I believe was a discovery. Your average Irish man and your average Irish woman, particularly on, shall we say, a peasant level, is not a person who moves a great deal. He's very static, and I found that nearly all the people who have come to me to play Irish parts in America, have put their hands on their hips, thrust up their heads, and have given such a volatile dancing performance that I have recognised immediately that this has nothing to do with this country. I think it was that strange, curious immobility of the early Abbey players that gave them a certain quality which is still inherent to a certain extent. Now if you are going to do plays which are setting the mirror up to that particular kind of realistic nature of the Irish people, this style, to a certain extent, must continue. The difficulty is to be a master of this style, and the next night to come out and play Shakespeare.

McKENNA. To get back to the six plays. I was going to say, without giving it any thought, I would have, as I said, *The Playboy of the Western World*. I wouldn't agree with the *Marat/Sade* – it was a great production, but I don't think it was a great play. Possibly *Mother Courage*; *The Fire Raisers*, by Max Frisch; *Andorra* by Max Frisch; the O'Casey plays – *The Plough and the Stars* and *Juno*. I think I've mentioned six at random.

LINEHAN. Why not have *Stephen D* and *Philadelphia Here I Come*?

KELLY. Why not *King of the Castle* and see what a good play it really is?

FITZGERALD. A national theatre is a national dilemma. It should be subsidised and as happens in most civilised countries except ours, it should also be free –

KELLY. Artistically free?

FITZGERALD. Artistically free. This is a dilemma which a democracy only can solve where you actually do give money to a theatre. Incidentally, the Abbey is not being built by government money. It's time we said quite clearly on this tape, and it should be printed somewhere in a tiny addendum that this is not a subsidised theatre. It is being built from the Funds of Suitors money, nothing to do with the government whatsoever; it's money robbed temporarily from the dead.

McKENNA. But allocated by the government, let's be fair.

FITZGERALD. Allocated on the unlikely basis that when the dead arise and ask for some of it back, the Abbey is gone for its tea.

McKENNA. What was the deadly thing you were going to say, Fitz?

FITZGERALD. What, in fact, is the Abbey? It is a limited liability company, run by old men. How can this Board understand the absolute need for a theatre to be (a) part of the establishment because the establishment is subsidising it, and (b) the essential point, outside the establishment because the theatre today should be able to criticise, analyse and show what the establishment is doing. This is the whole essence of theatre. If you have an establishment theatre, that's one problem, because the establishment is anti-theatre. But if you have an establishment theatre in which the establishment of forty or fifty years back is running things . . .! And no one can convince me that the astute, honest, patriotic and ever-living Ernest Blythe is not fully in control and will deny, if necessary tomorrow, anything that Tomás MacAnna has said.

MacANNA. I would like to speak as a producer of plays about the future of the Abbey, and I'm not committing anybody, I'm telling you something that I know, something that I know is going to happen. You said something some time ago that the national theatre should use all actors, all Irish actors, all Irish directors and set designers. I don't think it can do this at the one time, but it will do this, and I know that Barry and Fitz will work in the new national theatre. I look forward to the day when Fitz, inside looking out, will say, 'Those blasted critics, they were always against the Abbey!' This is going to happen, because something is happening which we have not been very much aware of. I am aware of it. The television screen has put before us in our drawing-rooms a reality that the theatre cannot imitate at all and should not try to.

EDWARDS. One is based on form, the other is based on accident or enlarged journalism.

MacANNA. Precisely. The stage, as we know it, has changed. It is no longer a place where you go, with the curtain rising to reveal a set attempting to show you such and such a house at such and such a time of the day, correct to its last detail. That day has gone; also the day of the play that assumes that the audience is not there and if they are there, they are looking through a keyhole at what is happening; that people are behaving like this in ordinary day life, so that the playwright leans over backwards to give the impression of reality. My own approach to anything I do on the stage is this. The stage is a stage, the audience are there, these are actors, these have something to communicate, and what they communicate is in the play they are doing, and to hell with any superficial trimmings of going or coming or this or that. We are going back to a Shakespearian stage, and that is right. Is our national theatre about to become aware of this? Yes, we are aware of this, and I'm speaking as a director of plays in our theatre.

We, Tomás MacAnna, the players, Frank Dermody, the artistic people in there are aware of it.

EDWARDS. I've been aware of this for thirty-five years, and look where I am now. In a feature in the *Irish Times*.

FITZGERALD. A practical suggestion. A national theatre should not employ actors for longer than a year or two years. The national theatre, as presently constituted, should respect its older artists and pension them off. In fact many of them are very brilliant, but you should never reemploy anyone for over a year or two years.

CASSIN. You believe in the stimulus of uncertainty?

FITZGERALD. Yes, and I also believe in the fact that actors should have the option of going out, and not leaving because they've been there for five years.

McKENNA. I think that certainly it's a bad thing to employ actors on a long-term basis, but I think it's been proved very valuable for holding a team together until they build a style. I think laying down time is dangerous. I think one actor can develop magnificently in two years, it may take another actor ten years to develop.

KELLY. I want to ask what I think is a dirty question. Tom McKenna, how long were you actually in the Abbey company?

McKENNA. Eight years.

KELLY. Well, as a working artist in that company, how frustrated did you get? Did you feel that you were fulfilling yourself as an actor in everything you played in the Abbey, or in anything you played in the Abbey?

FITZGERALD. Ah, that's a Seamus Kelly question.

McKENNA. The reason I left the Abbey was because I felt that in the style of plays that were being done I was not broadening in technique and experience. I think an actor should be a fully flexible, sort of athlete in his medium. He should be able to encompass within his own talent, as many styles or idioms as he can possibly manage, and I felt, when I was in the Abbey, that one of the reasons that I had to get out was that I was being trained in too narrow a field.

KELLY. Well, may I ask a supplementary question? Do you think you would have been so anxious to leave either the Gate or the Globe?

McKENNA. Well, I think eight years is long enough for any actor to stay in any company.

MacANNA. Will you come back?

McKENNA. I would be very happy to come back to the Abbey and play.

KELLY. Will the New Abbey let the exiles back?

MacANNA. Yes, of course they will.

McKENNA. I must say, the unfortunate thing is whenever it comes to criticising the Abbey, there's always been a very defensive attitude taken up both by the players and by the directors. This is a sort of immaturity. I remember, I never, when I was in the Abbey, was outraged personally when there was an attack on it, and I could never understand it. Yet I find, whenever I am at the Abbey still, that you say something honestly and openly about policy and things artistic and technical, and people are spitting at you on the street as if you attacked them personally.

EDWARDS. May I suggest that the reason for this is that the Abbey has been so long a standard of Irish nationality, that when people attack it, others get the impression that they are attacking Ireland.

FITZGERALD. As an old Marxist I know that this defensive mechanism is entirely due to long-term contracts; there's no question about this. I've seen people who couldn't act for skins and who are still in the Abbey after twenty or thirty years. There are people in the Abbey who have reputations based on repetition, who couldn't originally act, because if they could, they would have got better. Sybil Thorndike is a perfect example of an actress who can get better and better and better (even though her work doesn't amuse me vastly). The Abbey has people who have patently never been able to act, and I've been watching them for seventeen years. That is what's wrong – long term contract. When you attack an old Abbey actor who's been there since he was twenty it's an attack on his own personal property.

EDWARDS. Much as I agree with Fitz about the great danger of long-term contracts we now see the evidence of the awful danger of contract terms so short that nobody can establish themselves in any team or any kind of technique whatsoever, and, therefore, the answer lies somewhere in the centre. I'd like to know whether it is advisable for one of us to advise the Abbey to concentrate on being the national theatre in the smallest sense, or whether it is to take in the international scene, which I would have rather thought was the function of another theatre, such as the late, and to me, lamented, Gate.

McKENNA. This is a very interesting point, because I remember Mr Blythe talking to us when we got to a certain stage of plays being so sub-standard, that they became almost intolerable, and with the audience coming in in their tens and twenties. We said: 'Why can't we take some of the new playwrights in England like Osborne, Pinter and so on?' 'Well,' he said, 'there's a patent here', and this seemed to be an arrangement whether it was on paper or not. 'We have a patent whereby we will not encroach on the policy of the Gate Theatre.' Mr Blythe said this at the time when we suggested doing a wider range. In my presence. We were told that it was all right to do O'Neill, because he had Irish origins and this sort of thing, but going into the English theatre was bad. Well, now unfortunately, the Gate is not running as a permanent theatre which was fulfilling this most valuable function.

MacANNA. I would like to continue. I want to speak about a national theatre at which I worked: the national theatre of Iceland. It was opened about twelve or thirteen years ago and its repertoire consists in the main of worthwhile, Icelandic plays, but they also expand to embrace European plays. But side by side with this national theatre which has a very large subsidy from the government, there is a small theatre and it plays all sorts of Icelandic plays, all sorts of European masterpieces, and keeps the national theatre, the big house as they call it, on its toes. Now, the point I'm making is this. I think we must have competition. I think one way of making sure the Abbey will die is to have no other theatre in Dublin but the national theatre. If I were Minister of Finance tomorrow, I would subsidise the national theatre, but would make damn sure that quite a big subsidy went to another theatre in town. Hilton's the man I'd give it to definitely.

McKENNA. Hilton, I would like to ask you, as a man who ran a theatre very successfully, with a sort of broad outline of policy, how do you see the aims and the structure of a new national theatre?

EDWARDS. I still think a new national theatre should have its main accent upon the cultivation of Irish works. Because I don't see how, although it's possible theoretically you can get a company who can really develop both arts. I would like to see another theatre, better than our own Gate Theatre, subsidised and going on ahead now. But it is simply, gentlemen, a question of finance. As I say, I would like to see something like the Gate, developing, and getting finer and better, and I think you will find this, with a number of subsidiary companies going round, will be quite enough to satisfy the theatrical demand of the city. But the Abbey at the present moment has the ball at its feet, and has the money. This is why I am concentrating upon it as I don't think that any money is likely to be forthcoming for any other theatre at the moment.

LINEHAN. I'm afraid, we're running out of time. May I ask each of you for a short summing up statement? I'll start with you, Jim.

FITZGERALD. The vision of a national theatre should be that, first, it inspires playwrights by showing them what other playwrights are doing. We're a small country, we should be doing the plays of people like Brecht and Dürrenmatt as I've said before. Secondly, a national theatre should be a national theatre, not a repertory company. Third point. We must involve our theatre with our children from the age of about five up to university age. At the moment, the essential people to attack are the universities, and work back to the bases. In other words, all the universities in the Republic – and Queen's[2] – should get excited about what is happening in the Abbey. They should be circularised for their ideas, and we should also circularise the teachers, saying: 'What do you think should be done in the national theatre?'

McKENNA. Well, I would broadly speaking, endorse everything Fitz has said. I think there's a great need here and now, to bring in intellectual life into the Abbey Theatre, that is, bring people from the universities and encourage the new and better writers – and it has been very reassuring to hear Tomás MacAnna on this. I think that it is necessary that the confidence of the writers in the theatre field was restored and I think they've been lost to a great extent. The second important thing is that there must be a raising of the standards technically in the theatre, from the acting, production and design point of view. How these things are to be brought about I don't know, but these seem to me to be the pressing needs of the moment.

CASSIN. A national theatre should be a reflection of current ideas and attitudes of a nation. I think that's the first function of a national theatre. To help to do this writers must be stimulated, as has been said. Part of this, I believe, can be done by showing to them in your national theatre, important contemporary plays. Some of them may not have lasting value; I don't think that is important. I think to elaborate our own ideas, to learn more, we must see what's going on outside, as well as inside. I think the Abbey has become ingrown. I'm full of hope from what Tomás MacAnna said – I know that he speaks as an individual director. The Abbey, like every other institution, has been dying since the day it was opened. Sometimes quite justifiably – I'm not saying yes or no. The time will come, if MacAnna's ideas are carried out, when, with the help of God, people will be saying '*He's* old-fashioned.' Competition I think will always be there. You always have the compensatory factor. I'm certainly full of hope for this new theatre and for the Abbey; that we can see something new of techniques. I would like to know and to feel assured that there are at the hands of say Tomás and the other producers the full techniques which I think the theatre is due in this day and age. That I do not know, I don't know the inside of the theatre. But, once again, I'm full of hope for the Abbey, and if it fails this time, it should be given a pill.

KELLY. I stand over what I said before. I'd like them to run a classical rep., done classically as is done by the Comédie Française. To be also open, as the Gate was, to outside plays and progressive modern depth in every sense of the term. I'd like them to run a second company round the sticks of Ireland, and to run the first company outside Ireland from time to time, so that they would benefit in turn from seeing the theatre of the world. I would like them to establish some sort of a tutelary college for young Irish playwrights, who might, in the new dispensation of things, find themselves treated the way O'Casey was by the old Abbey, and gently done over so that they learn their trade.

EDWARDS. I should like a national theatre here to set a standard and cultivate the theatrical genius of this country, to manifest this particular genius, and if it is necessary in doing so (as I think it is) to bring in from time to time other influences, to stretch this and widen it, and enrich it. I think the main thing should be to set a standard whereby other theatres and companies and small experimental companies will turn round and, say, 'Look, this is what theatre means and should be.' Now this may be an almost impossible deal, but we know that in this and things like this, the academies are rather inclined to be conservative and to cling on to all the traditions rather than to be experimental. But this is what I should like to see. I should like to be able to turn round and say: 'This is the national theatre of Ireland; this is what is best in the Irish theatre, and this is how it should be done.'

LINEHAN. As the working man in the Abbey, Tom, the last word rests with you.

MacANNA. I look forward to an Abbey Theatre which will be the focus of intellectual life in Ireland. I look forward to an Abbey and Peacock Theatre which will be a medium of communication of this generation to itself and the coming generation; we should have a mirror, as it were, in which we will see reflected the intellectual life of the continent. I look forward to a theatre which will never settle down. It will be a place of youth and excitement. It'll never settle down to a humdrum succession of play upon play. In fact I earnestly look forward to a theatre with fresh young vital audiences in Gaelic and in English, rioting at least once a month.

NOTES

A round table discussion between Seamus Kelly, *Irish Times* drama critic; T. P. McKenna, actor and former member of the Abbey Company; and four directors: Hilton Edwards, Jim Fitzgerald, Barry Cassin and Tomás MacAnna. Edited by Fergus Linehan.

1. Literary, without which it could not be done: an indispensable condition, a necessity.

2. In Belfast.

Additional Bibliography*

'The Abbey', *Irish Times* (Dublin), 12 Aug 1938, p. 6 (editorial; this issue and the preceding and the following issues carry reports on the speeches and lectures made at the Abbey Theatre Festival).

'The Abbey', *Irish Times* (Dublin), 20 Feb 1963, p. 7 (editorial on the disgraceful state of affairs).

'The Abbey', *Newsweek*, 68 (1 Aug 1966) 82 (on the opening of the new Abbey Theatre).

'The Abbey Theatre', *Irish Times* (Dublin), 1 Apr 1919, p. 4 (praise of its work).

'The Abbey Theatre', *Irish Times* (Dublin), 28 July 1944, p. 3 (letters to the Editor on the general condition of the Irish National Theatre).

The Abbey Theatre Dramatic Festival of Plays and Lectures (Dublin: Cahill, 1938) (thirty-eight page souvenir brochure).

'Abbey Theatre, Dublin', *Building* (New York), 212 (23 Sept 1966) 81–8.

'The Abbey Theatre: Its Origins and Accomplishments', *The Times* (London), 17 Mar 1913, Irish Number, p. 15. Reprinted, with some additions, in *The Ireland of Today* (London: John Murray, 1913; Boston: Small, Maynard, 1915) pp. 131–7.

'Abbey Theatre Players', *Irish American* (New York), 14 Oct 1911, pp. 1, 4 (Abbey Theatre's first American tour).

'Abbey Theatre Subsidy', *Literary Digest* (New York), 86 (12 Sept 1925) 29–30 (by the Irish Free State).

'The Abbey Theatre: What Is Wrong with the Drama', *Manchester Guardian Weekly*, 32 (19 Apr 1935) 318 (on the Theatre's plans to produce more foreign plays for lack of Irish ones).

'Abbey's New Policy', *Evening Herald* (Dublin), 13 Aug 1935, p. 7 (of producing more foreign plays).

Alldridge, John, 'What's Wrong with the Abbey?', *Irish Digest* (Dublin), 29 (Feb 1948) 17–19 (an attack on the directors of the Abbey Theatre).

Allgood, Sara, 'The Story of the Irish Players: Not for Money', *Sunday Record–Herald* (Chicago), 4 Feb 1912, part 7, p. 1 (recollections).

'Au Revoir to the Abbey Theatre', *The Sunday Times* (London), 25 Jan 1959, p. 9 (to preserve a record of the Abbey Theatre before it was pulled down for rebuilding, some of its former illustrious members visited it to make a film).

'Aviation, Animals and "The Abbey"', *Illustrated London News*, 219 (28 July 1951) 153 (on the fire which gutted the Abbey Theatre on 18 July 1951).

Barrington, Maeve, 'Queen of the Abbey Theatre', *Irish Digest* (Dublin), 54 (Oct 1955) 29–31 (Maureen Delany and recollections of the Abbey Theatre).

*For a more comprehensive bibliography see E. H. Mikhail, *An Annotated Bibliography of Modern Anglo-Irish Drama* (Troy, New York: Whitston, 1981).

Bentley, Eric, *In Search of Theater* (New York: Alfred A. Knopf, 1953; London: Dobson, 1954) (includes a chapter on 'The Abbey Theatre').

Bergholz, Harry, *Die Neugestaltung des Modernen Englischen Theaters, 1870–1930* (Berlin: Bergholz, 1933) (includes discussion on the Abbey Theatre).

Blythe, Ernest, 'The Abbey Theatre and the Irish Language', *Threshold* (Belfast), 2 (Summer 1958) 26–33.

——, *The Abbey Theatre* (Dublin: The National Theatre Society, [1965]) (a brochure on the Abbey's policies).

Borsa, Mario, 'The Irish National Theatre', in *The English Stage of Today* (London and New York: John Lane, 1908), pp. 286–314 (survey).

Boyd, Ernest A., 'The Abbey Theatre', *Irish Review* (Dublin), 2 (Feb 1913) 628–34 (some radical change must be made in the conduct of the Abbey Theatre).

——, *Ireland's Literary Renaissance* (Dublin: Talbot Press; New York: John Lane, 1916; new rev. edn. New York: Alfred A. Knopf, 1922; reprt Dublin: Allen Figgis, 1968) (includes chapters on the Irish dramatic movement).

Bronson, Gerald, 'Dublin's Abbey – The Immortal Theatre', *Theatre Arts* (New York), 35 (Oct 1951) 36–7 (recollections by a playwright who saw the ruins of the theatre following the 1951 fire).

Byrne, Dawson, *The Story of Ireland's National Theatre: The Abbey Theatre, Dublin* (Dublin: Talbot Press, 1929; reprt New York: Haskell House, 1971) (survey).

'Chanel' [Clery, Arthur Edward], *The Idea of a Nation* (Dublin: Duffy, 1907) (includes 'After the Abbey Is Over', pp. 17–19, and 'The Philosophy of an Irish Theatre', pp. 48–51).

Chisholm, Cecil, *Repertory: An Outline of the Modern Theatre Movement* (London: Peter Davis, 1934) (includes brief discussion on the Abbey Theatre).

Clarke, Brenna Katz, *The Emergence of the Irish Peasant Play at the Abbey Theatre* (Ann Arbor, Michigan: UMI Research Press, 1982).

Colum, Mary, 'Early Days of the Abbey Theatre', in *Life and the Dream* (London: Macmillan; Garden City, New York: Doubleday, 1947) pp. 97–109.

Colum, Padraic, 'The Abbey Theatre Comes of Age', *Theatre Arts Monthly* (New York), 10 (Sept 1926) 580–4 (recalls the Abbey's early successful days).

——, *The Road Round Ireland* (New York: Macmillan, 1926) (includes a chapter on The Abbey Theatre).

Connery, Donald S., *The Irish* (New York: Simon & Schuster, 1968) pp. 234–8 (The Abbey Theatre).

Craig, May, 'My Abbey Debut', *Irish Digest* (Dublin), 34 (July 1949) 53–5.

——, 'May Craig Recalls the Abbey Days', *Irish Times* (Dublin), 10 June 1965, W. B. Yeats Supplement.

Curran, C. P., 'The Peacock Spreads His Tail', *Irish Statesman* (Dublin), 19 Nov 1927, pp. 255–6 (on the Peacock Theatre).

——, *Under the Receding Wave* (Dublin: Gill & Macmillan, 1970) (includes recollections of the early years of the Abbey Theatre).

Cusack, Cyril, 'Every Week a Different School', in *A Paler Shade of Green*, ed. Des Hickey and Gus Smith (London: Leslie Frewin, 1972) pp. 23–35 (recollections).

Dace, Letitia and Wallace Dace, *Modern Theatre and Drama* (New York: Richards Rosen Press, 1973) (includes a chapter on the Abbey Theatre).

Delany, Maureen, 'Meet Maureen Delany', *Irish Digest* (Dublin), 19 (Aug 1944) 55–6 (recollections by an Irish actress).

Dickinson, Page L., *The Dublin of Yesterday* (London: Methuen, 1929) pp. 87–9 (recollections by an English journalist).

Dickinson, Thomas H., *An Outline of Contemporary Drama* (Boston: Houghton Mifflin, 1927; reprt New York: Biblo & Tannen, 1969) (includes a study of 'The Irish National Theatre').

Duncan, G[eorge] A., *The Abbey Theatre in Pictures* (Dublin: National Press Service of Ireland, 1963).

Dunne, John J., 'I Treasure Those Theatre Programmes', *Irish Digest* (Dublin), 75 (Aug 1962) 81–2 ('Souvenirs of Exciting Nights').

Eglinton, John, 'Irish Letter', *Dial* (Chicago), 81 (Dec 1926) 496–9 (recollections by an Irish poet and critic).

Ellis-Fermor, Una, *The Irish Dramatic Movement* (London: Methuen, 1939; 2nd rev. edn, 1954; reprt London: University Paperbacks, 1967).

Fallis, Richard, *The Irish Renaissance* (Syracuse, New York: Syracuse University Press, 1977) (includes a survey of Irish drama).

Fallon, Gabriel, 'The Fays Made Abbey History', *Irish Digest* (Dublin), 30 (Mar 1948) 50–2.

——, *Abbey Theatre – Dublin, 1904–1966* (Dublin: The National Theatre Society, 1966) (a brochure to mark the opening of the new Abbey Theatre building in 1966).

——, *The Abbey and the Actor* (Dublin: The National Theatre Society, 1969) (a booklet on the historical background to what has come to be known as the Abbey Theatre acting tradition).

Fay, Gerard, 'Ructions in the Abbey Theatre', *Irish Digest* (Dublin), 59 (Apr 1957) 18–20 (recollections).

——, *The Abbey Theatre, Cradle of Genius* (Dublin: Clonmore & Reynolds; London: Hollis & Carter, 1958) (a history by the son of the Abbey actor Frank Fay, concentrating on the period 1902–8).

Fay, William George and Catherine Carswell, *The Fays of the Abbey Theatre: An Autobiographical Record* (London: Rich & Cowan; New York: Harcourt, Brace, 1935) (also contains 'List of First Productions, with Casts').

Flannery, James W., *Miss Anne F. Horniman and the Abbey Theatre* (Dublin: Dolmen Press; London: Oxford University Press, 1970).

——, *W. B. Yeats and the Idea of a Theatre: The Early Abbey Theatre in Theory and Practice* (New Haven and London: Yale University Press, 1976).

Fox, R. M., 'Maureen Delany Takes a Bow', *Irish Digest* (Dublin), 29 (Dec 1947) 21–3 (includes recollections of the Abbey Theatre).

Gaffney, Sylvester, *The Burning of the Abbey Theatre (or The Lament for the Queen's)* (Dublin: Walton, 1951) (ballad set to music).

Gogarty, Oliver St John, *As I Was Going down Sackville Street* (London: Rich & Cowan, 1937) pp. 282–5 (recollections of the Abbey Theatre).

Gray, Tony, *The Irish Answer: An Anatomy of Modern Ireland* (London: Heinemann, 1966) pp. 255–6 (note on the 'dreary but comfortable routine' at the Abbey Theatre).

'Great Days at the Abbey', *Irish Digest*, (Dublin), 77 (Apr 1963) 71–4 (recollections by actors J. M. Kerrigan and Arthur Shields).

Gregory, Lady [Isabella Augusta], 'The Irish Theatre and the People', *Yale Review* (New Haven, Connecticut), 1 (Jan 1912) 188–91 (how the Irish theatre came into being).

——, *Journals 1916–1930*, ed. Lennox Robinson (London: G. P. Putnam, 1946; New York: Macmillan, 1947; reprt in complete form, ed. Daniel J. Murphy, Gerrards Cross: Colin Smythe, 1978).

——, *Our Irish Theatre* (New York and London: G. P. Putnam, 1913; reprt New York: Capricorn Books, 1965; rev. enl. edn with Foreword by Roger McHugh, Gerrards Cross: Colin Smythe, 1972).

——, *Seventy Years 1852–1922*, ed. Colin Smythe (Gerrards Cross: Colin Smythe, 1974).

Gwynn, Denis, 'The Irish Literary Theatre', in *Edward Martyn and the Irish Revival* (London: Jonathan Cape, 1930) pp. 109–70 (survey).

Gwynn, Stephen, *Dublin Old and New* (New York: Macmillan, 1938) pp. 49–53 (on the Abbey Theatre).

Hamilton, Clayton, 'The Irish National Theatre', *Bookman* (New York), 34 (Jan 1912) 508–16 (discusses the aims and achievements of the Irish National Theatre Society).

Henderson, W. A., *1909: The Irish National Theatre Movement: A Year's Work at the Abbey Theatre* (Dublin: privately printed, 1909) (told in press cuttings).

Hogan, Robert, *After the Irish Renaissance: A Critical History of the Irish Drama Since 'The Plough and the Stars'* (Minneapolis: University of Minnesota Press, 1967; London: Macmillan, 1968) (an 'informal critical account').

——, *The Modern Irish Drama* (Dublin: Dolmen Press; Atlantic Highlands, New Jersey: Humanities Press, 1975–) (multi-volume survey through letters, memoirs and reviews).

——, 'An interview with Michael Conniffe,' *Journal of Irish Literature*, 6 (Sept 1977) 80–8 (with the Abbey actor).

Holloway, Joseph, *Joseph Holloway's Abbey Theatre: A Selection from His Unpublished Journal 'Impressions of a Dublin Playgoer'*, ed. Robert Hogan and Michael J. O'Neill (Carbondale and Edwardsville: Southern Illinois University Press; London and Amsterdam: Feffer & Simons, 1967) (covers the years 1899–1926).

——, *Joseph Holloway's Irish Theatre, 1926–1944*, 3 vols, ed. Robert Hogan and Michael J. O'Neill (Dixon, California: Prosenium Press, 1968–70) (selections from the later years of Holloway's 'Journal').

Howe, P. P., *The Repertory Theatre: A Record and a Criticism* (London: Martin Secker, 1910; New York: Mitchell Kennerley, 1911) pp. 42–51 (the Abbey Theatre).

Hudson, Lynton, 'The Little Theatre: The Irish Movement', in *The Twentieth Century Drama* (London: George G. Harrap, 1946) pp. 37–44 (survey).

Hunt, Hugh, *The Abbey: Ireland's National Theatre 1904–1979* (Dublin: Gill & Macmillan, 1979).

Jones, Robert Edmond, *The Dramatic Imagination* (New York: Theatre Arts Books, 1941) pp. 29–30 (recollections of seeing the Abbey Players).

Joyce, James, 'The Day of the Rabblement', in *The Critical Writings of James Joyce*, ed. Ellsworth Mason and Richard Ellmann (London: Faber & Faber, 1959) pp. 68–72 (condemns the Irish Literary Theatre for its parochialism).

Kavanagh, Peter, *The Irish Theatre; Being a History of the Drama in Ireland from the Earliest Period up to the Present Day* (Tralee, Ireland: Kerryman, 1946) (includes a brief chapter on the Abbey Theatre).

——, *The Story of the Abbey Theatre from its Origins in 1899 to the Present* (New York: Devin-Adair, 1950) (survey).

Kennedy, Maurice, 'Shining in Its Infancy', *Sunday Press* (Dublin), 10 June 1951, p. 9; continued as 'Those Early Days', *ibid.*, 17 June 1951, p. 9.

Kiernan, T. J., 'Lady Gregory and W. B. Yeats', *Dalhousie Review*, 38 (Autumn 1958) 295–306 (the Irish Literary Theatre).

Lane, Yoti, *The Psychology of the Actor* (London: Secker & Warburg, 1959; New York: John Day, 1960; reprt Westport, Connecticut: Greenwood Press, 1973) p. 201 (Abbey Players).

Lawrence, W. J., 'The Abbey Theatre: Its History and Mystery', *Weekly Freeman* (Dublin), 96 (7 Dec 1912) 11–12 (survey).

Leblanc, Gerard, 'L'Abbey Theatre: Une difficile naissance', in *Actes du Congrès de Nancy*, SAES (Paris: Didier, 1975) pp. 291–305 (the beginnings of the Abbey Theatre).

Letts, Winifred, 'For Sixpence', *Songs from Leinster* (London: Smith, Elder, 1914) pp. 40–1 (a poem commemorating the old days at the Abbey Theatre).

——, 'Early Days at the Abbey', *Irish Digest* (Dublin), 31 (Sept 1948), 8–11 (recollections).

——, 'Young Days at the Abbey Theatre', *Irish Writing* (Cork), no. 16 (Sept 1951) 43–6 (recollections).

——, 'When the Abbey Was Young', *Ireland of the Welcomes* (Dublin), 1 (July–Aug 1952) 9–11 (recollections).

Lunari, Gigi, *Il Movimento Drammatico Irlandese (1899–1922)* (Bologna: Cappelli, 1960) (survey of the Abbey movement).

MacAnna, Tomás, 'Nationalism from the Abbey Stage', in *Theatre and Nationalism in Twentieth-Century Ireland*, ed. Robert O'Driscoll (Toronto: University of Toronto Press, 1971) pp. 89–101.

McCann, Sean, ed., *The Story of the Abbey Theatre* (London: New English Library, 1967) (contents: Sean McCann, 'The Beginnings'; Anthony Butler, 'The Guardians'; Sean McCann, 'The Theatre Itself'; Catherine Rynne, 'The Playwrights'; Gabriel Fallon', 'The Abbey Theatre Acting Tradition'; and Donal Dorcey, 'The Big Occasions').

MacDonagh, John, 'Acting in Dublin', *Commonweal* (New York), 10 (19 June 1929) 185–6 (recollections by an Irish producer).

MacGowran, Jack, 'Waiting for Beckett', in Des Hickey and Gus Smith, *A Paler Shade of Green* (London: Leslie Frewin, 1972) pp. 97–104 (recollections).

McHugh, Roger, 'Frank O'Connor and the Irish Theatre', *Eire–Ireland*, 4 (Summer 1969) 52–63.

MacNamara, Brinsley, *Abbey Plays 1899–1948, Including the Productions of the Irish Literary Theatre* (Dublin: At the Sign of the Three Candles, [1949]).

McQuillan, Deirdre, *The Abbey Theatre Dublin, 1966–1976: A Commemorative Record* (Dublin: The Abbey Theatre, 1976) (a booklet celebrating the tenth anniversary of the new Abbey Theatre).

Malone, Andrew E., 'The Decline of the Irish Drama', *Nineteenth Century and After* (London), 97 (Apr 1925) 578–88 (very few Abbey playwrights give promise of important work in the future).

——, 'The Coming of Age of the Irish Drama', *Dublin Review*, 181 (July 1927) 101–14 (the Abbey Theatre's twenty-first birthday).

——, *The Irish Drama* (London: Constable; New York: Scribner's, 1929; reprt New York: Benjamin Blom, 1965) (survey).

——, 'The Early History of the Abbey Theatre', in *The Irish Theatre: Lectures Delivered During the Abbey Theatre Festival Held in Dublin in August 1938*, ed. Lennox Robinson (London: Macmillan, 1939; reprt New York: Haskell House, 1971) pp. 3–28.

Mikhail, E. H., ed., *J. M. Synge: Interviews and Recollections* (London: Macmillan, 1977).

——, ed., *Lady Gregory: Interviews and Recollections* (London: Macmillan, 1977).

——, ed., *W. B. Yeats: Interviews and Recollections* (London: Macmillan, 1977).

Mikhail, E. H. and John O'Riordan (eds), *The Sting and the Twinkle: Conversations with Sean O'Casey* (London: Macmillan, 1974).

Miller, Anna Irene, 'The National Theatre of Ireland', in *The Independent Theatre in Europe, 1887 to the Present* (New York: Ray Long & Richard R. Smith, 1931; reprt New York: Benjamin Blom, 1966) pp. 255–310 (survey).

M[itchell], S[usan] L., 'Dramatic Rivalry', *Sinn Fein* (Dublin), 4 (8 May 1909) 1 (berates W. B. Yeats for letting Maire Nic Shiubhlaigh go).

Mooney, Ria, 'Players and the Painted Stage', an unpublished manuscript, ed. Val Mulkerns, in Robert Hogan, *The Rise of the Realists, 1910–1915* (Dublin: Dolmen Press, 1979) pp. 115–18 (recollections).

Moore, George, 'The Irish Theatre', *Boston Evening Transcript* (23 Sept 1911), part 3, p. 8 (recollections).

——, *Hail and Farewell* (London: Heineman:/New York: D. Appleton, 1911–14) (recollections including background to the Abbey Theatre).

Moroney, Helen, 'The Most Exciting Day of My Life', *Irish Statesman* (Dublin), 4 (21 Mar 1925) 42–3 (recollections of a visit to the Abbey Theatre).

Na Mainistreach, Amharchann (ed.) *The Creation of the Abbey Theatre* (Dublin: Irish Tourist Board, 1966) (a twenty page pamphlet issued to mark the opening of the new building).

National Theatre Society, *Rules of the National Theatre Society Limited* (Dublin: Cahill, [1903]).

O'Casey, Sean, *Autobiographies* (London: Macmillan, 1963) (includes recollections of the Abbey Theatre).

O'Connor, Frank, 'The Abbey Theatre', in *My Father's Son* (London: Macmillan, 1968) pp. 145–78; (New York: Alfred A. Knopf, 1969) pp. 169–80 (recollections).

O'Connor, Ulick, 'Abbey Memories', *Everyman* (Benburb, Co. Tyrone), no. 2 (1969) 46–7 (recollections by actors Arthur Shields and J. M. Kerrigan).

O'Faolain, Sean, *Vive Moi!* (Boston: Little, Brown, 1964; London: Hart-Davis, 1965) (autobiography including background to the Abbey Theatre).

Ó Farachain, Roibeárd, 'The Second Spring: A Manifesto for the New Abbey Theatre', in the souvenir programme to mark the occasion of the opening of the new Abbey Theatre, 1966.

Ó hAodha, Micheál, *The Abbey – Then and Now* (Dublin: Abbey Theatre, 1969) (a monograph bringing the Abbey Theatre's history up to 1969).

O'Neill, Michael, 'The Diaries of a Dublin Playgoer as a Mirror of the Irish

Literary Revival', Ph.D dissertation, National University, Dublin, 1952 (by Joseph Holloway).

O'Shannon, Cathal, 'Abbey Memories', *Evening Press* (Dublin) 24 May 1957, p. 6.

Peter, John, 'Jack MacGowran on O'Casey and Beckett', *The Times* (London), 18 Mar 1967, p. 7.

Plunkett, Grace, *Twelve Nights at the Abbey Theatre: A Book of Drawings* (Dublin: At the Sign of the Three Candles, 1929).

——, *Doctors Recommend It: An Abbey Theatre Tonic in 12 Doses* (Dublin: At the Sign of the Three Candles, 1930) (a twenty-eight page booklet containing caricatures of actors and actresses in scenes from Abbey Theatre productions, 1906–30).

Pogson, Rex, *Miss Horniman and the Gaiety Theatre, Manchester* (London: Rockliff, 1952) pp. 8–13 (Miss Horniman's association with the Abbey Theatre).

Reid, B. L., *The Man from New York: John Quinn and His Friends* (New York: Oxford University Press, 1968) (includes several references to the Abbey Theatre).

Rice, Elmer, *The Living Theatre* (New York: Harper; London: Heinemann, 1960) pp. 75–8 (examines the decline of the Abbey Theatre).

[Robinson, Lennox], 'Abbey Players', *Evening Mail* (Dublin), 6 July 1911, p. 5 (interview).

——, 'The Birth of a Nation's Theatre', *Emerson Quarterly* (Boston), 13 (Jan 1933) 3–4, 16–18, 20 (background piece on the Abbey Theatre).

—— (ed.), *The Irish Theatre: Lectures Delivered During the Abbey Theatre Festival Held in Dublin in August 1938* (London: Macmillan, 1939; reprt New York: Haskell House, 1971).

——, *Curtain Up: An Autobiography* (London: Michael Joseph, 1942) (contains background to the Abbey Theatre).

——, *Ireland's Abbey Theatre: A History 1899–1951* (London: Sidgwick & Jackson, 1951; reprt Port Washington, New York: Kennikat Press, 1968) (the official history commissioned by the Abbey Theatre authorities).

——, 'Them Were the Days', *Ireland of the Welcomes* (Dublin), 3 (Nov–Dec 1954) 13–14, 30 (recollections).

Rocke, William, 'May Craig Recalls That Abbey Uproar', *Irish Digest* (Dublin) 53 (Mar 1964) 71–3 (*The Plough and the Stars*).

Rolleston, T. W., 'The Story of the Irish Players', *Sunday Record–Herald* (Chicago), 4 Feb 1912, part 7, p. 1.

Russell, George W., 'AE Talked to Shaw', *New York Times*, 7 Feb 1928, p. 12 (recollections).

'Ruttledge, Paul' [George Moore], 'Stage Management in the Irish National Theatre', *Dana* (Dublin), no. 5 (Sept 1904) 150–2.

Saddlemyer, Ann, ' "Worn Out with Dreams": Dublin's Abbey Theatre', in *The World of W. B. Yeats*, ed. Robin Skelton and Ann Saddlemyer (Victoria, B.C.: Adelphi Bookshop, for University of Victoria, 1965; rev. edn Seattle: University of Washington Press, 1967) (examines the behind-the-scenes political struggles to create the Abbey Theatre).

——, 'Stars of the Abbey's Ascendancy', in *Theatre and Nationalism in Twentieth-Century Ireland*, ed. Robert O'Driscoll (Toronto: University of Toronto Press; London: Oxford University Press, 1971) pp. 21–39.

——— (ed.), *Theatre Business: The Correspondence of the First Abbey Theatre Directors William Butler Yeats, Lady Gregory and J. M. Synge* (Gerrards Cross: Colin Smythe, 1982).

Sharp, R. Farquharson, 'The Dublin Theatres', in *A Short History of the English Stage from Its Beginnings to the Summer of the Year 1908* (New York: Walter Scott, 1909) chap. 20 (includes a history of the Abbey Theatre).

Shaw, Bernard, 'The Irish Players', *Evening Sun* (New York), 9 Dec 1911, pp. 4–5 (on *Blanco Posnet* and the Abbey Theatre first American tour).

Smith, Hugh, 'Twilight of the Abbey?', *New York Times*, 31 Mar 1935, section 11, p. 2 (the Abbey Theatre is passing through critical times).

Stage Design at the Abbey Theatre: An Exhibition (Dublin: Peacock Theatre, 1967).

Stalder, Hans-Georg, *Anglo-Irish Peasant Drama: The Motifs of Land and Emigration* (Bern and Frankfurt: Lang, 1977) (includes a discussion of the Abbey Theatre).

Starkie, Walter, *Scholars and Gypsies: An Autobiography* (London: John Murray, 1963) pp. 37–9 (recollections of the first production of *The Playboy of the Western World*).

Stewart, Andrew J., 'The Acting of the Abbey Theatre', *Theatre Arts Monthly* (New York), 17 (Mar 1933) 243–5 (Abbey actors are noted for naturalness).

Strong, L. A. G., 'The Old Woman Outside the Abbey Theatre', in *Dublin Days* (Oxford: Blackwell, 1921) p. 9 (a poem).

Synge, J. M., 'I Don't Care A Rap', *Dublin Evening Mail*, 29 Jan 1907, p. 2 (interview on the occasion of the first production of *The Playboy of the Western World*).

Tennyson, Charles, 'The Rise of the Irish Theatre', *Contemporary Review* (London), 100 (Aug 1911) 240–7 (the story of the Abbey Theatre).

'Two Actors Relive Great Days at the Abbey Theatre', *The Times* (London), 28 Jan 1963, p. 5 (recollections by Arthur Shields and J. M. Kerrigan).

Weygandt, Cornelius, *Irish Plays and Playwrights* (London: Constable; Boston and New York: Houghton Mifflin, 1913; reprt Port Washington, New York: Kennikat Press, 1966) pp. 19–21 (recollections of a visit to Camden Street Hall).

Yeats, W. B., 'The Irish Theatre', *Daily News* (London), 6 June 1910, p. 4 (interview with Robert Lynd).

———, 'The Irish National Theatre', *Pall Mall Gazette* (London), 9 June 1911, p. 5 (interview).

———, 'The Abbey Theatre', *Evening Telegraph* (Dublin), 28 June 1911, p. 3 (interview).

———, 'W. B. Yeats Looks Back; Ireland in the Early Days of the Abbey Theatre', *Irish Press* (Dublin), 14 Oct 1935, p. 9 (interview).

———, *Autobiographies* (London: Macmillan, 1955).

———, *Memoirs*, ed. Denis Donoghue (New York: Macmillan, 1972) (includes Yeats' journal, begun in 1908; and the first draft of his autobiography, begun in 1915).

Index

(The figures in parentheses after entry numbers indicate the number of references. Mc is treated as if spelt Mac.)